The Many and the Few

For Irving & Jean Richter, though this book has been known to you from the first edition, exhausted decades ago, we thought you might be interested in having a copy of this new issue just out. Sorry to have missed seeing you but we expect to be back in the States for a prolonged stay beginning next April.

Affectionately,

Dorothy & Henry Kraus

October 28, 1985.

The Many and the Few

A CHRONICLE OF THE DYNAMIC AUTO WORKERS

SECOND EDITION

Henry Kraus

With an Introduction by Neil O. Leighton,
William J. Meyer, and Nan Pendrell

University of Illinois Press
Urbana and Chicago

Illini Books edition, 1985

Introduction to the Second Edition, © 1985
by the Labor History Project of the
University of Michigan–Flint

© 1947, 1975, 1985 by Henry Kraus
Manufactured in the United States of America
P 5 4 3 2 1

This book is printed on acid-free paper.

Library of Congress Cataloging in Publication Data

Kraus, Henry, 1905-
  The many and the few.

  Includes bibliographies.
  1. General Motors Corporation Sit-Down Strike,
1936-1937.   I. Title.
HD5325.A82 1937.F5 1985   331.89'28292'0973   85-1193
ISBN 0-252-01199-6

To the auto workers,
whose courage, clarity, and resourcefulness
must continue to serve America

Contents

Preface to the Second Edition   *ix*

Introduction to the Second Edition   *xiv*

Introduction to the First Edition   *xxiii*

1936-1946: A Historic Parallel   *xxv*

1   Leavening the Dough   1

2   First Sitdown — A Dress Rehearsal   31

3   Rooting Out the Fifth Column   56

4   Strategy and the Rank and File   70

5   "Protect Your Jobs!"   86

6   Counter-Attack   106

7   Battle of Bull's Run   125

8   General Motors Breaks a Truce   146

9   Violent Crescendo   168

10   Union Wit versus Company Force   189

11   Capture of Chevy 4   209

12   Final Jitters   227

13   "Solidarity Forever!"   263

Preface to the Second Edition

The Many and the Few was first published in 1947, ten years after the great General Motors sit-down strike and over seven years after the book was written. In the introduction to the first edition I explained the difficulties that I had encountered in trying to get the book accepted. All of the publishers who saw it were in accord that though it had merit, it would not sell. "It is a hard fact," one wrote, "that the labor movement will not support books that should be of interest to it and the rest of the populace is even more uninterested." Another admitted that this judgment was undoubtedly a "form of censorship."

In the end my wife Dorothy and I decided that we would probably have to publish the book ourselves. But we learned that this would be very costly, and since we had little money at the time, we reluctantly put the manuscript aside. By 1946, however, our financial situation had improved, and so without losing any more time trying to contact other publishers, we proceeded to undertake publication of the book.

When the book appeared, we soon learned that printing was only one facet of the publication process. Distribution was just as vital an operation. We wrote to our many friends and especially to those still in the UAW or other CIO unions and were heartened by their response. But sales added up to only a few hundred of the bound copies, and we had already ordered an inexpensive cardboard-covered edition of 5,000. Although our Los Angeles printer had given us a short space of time to pay for these books, we soon realized that waiting for the locals to react to our letters would quickly exhaust the period of credit leeway.

My wife and I decided to go out to contact personally the UAW locals — the primary audience for whom the book was intended. I was delighted to learn that a number of the members had already read the book and were prompt to make their observations about it, often couched in terms that were as acute as those of any professional critic. For me this was an exciting corroboration of that independence of spirit and expression that I had seen grow up so strongly among these auto workers in the tough struggles that they had conducted, in their strikes and in their subsequent dealings with the supervisors. Though they sometimes expressed disagreement with the book on some point or other, the positive note must have prevailed, since over 4,000 copies were ordered as a result of this safari. Among the locals that received large shipments running into the hundreds of copies were many of the most prominent in the UAW: Ford Local 600; West Side Local 174; Hudson Local 154; Chevrolet Flint Local 659; Tool and Die Locals 155 and 157; and many others.

A "broader public" never existed as far as this first edition was concerned. Reviews in other than labor or leftwing journals were rare. This result was in striking contrast with the reaction to a French edition, which appeared shortly thereafter (on the recommendation of a well-known sociologist, Daniel Guérin, in his *Où Va le Peuple Américain?*). In addition to labor and "progressive" commentators, it also interested spokesmen of wider audiences, such as the important liberal Catholic author Jacques Madaule.

Academic notice of the book in the United States was slow in coming, paralleling the very gradual realization of the full significance of the organized labor movement as something worth studying professionally. My wife and I were already living and working in Paris when we began to hear by second-hand report that *The Many and the Few* had become a kind of classic to this group, though unfortunately this occurred when it was already out of print! I recall one letter that was rerouted to me from an economics professor, who wanted to purchase fifty copies of the book for his students — "at the usual reduction."

It was some years later that I made contact with Professor Philip P. Mason of Wayne State University, when my collection of documents entered his remarkable Labor Archives. I learned from him that the subject of labor had by then attained such importance in academic circles that there were dozens of labor historians established in the universities. Needless to say, *The Many and the Few* was known to them, and soon their students began to contact my wife and me about their theses (which were probably inspired by the book), dealing with such subjects as the role of women in the strike; inner-plant organization of the sit-down; its problems of discipline; even a query on theatrical performances during the strike, a theme that must have been prompted by one fleeting incident in the book.

It was gratifying to find that the scholars that I began to meet or read had done some original thinking about *The Many and the Few*. Rarely was their viewpoint similar to the one we had known in the early days — that of an almost automatically unfriendly reaction. Nevertheless, the charge of "lack of objectivity" that was at times leveled against my book surprised me, since it showed a failure to take into account certain factors surrounding the writing of such a work. As an active participant in the great struggle and as organizer-editor of the union that led it, it would have been impossible to have recorded this chronicle from the inside of one of the two great forces that were involved in the conflict without taking sides. The alternative would have been to sacrifice its force, its passion, its special truth. I had, moreover, pointed to important gaps in the range of subject matter that was handled in the book, explaining how I had "started by writing a general history of the United Auto Workers" but had for explicit reasons "decided to defer its publication" to a later date. Six chapters still exist in typescript of this effort, as well as many unworked notes, including fifty oral histories (done before the term existed perhaps) that I took of UAW leaders and other activists back in 1938. Some day this material will join the Labor Archives or perhaps find another type of outlet.

It is most heartening, meanwhile, that the University

of Illinois Press should have decided to reissue *The Many and the Few* and that the initiative for this should have come from labor historians, three of whom have collaborated in writing a new introduction. To all of these, and to the many others who over the years have expressed the desirability of a reissue of this book, I extend my appreciation.

Henry Kraus

Paris, France
March, 1984

Introduction to the Second Edition

The reissue of *The Many and the Few,* Henry Kraus's narrative of the Flint, Michigan, sit-down strike of 1937, is a sign of the ongoing strength of the current trend among social historians to further working-class studies. Not conventional oral history (though many individuals speak in its pages), the book is the first and only comprehensive attempt by a class-conscious participant to describe a forty-four-day strike that many acknowledge as pivotal in the unionization of labor in twentieth-century America. *The Many and the Few* recreates the drama as it was actually played, from the prologue in 1934, when industrial strikes, challenging the open shop and craft unionism, swept much of the country, to the climax in 1937, when General Motors was compelled to accept the United Auto Workers (UAW) as the automobile industry's sole bargaining agent. This was the time when auto workers dared everything — and came close to winning it all.

Within a year of the sit-down strike, wages in the auto industry increased by $300 million; the UAW had grown from 30,000 to 500,000 members; and the union had written agreements with 4,000 automobile and auto-parts concerns. Throughout the nation sit-down strikes became the way to organize: teachers, WPA workers, artists, busboys, bellboys, municipal employees, clerks, and stenographers joined with cooks, steel workers, longshoremen, garment workers, fur workers, lumberjacks, and sharecroppers in such strikes. Black workers began to be organized, and working women were admitted into industrial unions other than the textile and needle trades, where they were already accepted.*

Today virtually all labor historians recognize the centrality of the Flint sit-down strike to subsequent labor and corporate developments. Several major books about the strike are regarded as standard histories of the period. Sidney Fine's *Sit Down* uses standard historical sources to describe and analyze the strike. Peter Friedlander's *The Emergence of a UAW Local,* an individualized oral history, describes the development of a single local in Detroit in the 1920s and 1940s. August Meier and Elliot Rudwick's *Black Detroit and the Rise of the UAW* describes the role of black workers in building a political coalition that arose from the organizing drives of the auto workers. Wyndham Mortimer's *Organize* is an informative, personal account of a machinist turned labor organizer who was a UAW vice-president at the time of the Flint strike. Richard O. Boyer and Herbert M. Morais's *Labor's Untold Story* includes a documented account of the effects of the strike on the entire labor movement. Art Preis's *Labor's Giant Step* is a significant political polemic. Bert

*Richard O. Boyer and Herbert M. Morais, *Labor's Untold Story* (New York: United Electrical Radio and Machine Workers of America, 1972), 390.

Cochran's *Labor and Communism* is a sectarian analysis of the role of the left in the labor movement of the 1930s and 1940s. Roger Keeran's *Communist Party and the Auto Workers Union* presents a balanced account of the role of the Communist party in the leadership of the auto-industry organizing drives. One should not overlook Gerard Zilg's massive and well-documented investigation of the role of the Du Pont Corporation in the ownership of General Motors during this crucial period — *Du Pont: Behind the Nylon Curtain.* The role of the Reuther brothers, Walter, Roy, and Victor, in this critical period of trade union organizing is told in Victor Reuther's biographical account, *The Brothers Reuther.*

However, all of these accounts have been produced by individuals whose varying distance from the moment-by-moment, day-to-day events is evident and acknowledged. This same distance is reflected in the documentary films of the strike. *With Babies and Banners* portrays the contributions to the strike by women who organized and joined the Flint Women's Emergency Brigade, but its several factual lapses are the result of the filmmakers themselves reconstituting events in the late 1970s that had occurred forty years before. The British Broadcasting Corporation's *Yesterday's Witness in America: The Great Flint Sit-Down* (1980) used interviews with the people who had taken part in the strike but had to portray the period of upheaval in American working-class history not only through the prism of receding time but also across geographical space and cultural differences.

Only *The Many and the Few* has been written by a scholar who was himself an activist and a participant in the strike. Kraus helped to shape the events he wrote about. As the editor of the UAW's first newspaper, *The United Auto Worker,* and of the Flint strikers' only local supportive publication, *The Flint Auto Worker,* Kraus found his journalism being tested constantly. What *The Flint Auto Worker* reported had to withstand the scrutiny of the auto workers themselves and to survive the ever-vigilant nitpicking and distortions of the national establishment press and hostile local opinion-makers.

The Flint Auto Worker came to serve Kraus in the same way that personal field diaries serve the social scientist: he had in his possession an invaluable document of record. Thus, although *The Many and the Few* was written after the strike (during 1939 and 1940) and was not published until 1947, Kraus held a reliable means to check his own and others' recollections. It therefore seems natural that practically every serious piece of writing about the Flint strike refers to *The Many and the Few.* It is also not surprising that in 1971 Wyndham Mortimer, first vice-president of the UAW and the initial organizer of Flint's pre-sit-down strike organization, dedicated his autobiography not only to Robert Travis ("the real leader of the 1937 GM Sit-Down Strike, and the most brilliant strategist the UAW ever had") but also to Henry Kraus, "whose services in the UAW, much of it without pay, were greater than many in the union's top leadership."*

The Many and the Few can be read with a sense of discovery by all who are troubled by the desperate uncertainties of today and tomorrow. Bring to this chronicle an urge to try to figure out how we have gotten here

*Wyndham Mortimer, *Organize* (Boston: Beacon Press, 1971), v.

from 1937. How did we lose so much? When did the labor movement begin to regress to its present, almost exclusive concentration on wages, fringe benefits, and pensions, that is, on "economism," which in 1937 was merely the non-negotiable bottom line that was necessary to insure an entirely new way of life? What are the relationships between this economism and racism, the erosion of class consciousness, and chauvinistic nationalism? Kraus does not answer all of these questions: no book written that close to 1937 could foresee the limitless extent of questions like these. However, readers can pursue scores of suggestive clues in *The Many and the Few*.

Kraus does not conceal the ruinous factional struggles that cropped up from the start of organization in the automotive industry and elsewhere. In the course of these fights visionary labor leaders were transformed into political supporters of welfare capitalism: the leaders of the CIO and the UAW aligned themselves with the New Deal programs of the Franklin D. Roosevelt administration. These programs ameliorated the harshest consequences of the business cycles that had characterized laissez-faire capitalism by giving the workers the right to strike and providing financial benefits during economic hard times.

But these programs came with price tags for the labor movement as well as benefits. The first was the mass intervention of the government into the entire field of labor relations during World War II, from controlling wages through mediation-arbitration to the proscribing in many cases of the right to strike. This was best demonstrated by the passage of the Smith-Connally Act of 1943. The second price tag came in the form of huge profits made by the corporations as a result of government-enforced wage controls and cost-plus contracts. Real wages did not keep pace with inflation, and the result was worker discontent, wildcat strikes, and the unwillingness of the AFL's and the CIO's leaders to budge from their support of the no-strike pledge. Consequently leadership authority over the rank and file was damaged. The third price tag was the changing political climate occasioned by the return of economic stability, the federal regulatory agencies headed by industrialists, and the lack of organized labor's ability to check these corporate leaders. At the state level conservative antilabor forces managed to stop the progressive movements of the 1930s and to check any new moves for social reform. This rightward drift was further complicated by those leaders on the left who unstintingly supported the CIO policy of national unity, increased production, and the no-strike pledge, even when conditions of a national emergency were no longer present. The left became increasingly isolated in the postwar period, but only partially because of their own lack of sensitivity to rank and file workers' needs. More important, the left and Communists in particular became the target of those who sought to exploit the growing distrust of the Soviet Union and the anti-Communist hysteria of this period in order to gain unchallenged control of the labor movement.*

Even before the formal onslaught of the McCarthy inquisitions in the early 1950s, anti-Communism had become the official orthodoxy of the labor movement and

*Roger Keeran, *The Communist Party and the Autoworkers Unions* (Bloomington: Indiana University Press, 1980), 235-37.

many of the key figures in the organizing drives of the 1930s and early 1940s were driven from leadership positions or coopted by the new right-leaning leaders. By 1949 the labor unions were avowedly anti-Communist: the CIO expelled eleven of its unions that year — United Electrical Workers; Fur and Leather Workers; Mine, Mill and Smelter Workers; International Longshoremen and Warehousemen; United Farm Equipment Workers; Food, Tobacco and Agricultural Workers; United Office and Professional Workers; United Public Workers; American Communications Association; National Union of Marine Cooks and Stewards; International Fishermen and Allied Workers. This frenzy of purging within the ranks of organized labor has yet to be fully studied.* *The Many and the Few* is an excellent guide to starting this much needed social archaeology.

No other reporter of the period has drawn the necessary conclusions from the fact that the General Motors Corporation was merely one production unit (albeit its most profitable one!) in the vast empire of the GM's real owners: E. I. Du Pont de Nemours of Delaware. Decisions concerning GM plants throughout the United States were made by Du Pont officers; GM corporate board seats were held by Du Pont appointees (who were family members); and GM contracts with the UAW after the strike were signed by Du Pont attorneys. Formal separation of the two corporations came only with the divestiture of the millions of GM shares by the Du Pont Corporation

*Stanley Aronowitz, *Working Class Hero* (New York: Pilgrim Press, 1984), 214. The author also states that as of early 1984 no comprehensive study has been made of the fate of the eleven unions expelled from the CIO in 1949.

some twenty years later, in the 1950s. GM politics, as Kraus shows, were manufactured by Du Pont and were forced on the working men, women, and children of Flint by the corporation's surrogates in every cultural, educational, and political institution in the city.

Any reader who has worked and lived in a company town like Flint will be struck by the insight Kraus reveals when he lays open the efforts of General Motors "to secure control over the chief organs of community life and authority. . . . All the more subtle influences were exploited in the service of the great corporate Personality. There was a mammoth company settlement — euphemistically named The Industrial Mutual Association (IMA) — which in a thousand ways — through classes, clubs, sports leagues, choruses, orchestras, dances, activities for the worker's children, his wife and old folks — multiplied the hidden ties between man and company" (5, 6).

From the union's experiences and from federal reports Kraus documents that with few exceptions (notably certain church and professional figures), every law officer, politician, and civic personality — supplemented by company-paid spies and armed thugs — was arrayed against any manifestation of pro-union sympathy. These are invaluable insights for those who want to explore the nature of "community" in the United States during the period of burgeoning industrialization that was coterminous with the rise of the auto industry. It is clear that *The Many and the Few* is the preeminent *casebook* of the sit-down strike. It is a guide through a protracted trauma that succeeded because the forty-four days and nights were conceived as manageable by "ordinary" workers of good will and common sense. How did this come about? How were these days and nights actually managed by men confined within company property? Away from family, friends, lovers, churches, and bars — how did collective responsibilities arise; how were discipline, hygiene, group- and self-education organized? What a wealth of homely, yet gigantic problems had to be solved by men and women who were new to the tasks, but found themselves equal to them.

The Labor History Project of The University of Michigan–Flint is proud to have played a part in restoring this long-lost handbook of confrontation with the realities of a struggle for power and human dignity to the readers for whom it was originally intended — the autoworkers and working-class people everywhere. Moreover, it will be available to newer generations now isolated from an intimate understanding of these events. Titanic struggles are again in the offing as labor throughout America is under attack by corporate-led efforts not seen since the 1930s. *The Many and the Few* demonstrates to working-class people how and what had been accomplished in those historic forty-four days at Flint in the winter of 1937. The lessons for today are all there, plain and clear.

Neil O. Leighton
William J. Meyer
Nan Pendrell
The Labor History Project of
the University of Michigan–Flint

Introduction to the First Edition

If there is any one paramount characteristic of books on American history, it is that they are not histories of the people. Histories of the generals, the diplomats, and the politicos there are plenty; histories of the people — the plain people — there are few.

This is no accident. It is part of the great conspiracy which consists in drawing an iron curtain between the people and their past. The generals, the diplomats, and the politicos learned long ago that history is more than a record of the past; it is, as well, a source from which may be drawn a sense of strength and direction for the future. At all costs, that sense of strength and direction and purpose must be denied to the millions of men and women who labor for their living. Hence, the record of their past achievements is deliberately obscured in order to dull their aspirations for the future.

The Many and the Few is an important contribution to the cause of smashing the iron curtain of cultivated ignorance. It is a simple story of simple people who battled and defeated the most arrogant and powerful citadel of monopoly in the history of the world. It is the story of their sacrifice and their heroism, written by one who shared their struggle with them. But it is more than a record of a great triumph of the people; it is a herald of the future, when the common people shall fully possess their heritage.

George F. Addes, *Secretary-Treasurer*
R. J. Thomas, *Vice President*
UAW (CIO)

1936-1946: A Historic Parallel

Though the events described in this book are now a decade past, it would be missing its point entirely not to see the vital contemporary context into which they fit. There have of course been numerous minor shifts and changes in the contending forces. But the essential lineup remains today pretty much the same as it was in 1936.

Perhaps no single episode during this decade did more to tip the scales to the side of progress than did the great General Motors sitdown of January 1937. The victory obtained here gave rise to a union impulse unequalled in our history, bringing new millions of workers into the organized effort against reaction while also wakening other segments of the people to spread the struggle over an ever-widening circumference. More recently, the emphasis of the great dispute shifted to an international scope, in which the more spectacular domestic aspects were submerged. But the end of the war reopened the old conflict as labor, fresh from its unprecedented accomplishment during the emergency, found itself faced by a fundamental challenge.

This book frankly takes its stand in the continuing contest through seeking to assist the working people in acquiring a "sense of strength and direction and purpose." The author regrets that what influence it might have is under the special handicap of all "labor" books. For though radio and press have to some extent recognized the tremendous new importance of the union movement, it is a fact that our book literature hardly reflects. The reading public apparently remains still strongly allergic to such books and the general ignorance of labor fact and history is abysmal.

It is possible that reading tastes have not yet had time to catch up with the rapidly evolving subject. However, the author's experience with publishing houses would indicate something like a vicious circle operating to keep this situation at status quo. Of the few national publishers that saw this book, all were agreed that it had merit. Yet all were equally insistent that it would not sell. "It is a hard fact," the words of one put it for all alike, "that the labor movement will not support books that should be of interest to it, and that the rest of the populace is even more uninterested." Another admitted honestly that this prevailing judgment was undoubtedly a "form of censorship."

This state of affairs is not very encouraging to the growth of a labor library. It places a great burden on those writers who are courageous or perhaps foolhardy enough to seek to evade it as well as on the labor movement which suffers from not getting its story properly told. Clearly, the unions must vigorously support every legitimate effort toward that end. But the labor writer must also accept the obligation to do a creditable technical job. For indifference to manner of presentation of many such books in the past has certainly been an element in the failure of the subject to attract more friends.

Accordingly, in writing the present book, the author put the accent on drama, on those terms of emotion and conflict and expectancy which a reader understandably demands of any book. Having started by writing a general history of the United Auto Workers, he decided to defer its publication and to expand instead on this one chapter in that history — a major one, to be sure, and one which contained within its limits an astonishing, a symbolic richness — in order to attain a narrative unity that would heighten the excitement and readability of the book.

Some readers will possibly be disappointed by this selection. This may be true particularly of auto workers from Chrysler, Ford and other companies besides General Motors, who will consider their story and their contribution just as important as the one recorded here. There can be no doubt that a complete history of the nation's most exciting union should be available. But for this first book the argument made above has prevailed.

Strict choice has played its role even within the bounds of the condensed subject. For there were thousands of workers directly engaged in the General Motors sitdown and of these, hundreds who made a measurable contribution. The author clearly had to keep the number of actors to a minimum, to avoid confusion. And his major concentration on Flint — the vortex of the struggle — was buttressed by pretty much the same considerations as guided the producers of such excellent films as *The*

Story of GI Joe or *A Walk in the Sun*. In each of these films, despite a rigidly confined sector of action, a powerful impression of the whole great war was nevertheless obtained. More names might have been mentioned in the book perhaps, but there is hardly anything that makes more tedious reading than a list of names!

The author cannot even take space to thank individually the great number of people who have made personal material available for this story, but he does so collectively, with deep appreciation. His own file of documents in excess of 10,000 pieces has, moreover, supplemented this more immediate data. All this, too, added to the problem of selection but at the same time it facilitated the task of avoiding the searing factionalism that has existed in the UAW for years, aiding the author in hewing to a firm policy of treating individuals and groups in light of their actual contribution. This book has no hero or heroes; it is a story of the rank and file.

The question of interpretation rose most sharply perhaps in the treatment of such an individual as John L. Lewis. The author would certainly not excuse the conduct of this man during the war nor his surrender of principles which he did much to energize in the early days of the CIO. Yet he does not regard the outstanding role played by Lewis in this narrative, based as it is on incontestable fact, as a contradiction. It is his firm conviction that the social entity rather than the individual is the determining factor in history. When Lewis divorced himself from the new movement which he helped found, he quickly lost his place as a leading creative force in American labor. On the other hand, the CIO in losing Lewis did not sacrifice its fundamental character. Under Philip Murray and his co-workers, it has continued to grow along the lines described in this history, attaining new heights of influence and prestige.

As for Homer Martin, this book confines itself to what was known about him at the time. Of his subsequent treacheries, the full details will later be told.

The fact of organized labor's new power is now accepted by all, even by those who are seeking to curb or trim its growth. Such people do not (or do not *wish* to) see this strength as a positive element in the continuing upward swing of our country. Yet the war demonstrated conclusively that labor's contribution in skill and devotion was greatest where workers were part of a conscious unity. But even during the nation's emergency, unfortunately, this creative collective power was far from fully utilized. It will not be ignored indefinitely.

H.K.

San Pedro, California
February, 1947

1

Leavening the Dough

On a bland, early June day in 1936 a man of unexceptional appearance parked his Dodge car near a modest downtown hotel in Flint, Michigan, got his bag off the rear seat and carried it into the lobby.

"I want a room by the week," he told the clerk. "How much will it be?"

"Well, we can give you a room for fifteen, eighteen or twenty-one dollars," the clerk replied.

"Fifteen will be all right," the man said and he took the pen from the clerk's hand to sign the register.

The clerk took the pen back, glanced at the name on the register and pushed a button on the bellboard. "Okay," he said. "I'll have the boy down in a minute."

It was evident from the clerk's reaction that the name on the register had meant nothing to him. With a frozen smile he looked at the newcomer, perhaps wondering in a casual way what his business was in Flint. There was little in the man's appearance to indicate for certain. He was a man of fifty, above average height, well built. Somehow you couldn't take him for a salesman. He was too quiet-looking, had nothing breezy or showy about him. He was dressed neatly, though definitely for utility. His deep blue eyes, covered by glasses, had an intellectual cast to them: maybe the man was a technician, in Flint on a matter for General Motors. That was more likely, though it happened not to be true, either. Indeed, if the clerk had shaken hands with the newcomer he could hardly have reached such a conclusion. For he would have found the palm taut and calloused, hallmarks of the workingman.

While the stranger's entrance into Flint was unnoticed, it did not long remain so. Somewhere, in well-appointed offices and behind shut doors, there was a stirring because of it and the following morning, when the modest man came down from his room, there was an individual sitting in an armchair in the lobby waiting for him. When he went through the front door, the other put his paper down and followed him out into the street. And thereafter, he or one of two others always managed to be with him. Even if the stranger got his car out of the garage and went driving to some section of the city, the other men had a machine conveniently parked in which they could tail him, see where he went, and more important, note whom he saw.

One day the newcomer became conscious of this constant shadowing and he was amused. He was no criminal, had never spent a day in jail, and yet he was not surprised at the attention he had attracted. It struck him as funny how during the first few days he must have unintentionally befuddled his followers. For he had spent many hours touring the city, usually by foot and seemingly without aim. Slowly, methodically, he had gone into every district, noting how people lived, what kind of houses they had, where the great factories of General Motors were located. He had appeared interested in everything and the men who had shadowed him must have had difficulty trying to make sense or system out of the things that attracted his attention.

Viewed superficially, the city of Flint in 1936 gave little indication of its importance. Its single commercial artery, Saginaw Street, was the typical smalltown Main Street, to which half a dozen multi-storied buildings strove futilely to give a metropolitan air. One was amazed to learn that the population of Flint was over 150,000. Only when one went a mile or two to the east and west of Saginaw— over to the astonishing industrial piles that made up the Buick and Chevrolet factories—did one begin to realize the source of Flint's greatness and the reason for its fame.

Yet Flint had been a place of mark for almost three-quarters of a century. Located on the Grand Travers (ford) of the Flint River which flowed through miles of Michigan's rich pine forest, the city's lumber mills became noted in the period before the state's magnificent wooded resources were exhausted by reckless exploitation. Carriage and wagon works grew up as an auxiliary to this industry and as a result of the highly developed assembly methods that were evolved, Flint's output in wheeled conveyances gave it the title of "The Vehicle City" long before General Motors was an inspired idea in the brain of the daring and romantic Billy Durant.

But the real prominence of Flint dated from the birth of the automobile and particularly from the founding there of the Buick Company in 1904. Not everyone looked upon the marvelous new vehicle with favor. Wall Street did not for several years regard it as a worthwhile financial risk. But the early successes of Oldsmobile and Buick and Ford swiftly established the brilliant career of the automobile and the cities of its origin grew with the dizzying crescendo of western mine centers or the boom oil towns of Oklahoma.

The population of Flint doubled every five years from 1905 to the middle of the twenties when the auto industry attained its apex of development. Workers poured into the city from the defunct lumber centers of the state; from the exhausted mines of the coal industry; skilled craftsmen came from the east, lured by double the wages paid for similar work. But chiefly the workers swarmed in from the small, mortgage-ridden farms of Michigan and the nearby states or more distant Missouri, Arkansas and Kentucky. Flint's new population was basically rural in origin.

The factories of General Motors spread phenomenally meanwhile until city and corporation became like linked reflexes in one of Professor Pavlov's experiments. You couldn't mention one without bringing the other to mind. With four of every five of the city's family heads working for it, General Motors' production records were the very barometer of life for Flint. When its five great plants were booming the city was energized but when they were shut down its vital currents grew sluggish. The latter effect was yearly noticeable at layoff time while during the great sitdown of January 1937 the average slump in business was calculated to be 50 percent or more. Stores were deserted, rents went unpaid, the banks were drained of their deposits and only the dispossess courts and the welfare stations were doing a rushing business.

4

And reciprocally, Flint was more than just an important General Motors city. It was the heart-and-nerve center of the vast combine. Creator of fortunes, incomparable benefactor to the chosen few, prize milch-cow of America's most patrician family, the du Ponts,* whose 10,000,000 shares of GM stock assured them a one-fourth cut of the corporation's unabating profits,whatever happened in this central city of the corporation, in this nondescript over-size village, reverberated throughout the financial capitals of the nation.

It was to be expected, in a city so crucial to its prosperity, that General Motors should make every effort through its resident representatives to secure control over the chief organs of community life and authority. And such indeed was the case. Political hegemony was assured through the occupancy of the leading posts by past or present company officials or by substantial stockholders. In June 1936 this was true of the city manager, the mayor, the police chief and a score of lesser public servants. The one daily paper and the local radio station were likewise firmly under control as the United Auto Workers learned when it sought to buy time for a broadcast and space for an advertisement. The city's atmosphere reeked with sycophancy in behalf of the corporation, a fawning which did not halt at the pulpits or even at the schools and was prompt to assume the character of rabid partisanship in a crisis.

All the more subtle influences were exploited in the service of the great corporate Personality. There was a mam-

*Lammot du Pont was chairman and three other du Ponts and a son-in-law were members of the GM board of directors; seven du Ponts and four Morgans were members of the 14-man commanding finance committee of the corporation.

moth company settlement* which in a thousand ways—through classes, clubs, sports leagues, choruses, orchestras, dances, activities for the worker's children, his wife and old folks—multiplied the hidden ties between man and company. The latter's petty beneficence was in fact almost inescapable, as UAW's Wyndham Mortimer once explained in a cogent phrase: "Like the old southern slaveholder, they [GM] will do almost anything for their victims except get off their backs!"

Yet, despite the corporation's vast joy and welfare program, dissatisfaction was rife among its thousands of workers who complained bitterly of the speedup and insecurity and of their relatively low annual wage.† The depression was still bitter to memory and the recovery had been inadequate to erase the bad taste. The city's housing condition was frightful with substandard ramshackle dwellings of the 1910 period renting at exorbitant rates. According to a survey, half or more of the homes in a number of workingclass districts had no private indoor toilet, bath or hot running water. Constantly on the borderline of want, the worker was further forced to bear the burden of his usually prolonged seasonal inactivity through a compulsory layoff loan system, the money being deducted from his earnings upon his return to work. This procedure cut his inadequate earnings by 10 percent or more and incidentally saved the corporation tens of thousands of dollars yearly in relief taxes.

Small wonder, consequently, when Vice-President Wynd-

*Euphemistically named the Industrial Mutual Association (IMA).
†The average annual earnings of auto workers for 1936, after three years of "recovery," were still only $1,294, or less than $25 a week.

ham Mortimer of the United Auto Workers came to Flint, that the corporation set spies on his trail and took other steps to check his activities. Though largely of rural derivation, Flint workingmen had often in the past shown strong union tendencies. Even during the depression, when two or three men were walking the streets for every one with a job, resistance to the continuing wage cuts and speedup had not been unknown. Thus, in early July of 1930, the workers of Fisher Body No. 1 led by a Communist-inspired union had struck, marching into the heart of downtown Flint bearing a banner:

IN 1776 WE FOUGHT FOR LIBERTY;
TODAY WE FIGHT FOR BREAD.

Ten years ago the word "union" had not yet attained respectable status in our vocabulary. A union was quite widely considered a foreign thing which could only be foisted upon American workers by guile or violence. This was very much stressed throughout the great sitdown in Flint since a number of its organizers came from the outside. But this circumstance, a result of the corporation's ruthless treatment of active unionists within its plants, tended to obscure the secret ferment which continued ceaselessly to boil among the rank and file workers and without which no strike could possibly have been successful.

An example of this undercurrent, only by chance brought to light, was the movement developed over a short period in 1935 by a group of workers in the camshaft department of the Flint Chevrolet factory. There was no union involved and yet the workers organized a most effective campaign aimed at reducing the speed of the line. The thing started when the management sought to take advantage of the natural tendency for higher working efficiency in the first half of the day to insist on an equal productivity in the second.*

"We brought it on ourselves," one of the men told his co-workers reproachfully. "We gave them 118 shafts every day and we did it day after day. Then they asked for 124 shafts a day and like a lot of damn fools we ran that many. When they asked for 124 a day we should have run around 120 and told them we couldn't get any more. The company has us right where they want us."

Nevertheless, the men determined to do something about it. At least they might keep the management from further raising the required output beyond the new figure.

"Any man who runs over 124 every night is only cutting his own throat," said Elmer O'Brien.

This was the word that spread swiftly through the department. The men also admonished each other to turn in an equal number of shafts during each of the two shift-halves, to remove the chief speedup lever of the supervision. Leon Witham, the pickup man, watched this detail carefully. When he went around gathering the shafts at the lunch hour he found one worker who had completed 70 shafts. He took only 62 of these and left the remainder, saying: "You have turned in 62 and that's enough."

Other men, if they ran past the prescribed figure, would hide the excess shafts in the rack beneath the machines, covering them with rough stock. Witham checked on the

*All details of this interesting incident are quoted from a confidential account, based on reports of company spies, which the personnel director prepared for the plant manager.

men every hour asking them how many shafts they had completed and passed the information along. In this way they were able to keep a steady and equalized pace and to resist further speedups.

Despite its constant, frenetic cries against "outside agitators" during the strike, General Motors never had so naïve a viewpoint of the natural trend toward mutual self-help among its workers. Every move of the Chevrolet camshaft incident was brought to its attention by an individual who was designated in the company report as "Machine Operator No.8004." This spy not only reported the talk and actions of the men but tried to do what he could to scotch their rudimentary solidarity. He warned them to "knock the production out and forget about trying to set an amount for each man to run," refusing to be lined up himself. On one occasion his opposition almost resulted in a fight between himself and one of the organizers of the anti-speedup action, William Johnson.

Following the crisis, through all of which General Motors had continued to pay dividends out of its enormous reserves,* the early NRA organization impulse found Flint seething with excitement. In the model changeover period of 1933 a strike of skilled tool and die workers led by an independent union originated in Flint and quickly spread to Detroit and other centers. It was not until the new season opened in early 1934 that the American Federation of Labor took the lead in organization efforts with auto workers flocking into its federal locals by the tens of thousands. Demanding the "recognition" supposedly assured

*For the 1927-1937 decade, including the deep depression years, GM's average earnings were $173,000,000 a year. This record established the corporation as the world's greatest money-maker.

them by the NRA code, these workers threatened a general strike of the industry when General Motors and other corporations refused to honor the national law.

Flint was once more the hot spot. Its workers were ready to take things into their own hands and the AFL leaders toiled early and late to prevent any spontaneous action which might lead to a nationwide tie-up. Postponement followed postponement; intervention of the government and even of President Roosevelt could not prevail on the corporation leaders who refused adamantly to as much as meet the representatives of the workers. AFL President William Green sat cooling his heels in General Hugh Johnson's NRA vestibule while the guardian of the Blue Eagle conferred with company officials. "We have simply been waiting like the bride at the church," Green told reporters after the manufacturers had left.

The enraged workers in Flint and other centers prepared resolutely for strike action. Reluctantly did the AFL leaders allow the realism of mass meetings and renewed strike votes and even more immediate arrangements to add to the explosiveness of the situation. The workers were so literal-minded. For example, those at the Flint AC Sparkplug plant wanted to know whether when they walked out at 9 a.m. on the designated day they should ring the time clock!

Union headquarters in all centers were seething with activity. Workers continued to join in increasing thousands. A staggering total of 20,000 in Flint alone designated their allegiance to the AFL during those climactic days. It was plain why they joined—to take part in the proposed strike. But the Federation leaders still hoped passionately for a peaceful way out of the threatening crisis. Finally it arrived, in the form of a wire from President Roosevelt asking for a further postponement and calling for one more "conference."

The auto workers' delegates returned to Washington where with pathetic trust they discussed their problems with the gracious chief executive, telling him in concrete terms of the wretched conditions under which they worked and lived. One spokesman exploded the myth of high wages that clung to the industry, setting the average income for the year past at less than $800.

"Mr. President," he asserted with affectionate intimacy, "you know and we all know that no family can maintain a decent standard of living on wages like these. I feel that I must tell you that the homes of my neighborhood are hovels, rooms without carpets, walls without paper, no modern conveniences and children undernourished...."

Each reporter repeated assurances of his own personal faith in Roosevelt. The attitude of the auto workers toward the President those days bordered on the mystical. One of the delegates presented him with an honorary life membership in his local. And another confidently asked him to issue a "proclamation freeing the workmen in the auto industry of the oppression of their overlords."

But the powerful, self-willed automobile manufacturers would not budge. And the AFL leaders sacrificed one demand after another, finally giving up the key point of recognition also. When this was understood by the workers of Flint, Detroit and other centers they made bonfires of their union books. And company unions, "legalized" by the settlement, flourished as never before.

Only in secondary automobile centers outside of Michigan did the new union movement remain alive during this disastrous season, but almost always as the result of an aggressive strike conducted by the rank and file and usually in defiance of the timorous AFL officialdom. Vigorous locals sprang up in Milwaukee, South Bend, Cleveland, where Wyndham Mortimer led; and Toledo, where George Addes, also of later UAW fame, won his spurs. The only substantial organizations establishing themselves in the center of the industry during two bleak years were independent of the AFL, one of which was founded by R. J. Thomas and Richard Frankensteen; in another, John Anderson was a key figure.

That the auto workers of Michigan remained responsive to organization efforts despite their shattering disappointment with the AFL was accountable to the intolerable conditions that continued to prevail in the plants. The situation was signalized in a remarkable report which a government committee headed by Leon Henderson made in 1935:

Labor unrest [in the automobile industry] exists to a degree higher than warranted by the depression. The unrest flows from insecurity, low annual earnings, inequitable hiring and rehiring methods, espionage, speedup and displacement of workers at an extremely early age.

The Henderson committee showed little of the allergy of official bodies to terms concretely descriptive of the human realities. It did not hesitate to pierce to the heart of the auto worker's lot, summing it all up in the one word—fear. Fear of losing one's job, fear of the foreman, fear of company spies, fear of old age. Workers came to the hearings incognito and after testifying ran from the chamber like hunted criminals to escape the dreaded lens of the news photographer. Some came "trembling" to the committee, asking "for assurances that their testimony would be kept confidential." But "they were determined to tell their story, nevertheless," Henderson reported:

So often did it occur, that it must be here recorded, witnesses, whose economic plight was tragic, need must be interrupted by us to stay the well of tears that surged within them. There were times when the deep feeling of despair transcended our best efforts.

The independent unionizing movement led by Thomas and Frankensteen, for a few months flaring to astonishing strength, had one fatal weakness: the spiritual attachment of many of its members to the pernicious, self-defeating philosophy of Charles E. Coughlin. The prestige of the radio priest, who had not yet proclaimed his preference for Mussolini and Hitler, was fabulous at the time. Many a militant unionist was enmeshed in Coughlin's somber oratory. A number of auto locals endorsed his 16-point program, sponsored the National Union for Social Justice and contributed to the Shrine of the Little Flower's radio fund. Under sway of the priest's weekly talks, auto workers became emotional proponents of the silver standard and looked upon the World Court as the Fountainhead of Evil.

Coughlin was not too enthusiastic over the spectacular rise of the new union and, as it continued to grow unabatedly, he became worried by the competition it might put up for the loyalty of his followers as well as by the danger of its getting out of hand. These fears were substantiated when, on his demand that the union affiliate with his own organization, R. J. Thomas led a successful fight against the tie-up. But the priest continued to offer autocratic directions to the union. Thus, he would emphasize a false dualism of interest between banker and industrialist, urging the workers to form a united front with the latter against the former.

"If you are contemplating a strike," he advised peremptorily, "do not enter it unless it is on a sound economic basis. Demand not only a lessening of the profits of the greedy stockholders but also an increase in the selling price of automobiles."

But when the union struck the Motor Products plant in the autumn, the relationship of the priest's theory to his practice was brought into sharpest focus. Despite repeated requests by the workers, he persistently failed to raise his voice in their support. Police guns and gas, aided by scab-herding of the AFL, drowned the strike in terror and confusion. The new union receded thereafter. But thousands of auto workers had meanwhile been delivered from one more yoke that saddled their untested strength.

Experience of the auto workers with the inept AFL leadership gave birth to a strong movement within the remaining locals for a national organization, democratically controlled and based on industrial unionism. Having been steadily harassed by demands of the 57 varieties of Federation crafts, each for its pound of flesh, the auto unions found no difficulty picking sides when the Committee for Industrial Organization was set up in October 1935 within the AFL by the miners, the clothiers and other industrial-minded unions. In May 1936, when the auto workers were given control of their own union they established formal relations with the CIO and hence soon after came under the AFL suspension of all such affiliates. However, this action of the Federation executive council worried the new leaders of the UAW little. With an aplomb that might have fitted a more modest task they went to work. Yet their job was truly mountainous. In Detroit the total strength of the UAW was slightly more than 1,000 out of a possible 250,000 or more. Even the addition of the Frankensteen-Thomas groups and other independent unions did not substantially affect the magnitude of the task. In Flint there were few more than 100 members out of over 40,000 eligible and a great many of these were stoolpigeons, according to data later released by the so-called LaFollette Committee.* But scores of volunteer organizers, encouraged by an honest and determined leadership, went to work. Board Member Frankensteen took over directorship of the Detroit area for the UAW; Board Member Walter Reuther set to work in the great organizational desert of Detroit's Westside.† A concerted effort led by organizer John Anderson was aimed at the skilled workers during the retooling period. Second Vice-President Ed Hall went into Indiana to organize General Motors feeder plants and First Vice-President Wyndham Mortimer went to Flint to launch his fateful activities.

*Subcommittee of the U. S. Senate Committee on Education and Labor (Chairman, Robert M. LaFollette, Jr.), established by Senate Resolution 266: "A resolution to investigate violations of the right of free speech and assembly and interference with the right of labor to organize and bargain collectively."

†There were fewer than 100 members in the now renowned Westside local when, in September 1936, it was formed of plant units including such giants as Ford, Ternstedt, Cadillac and Kelsey-Hayes.

15

If outside spies did not worry him, those operating inside the union proved Mortimer's most formidable early obstacle.

The work of the union stoolpigeon is varied and that of the spies active in Flint at the time was a model of disruption and synthetically-produced turmoil. General Motors spent half a million dollars a year for industrial spies and a large portion of this money went to Flint. Service for this outlay was richly indicated by the union's minutes which Mortimer studied carefully. They redounded in charges and counter-charges, in demands for audits and resignations, in special elections, investigations and dual movements. At meetings the practice of the stoolpigeons was to bedevil each discussion with parliamentary minutiae, dragging the sessions out interminably to discourage attendance. To hide the inner void a great display of superficial activity was put on with a full panoply of committees incessantly preparing ambitious plans which merely supplied fresh material for further endless discussion and sabotage.

While ostensibly offering to assist Mortimer in his organization work, the Flint stoolpigeons sought merely to be assigned leading tasks in order to assure that they would not be accomplished. Thus when Mortimer asked for a committee to take charge of distributing the international journal at the plant gates the two who immediately responded were "Frenchy" Dubuc and Dick Adlen, the former a Pinkerton stoolpigeon and the latter a Corporations Auxiliary spy. No wonder that Mortimer was soon hearing that the men at the plants weren't receiving the papers. On investigation he discovered that most of the bundles had simply been thrown down an old elevator shaft in the union headquarters building. Others were subsequently picked up in a boxcar on a Pere-Marquette siding. And the remainder had been sold for scrap.

One day Delmar Minzey, the local chairman and a dubious character, at best, "announced" that new members recruited by Mortimer must be "investigated" before being allowed to join. It was an old rule in Flint, he told Mortimer, and each plant unit of the local had its "investigating committee." That at Chevrolet, for example, happened to be headed by stoolpigeon Dick Adlen. At AC Sparkplug, Minzey himself was in charge.

"You see, we got a lot of stoolpigeons here," Minzey explained, "and we got to be extra careful that they don't get into the union."

Mortimer acted mildly skeptical.

"Well, how do you tell a stoolpigeon when you see one?" he asked. "Because I think we've got plenty of them in the union already."

Minzey wasn't very helpful on that score. Another basis for exclusion, he continued, would be for harboring communistic ideas. Mortimer patiently explained that that too was inconsistent with the union's new policy and was besides in violation of the UAW constitution which provided explicitly that there should be no discrimination against workers for their political beliefs.

"The only criterion for membership in our union," he declared, "is that a man works in an auto plant. We're conducting an organizing campaign not a witch-hunt."

Mortimer soon enough realized that if he was to have any success at all in his work he would have to exclude most of the present union members completely from it. This meant setting up an entirely independent apparatus. He took exclusive charge of all membership records, had the combination of the safe changed, opened a separate banking account and discharged the office girl. Those he recruited were told to remain away from union headquarters. In this way he laid the basis for a new, uncontaminated leadership in the plants, a factor that proved crucial at the time of action.

He conducted his campaign almost entirely door-to-door. And he found the attitude toward the union surprisingly good considering past disappointments. Yet the workers were variously pessimistic about its chances of staging a comeback. Two things kept coming up. One was just a general mistrust and fear; the other, contempt for the AFL to which the UAW, though under suspension along with other CIO internationals, was still formally affiliated. Suspicion—the result of years of stoolpigeon activity—had reached the stage of a mania among Flint's workers. The usual remark was that you couldn't trust your best friend; you couldn't even trust your own brother. As for the anti-AFL prejudice the suspension of the CIO unions by the Federation that summer actually proved a boon to the Flint union drive. It helped if you just completely denied any tie-up with the ill-reputed AFL.

On the other hand, the close association of John L. Lewis with the CIO sometimes proved embarrassing when former miners made uncomplimentary references to the autocratic methods of the United Mine Workers head.

As Mortimer's efforts took him frequently into the workers' homes the attitude of their wives became important.

Often they were antagonistic. Some would stomp out of the living room when he introduced himself and would sit brooding in the kitchen. If they remained they might break into the conversation:

"Now my husband ain't going to start monkeying with the union and get himself fired!"

Mortimer would try to bring the women into the discussion. After a while he would ask them to arrange little gatherings for their friends.

"You name the night," he said, "and I'll see to it that you have a gallon of ice cream here and some cookies. Or maybe you'd prefer doughnuts and cider."

These little family parties proved awfully popular. The woman of the house became involved through the chief function that she knew. Readying the house for the party and dishing out the sweets were a more intimate approach to her than any argument. But the discussion itself became much freer and more friendly. The workers seemed to be starved for talk. And Mortimer was well suited to invite their confidence. A man of mature years, quiet, human and patently trustworthy, it was hard to regard his interest as intrusive. And yet if the inevitable question— "What are you getting out of it?"—would arise, his forty years as a worker and his social viewpoint held him in good stead. He would tell of the blind alley that the unions of Cleveland, Toledo and the other places had ended in, due to the competition of the unorganized centers of Michigan.

"So you see our object is really selfish," he would say. "I don't claim to be a new Moses that's going to lead you out of the wilderness because I know that unless you do that yourself it'll never be done. However, I can tell you how we did it at White Motors or Studebaker or Toledo-Chevrolet and that ought to be some help."

The secret of Mortimer's effectiveness as an organizer was his own profound belief in unionism. This faith had come to him by a sort of heredity, his father having been a stanch union man before him, a leader of the Knights of Labor in the all-Welsh community of central Pennsylvania where Wyndham was born. The son had himself gone to work in the mines at the age of twelve. Soon after, the United Mine Workers began to organize in this district and he and his two brothers were among the first to join. And from that day he had—whether as coal miner, railroad brakeman, steel worker, or machinist in the White Motor plant of Cleveland—always either belonged to a union or done his best to build one where it was lacking. "A worker just isn't complete without a union," he would sum up to his listeners. "He simply isn't an entity."

To reach a wider group than was possible through personal contact Mortimer began soon to write a weekly letter which was eventually mailed to some 7,000 workers. There was a homely simplicity about these letters that went straight to the heart of the workers' problems:

What does the future hold for you as a worker in the automobile industry? Does it offer you security? Do you face the future confident and unafraid? When your children come out of school is there a place for them in the present scheme of things? What has become of your aged parents—are they too thrown aside to live as best they may after a lifetime of hard labor? Do you think the boss will be kinder to you than to them? Is the wife you promised to love, honor and cherish able to enjoy the good things of life she is entitled to? Is she not as precious to you as the employer's wife is to him? Are your children not as sweet and lovable as his? Why, as an American, do you permit this intolerable discrimination against you and yours?

Slowly Mortimer's efforts were rewarded. It was a process of breaking the hard ground, of *leavening the dough*, as he himself put it. A few men joined the union and then they got their friends in. It was exciting to see the change that came over them once the barrier was down, how eager they were to spread the message. Mortimer would have to caution them. "You're not going to be any help to the union or yourself if you get fired," he would tell them.

But to the workers the union meant extraordinary release. Momentarily the cruel conditions under which they worked and lived could be forgotten. The outrage that had been choked within them for so long found a vent in this real thing that brought hope and the opportunity to participate toward the accomplishment of actual goals.

Yet for each zealot there were several others in whom every variety of doubt locked the capacity for action. Mortimer recognized the signs. Though expressed in sarcasm or apathy, he knew that such negativism was often hardly a mental thing but rather the product of physical exhaustion, of sheer muscular and nervous collapse.

There was, for example, one family in which the father was no longer on speaking terms with his son, a bitter young chap of eighteen, who had shamed his parent by refusing to sign the application blank Mortimer had offered him in the latter's presence. The boy worked in the press shop at Fisher Body No. 1, a department into which Mortimer was especially eager to get a wedge.

One afternoon, following work, the union leader—after

making the usual circuitous detours to throw off his devoted followers—called on the old man, a Buick employee, to pick up some signed membership cards and an article for the union paper. As he entered the house, he found the son sprawled out on the bare living room floor, unwashed and still in his factory overalls. It was a familiar enough sight for Flint. The young man lay motionless while Mortimer and the father carried out their business.

He was not asleep for now and then he would suck in a deep quivering breath that tautened his frame and which sounded strangely like the sighing of a child after an access of tears. Mortimer noted the skinny arms of the boy—he was too young and light for the heavy press room work. His thin face was bloodless and his biceps muscles kept twitching in a helpless tic.

In the next room the mother was laying the table for supper. The house was tiny. It was one of Flint's typical workers' dwellings: one story; diminutive rooms reeking of mold; the wallpaper discolored from age; the ceiling low, hardly a foot above one's head when one stood up; the whole structure so rickety and fragile that it creaked from end to end at any step. There was no bath and only an outhouse toilet. Yet an heroic attempt had been made to make the place look tidy while a pot of ferns, a couple of headrest doilies and some cheap knickknacks gave a few pathetic decorative touches to it.

The woman brought in a platter of meat and potatoes and set it on the table. Mortimer had to sit down with the family. He knew there was no use trying to refuse their imperious hospitality. "Okay, I'll have a cup of coffee," he said. The boy continued to lie on the living room floor.

The mother went to him, stood over him concernedly. "Son, don't you want to get some supper?"

The boy didn't answer. The father raised his voice self-consciously to Mortimer and filled a plate for him despite his protests. The woman took her place but kept looking over to her son.

Suddenly the latter rose to his feet and clattered through the hallway and kitchen, out to the "washroom" on the back porch. In a moment those at table could hear him retching and vomiting. The woman looked up at her husband but the latter avoided her eyes, continuing to eat with determined concentration.

"He'll be all right now," he said at last. "I used to be the same way." It was as much as to say that this was normal and to be expected.

Mortimer wanted to reply. He felt like saying: "Yes, but what a way to live!" But it sounded preachy to him. You didn't have to preach to these people. When the moment of choice arrived, they would most certainly be on the right side.

The oppression of incredible working conditions, the effects of the implacable speedup, met Mortimer at every hand. During July, a torrid heat wave sent the thermometer boiling over 100 degrees for a week straight. But the assembly lines pounded away mercilessly while the workers fell at their stations like flies. Deaths in the state's auto centers ran into the hundreds within three or four days and the clang of the hospital ambulances was heard incessantly as they dashed to and from the factories in Detroit, Pontiac and Flint.

Shortly after, the layoffs began and the corrupt system

of favoritism prevailing in all plants attained its crudest expression. Mortimer's contacts told him how foremen began dramatizing their power over the life and security of their workers. Shrewdly they would allow themselves to be caught "accidentally" squinting at one man or another to give the impression that they were trying to decide whom to lay off next and whom to keep. One worker from the Chevrolet plant put it down on paper for the organizer:

Men eye each other with distrust and compete in their efforts to maintain their places. Every bad quality of a human being comes out at this time, and every man is deliberately made an enemy of the others by this trickery of the company. A union would shorten hours and increase wages, true enough. But with its guaranty of seniority, it would at one stroke wipe out the distrust and competition between workers which makes life in Plant 7 so miserable.

There was an old chap, Tommy Morris, who worked on the flywheel stamping job at Chevrolet No. 4. The job required the lifting of 300 fifty-pound flywheels twice an hour for the nine-hour day: a total of 135 tons of lifting. Tommy Morris was beginning to find the work exhausting but he kept up with it by a frantic and abnormal exertion. One day, something seemed to give way about Tommy's lower spine. He felt an excruciating pain in the sacro-iliac region that almost doubled him over and he could hardly straighten out again. Frenzied because of his advanced years and the fear of permanent layoff, the old man continued working anyhow though the agony almost caused him to lose consciousness at every lift. Finally, however, the desperate old worker was bent into an inflexible stoop —his condition was noticed and he was forced to quit.

Worry drove him temporarily out of his mind. But production went on as usual in Tommy's department with two young fellows having been hired to fill his place.

As things began to stir the stoolpigeons grew frantic. Mortimer had to change hotels because spies got rooms on both sides of his and then he discovered that the manager of the new place listened in on his telephone conversations. Always there seemed to be hidden eyes following one's least action, eager ears listening for one's most trivial word. It was part of the pervading fear atmosphere of Flint. Those who were active here during this period developed the habits of extreme caution, of turning one's head repeatedly to look behind one, of whispering in public places—practices that would be inadvertently continued for some time after leaving the city.

Meanwhile the spies in the local dropped even the attitude of coöperation. They demanded that Mortimer turn over the names of all new members to them, insisting that they would not be regarded as legitimate unless approved by themselves. And the local treasurer complained that the union wouldn't have a treasury shortly unless expenditures were cut down. Mortimer had to laugh out loud at that one, not only because every cent of the outgo came from international funds but especially because of the unintentional humor in this reference to the local's account as a "treasury." There had been exactly $24.41 in this account when he had arrived. And the debt owing on unpaid rent alone for union headquarters was $700. But what the treasurer was actually after was a report of Mortimer's secret international account which would have revealed the extent of his organizational success.

Next the stoolpigeons tried anonymous threats against Mortimer, letting it be known that unless he gave up his efforts he would be "carried out of town in a pine box." But Mortimer announced that he was too old to scare easy. It appeared that the union enemies were doomed to failure when they received help from an altogether unexpected source.

Homer Martin's meteoric career used to amaze people. A Baptist preacher, with a parish in Leeds, Missouri, an industrial suburb of Kansas City, the new era of Franklin Roosevelt had found in him a fiery, if sometimes irresponsible, champion. As the result of sermons delivered in behalf of the workers in the Leeds Chevrolet-Fisher Body plants, Martin was relieved of his pulpit by the conservative church board. He promptly got a job among the workers he had supported but was fired within a few weeks for union agitation. Thereafter, he took up his organizing work on the outside.

The tedious, day-to-day tasks of the union organizer never sat well with the volatile ex-preacher who for two years made no special mark for leadership. However, his remarkable talent as a speaker finally asserted itself when in 1935 the international union was established. AFL President William Green insisted on appointing the new union's president, arguing that the auto workers were too "inexperienced" (privately the Federation men used more uncomplimentary language) to fill such a post from among their own numbers. Then word of Homer Martin began to get around, about his pulpit background, college training and athletic career. Why these details were considered decisive for the particular job, especially in light of Martin's woeful lack of working experience in the industry, the auto worker representatives did not at the time stop to ask themselves. They heard him on the platform—"Boy, can that baby talk!"—and were convinced that destiny had found its man.

Martin was himself conscious of his lack of pertinent background for his new job yet he did little to make up for it by study. All during his union career his malaprop remarks were the despair of his colleagues. Typical was the case involving a Chrysler worker at a meeting which, as international editor, I happened to attend with him. After the meeting this worker came to the platform, highly pleased with Martin's oratory and wanting to shake his hand. While waiting his turn he engaged in conversation with me, expressing only one doubt about the new union —that word "international." Somehow it had a communistic ring. I wanted Martin to quiet these fears and in introducing the worker to him said leadingly:

"Homer, this brother would like you to explain the meaning of the word 'international.' Does it mean we take workers in from other countries?"

Martin, tall, handsome, well-built, smiled his best Hollywood smile. "Brother," he said with dramatic emphasis, "it means we can take them in from *all over the world!*" And he spread his arms wide.*

Because of his own shortcomings, Homer Martin was peculiarly sensitive to the competition of other leaders of the UAW. Perhaps above all others he feared Wyndham

*Actually the term "international" was originated to cover unions with members in Canada as well as the United States or its territorial possessions.

Mortimer and particularly feared what was antithetical in Mortimer's character to his own. This feeling soon extended to men who were known to be friendly to Mortimer as in the case of Walter Reuther who for six months was forced to do his crucial organizational work at his own personal expense before Martin agreed to put him on the union payroll.

Yet it was Martin's own idea that Mortimer should go to Flint, hopeful that he would break his heart and career assailing that redoubtable GM fortress.* He was greatly surprised when his first lieutenant accepted the assignment with enthusiasm. This feeling changed to trepidation when Mortimer's reports began to indicate the possibility of success. Martin grew frantic as these reports became increasingly optimistic. At this juncture the assistance of the stoolpigeons of Flint was offered him and the UAW president accepted it, lending a sympathetic ear to the complaints of these men that Mortimer was building a "Red Empire" in Flint and that he shunned the "coöperation" of all "honest" union members.

Martin, who had secretly taken up with a group of expelled Communist elements† who later became very prominent in his factional, union-splitting activities, also designated several of their number to spy on Mortimer while professing agreement with his policies. Because of their background, these individuals were considered experts in scenting out supposed "Red" procedures.

A Flint delegation finally appeared at Martin's instiga-

*Such statements, which might sound like casual assumptions, are always based on fact, often involving the subsequent testimony of those immediately concerned or of individuals close to them.

†Followers of Jay Lovestone.

tion before a secret session of the UAW general officers and presented their charges. Martin had conveniently failed to notify Mortimer of the meeting and when the UAW president promptly expressed his determination to remove his first vice-president from Flint, the other officers hit the ceiling.

"Now, wait a minute!" Ed Hall boomed.

Close to fifty and with Mortimer one of the few older men in the union leadership, the second vice-president had spent his life working in the Milwaukee auto plants and never lost the average worker's hatred for subterfuge. He was stout, gravel-voiced and boisterous and carried the colorful language of the factory into his union work. But it was more than mere words that made him a formidable antagonist.

"How many members did *you* bring in last week?" Hall grilled the Flint delegation, asking each of them the same question in turn. The entire committee could not account for a single man. Whereupon Hall let out a stream of characteristic invective and even mild-mannered George Addes was roused to utter his most extravagant cussword.

"Son-of-a-pup!" he exclaimed. "You've got a lot of guts coming here and asking us to move Mort out when he's actually doing a job up there while you guys are just sitting around making things hard for him!"

The secretary-treasurer, a former metal polisher, was twenty years younger than Hall and much different in other respects. He was quiet, almost shy, and assumed the dignity of his position as though born to it. His flair for union detail amazed everyone and he swiftly established his department as the smoothest-working in the international. This freed him from exclusive concern with office duties and allowed him to keep pace with the union's outside activities. Addes was to play a significant part in formulating the general strategy throughout the great sitdown.

The officers were of a mind to overrule Martin on the question and sent the Flint delegation packing. Mortimer arrived in Detroit and the battle that took place almost came to physical blows. Martin's secretary, when called in, inadvertently revealed damaging details of the former's plot against Mortimer. The UAW president suddenly broke down and wept.

"You must think I planned the whole thing, Mort."

"Well, Homer, if you were in my shoes, what would *you* think?" Mortimer replied.

Despite this outcome and the continued support of Addes and Hall, Mortimer decided to leave Flint—"to keep peace in the family."

"I can't fight General Motors and the president of the UAW as well," he told them. "All I ask is that we send a good, dependable man up to take my place. I won't stand for the Flint auto workers being sold down the river because of this."

"How about Bob Travis?" Addes proposed.

"Okay," Mortimer agreed. Travis was the man he himself had wanted to recommend. Martin had had other plans but he was so delighted to get Mortimer out of Flint that he fell in eagerly with the suggestion.

And the first serious rift in the UAW leadership, forerunner of the intense factional struggle that later began to plague the union, was for the time being patched up.

2

First Sitdown — A Dress Rehearsal

EVERYBODY liked Bob Travis, a personable young organizer from Toledo. Though still on the bright side of thirty, he had close to a decade of automobile production experience behind him. Strictly the extrovert, the depression had given Travis a serious turn, sobering his get-rich-quick dreams which had prior to 1929 inspired so many American youths. During the violent Toledo-Autolite strike in 1934, though employed at the Chevrolet factory, Travis had gone down to the other plant to have a look. When he arrived a fight was on with the militia who had driven the pickets from the factory gates. Darting from behind telephone poles, the pickets whipped stones down the hill. The troops retreated and the pickets ran forward. Travis knew little about the issues of the strike but suddenly the resentment of blasted hopes, of five years of misery and inadequacy, rose up in him and he began running with the strikers toward the factory.

He was a union man thereafter, becoming active in the organization of his own plant and in the strike there the following year, when the first unequivocal victory against a General Motors unit by a union was recorded. It was a fitting background for his new assignment and the young organizer soon proved that the general good opinion that was had of him was not misplaced. But the Flint stool-pigeons were given a rude awakening when on Travis' arrival he immediately let it be known that Mortimer's entire organization plan—including the methods of secrecy to which they so strenuously objected—would be retained intact.

It was in fact one of Mortimer's secret groups, that at Fisher Body No. 1, which soon after blew the lid off, setting the pace for the exciting events that followed. Such a development would have been next to impossible if Mortimer had confided in leaders of the old union clique in the plant. One of these, Harold Hubbard, had confessed membership in the infamous Black Legion that summer and had implicated several others. Testifying under the Hollywood cognomen of "Mr. X" before a one-man secret grand jury, Hubbard had told some hair-raising tales and incidentally named as Black Legionnaires these Fisher One union men: Plez Carpenter, ex-president; Bert Harris, former trustee; and Jerry Aldred, who was more recently a company union representative.*

The secret union nucleus at Fisher One was of an entirely different character. It included an exceptional group of men whose presence in the plant at the particular time was one of those lucky "breaks" which helped bring the union's stupendous task into the realm of possibility. At the center of the group were three friends—Bud Simons,

*The two last-named men later became identified with Homer Martin's anti-CIO activities and eventually split off with him to help form the fragmentary UAW-AFL.

Walter Moore and Joe Devitt—political left-wingers who would undoubtedly have been barred from membership as "Reds" if President Minzey and the old union clique had been allowed to "investigate" them. Fortunately for the union's future this did not occur.

Like the majority of Flint workers the three friends stemmed from the land, all being sons of small farmers. Simons came from southern Indiana, Devitt from South Dakota and Moore from Montcalm County, Michigan. Later events threw Simons into greatest prominence but the other men always remained a strong support to their excitable friend, Moore particularly often pulling him out of hot water. Part of Simons' difficulty with people was his pride. It was a trait that had early manifested itself and finally launched him on a wayward career.

It was when he was a junior in high school and his class was planning a banquet. Each student was required to pay five dollars for the honor of attending. Young Simons knew the condition of his family's exchequer. His father had found it necessary years back to get a job on the railroad to supplement the skimpy earnings of his 40-acre farm. What if you didn't have the five bucks to pay? Bud asked the teacher bluntly. The lady flushed with anger at the impertinent question.

"You've always been a disgrace to this school, Berdine!" she exclaimed.

Young Simons couldn't find it in him to return to class after that. However, when he left school and home as a result of this little incident it was to discover that the outside world was hardly more considerate of the underprivileged.

He obtained a job working on a farm for the bountiful sum of three dollars a week. And yet one day his employer told him that he would have to reduce his pay to $2.50. Simons didn't say a word. He merely slid down from the hay wagon and walked off. That was his first strike—strictly a one-man affair. But somewhat later he ran into something of a more professional nature along that line. Once while working in a plant at Des Moines some of the men suddenly began running through the shop shouting: "Strike! Strike!" Before he knew it Simons was walking out with the rest of the workers. The strike, he discovered, had been called by the IWW. It didn't last long but the incident aroused Simons' curiosity about unions and the like and thereafter he always looked for newspaper items about the "Wobblies."

Simons travelled all over the country and worked at all kinds of jobs. He even spent a short period in the coffee fields of Mexico. Then he went back home and married the girl he had left there. Hazel was the daughter of a coal miner, a strong union man. In fact, a thorough-going union consciousness was about all the dowry she brought the young itinerant. She was a mere kid when she married Simons, being only sixteen, but she had already worked for a year in a ball bearing factory after completing her tenth year in high. The Simonses proved to be a well-matched couple. Both strongly endowed with the independent spirit, the motto of their early married life ran: *"When you fly out of the nest you go where it is best."*

The Simonses settled in South Bend when Bud got a job at the Studebaker plant where he worked fairly steadily from 1925 to 1928. During the slack months Hazel would take their first son and return to her folks while Bud scoured all of northern Indiana for work. The family finally ended up in Grand Rapids where Bud obtained employment at Hayes Body. It was here that his friendship with Walt Moore and Joe Devitt began. At the time the country was at the brink of the depression but everybody thought that prosperity would last forever. The couple bought a five-room bungalow and put every spare dime into it. The family was growing apace and the acre lot gave the kids plenty of room to play. There were also peach trees and flowers on the property. It was all very lovely. Then the pit opened. Bud lost his job and they had to give up the home and go on relief. The welfare gave them a dilapidated shack to live in. One day a gas leak started a fire and the old hut burnt down to the ground with all the family belongings in it. The neighbors, the welfare and the Red Cross gave the destitute folks a few things with which to start housekeeping again but it was a dismal beginning.

In 1934, when things began picking up again, the three friends brought their families to Flint. Here they joined the AFL and when that organization's ill-fated spurt ended, they became active among the relief workers during the long seasonal layoffs. While thus engaged they often received anonymous threats but never thought of the Black Legion until the big exposé occurred in 1936. Then suddenly everybody realized the source of those mysterious goings-on that had been fearfully whispered about for months in a number of the automobile centers of Michigan, the tales of night-rides, whippings and worse.

The anti-union character of the Black Legion was somewhat obscured by its fundamentally much broader and often more spectacular program which extended all the way from chastising unfaithful husbands to plans for annihilating all Jews, Catholics and Negroes or even national insurrection. Its activities in the unions, moreover, were of such a nature as to make it difficult frequently to distinguish the Black Klansman from the common stoolpigeon. In Detroit, for example, the Legion conducted a "courtesy" service which made available to personnel departments the names of "Communists"—actually leading union members—working in the respective plants.

The accidental baring of a Legion trigger man who then implicated a number of his co-workers in an endless assortment of murders and other crimes blew the dam loose in the spring of 1936. Dozens of municipal and county officials were involved before the investigation was suppressed. The whole immediate result was that a few of the small fry took the rap. But the great public outcry that accompanied the astounding, if incomplete, revelations drove many fascist-minded individuals in the rockribbed Republican state scurrying for cover, making possible the election of liberal Frank Murphy as governor the following November. And for the UAW it proved another significant factor in a long chain of favorable circumstances that opened the way to its brilliant successes of that memorable first year.

Connections between the Black Legion and certain automobile manufacturers in Detroit and Pontiac were indicated before the burrowing for facts was effectually halted. That General Motors had not ignored the union-quelling designs of the Black Klan was revealed in a crucial detail thrown up at hearings conducted early in 1939 by the La Follette Committee. The hearings went into the operations of a so-called "Special Conference Committee" which GM had formed in 1936 in company with representatives of Standard Oil, U. S. Steel, Westinghouse, du Pont and other major corporations, for the purpose of formulating a program for fighting the rising threat of the CIO.

In May 1936, the investigation disclosed, William B. Foster, advisory director of the service department of E. I. du Pont de Nemours & Co., requested E. S. Cowdrick, director of the "Special Conference Committee," to obtain for him information concerning "The Sentinels of the Republic," the notorious pro-fascist organization. Cowdrick canvassed his constituents. Among those replying was Harry W. Anderson, GM vice-president in charge of personnel. A copy of Anderson's letter was published in the files of the LaFollette Committee:

Dear Mr. Cowdrick: With reference to your letter of June 1, regarding the Sentinels of the Republic, I have never heard of the organization. Maybe you could use a little Black Legion down in your country. It might help.

At Fisher One in Flint, the center of the city's Black Legion activity, evidence of a tieup with the supervisorial staff was not lacking. Marie Schlacter, an employee who was later active in the union, made a startling discovery one Saturday afternoon. She was in the plant late and on her way out she ran upon Nellie Compton, a forelady, and a group of foremen busily engaged in sewing and trying on black hoods and robes. Marie tried to run off unobserved but she was seen by the forelady. This woman—whose standard reply to stated grievances of her female workers was: "They'd like to have ice water in hell but they don't get it!"—half frightened the poor girl to death and gave her a long layoff as a warning to keep silence over what she had seen, an admonition which Marie observed until the union came.

Bud Simons and his friends greeted the opening of the union drive in Flint with a burst of activity. Working fervently though carefully, they laid the union foundations in their own departments and moved slowly outward. Included with the early converts were Harry Van Nocker, Jay Green, Clayton Carpenter, Vic Van Etten and others, all later active in the strike. Among the women Marie Schlacter and Pat Wiseman were promptly involved. First steps were confined to such things as pasting stickers on the bodies. Foremen tried to spot these and scraped them off but that in itself was a dramatic admission of the union's existence in the plant. And often one of the stickers with a leading slogan on it would go down the entire line, silently regarded by the workers.

The first break in the shop occurred among a group of non-union tinners. The management by a typical speedup procedure that was very much used that season had withdrawn one man from a team of five and told the four remaining men that they would have to turn out the same amount of work. Bud Simons got wind of this and began working quietly on the tinners. Finally they hung up their torches and went into the office to protest. Simons arranged to see them outside at lunch time. He took a flyer.

"Now look," he told them, "I don't know any of you guys from Adam but I think I can trust you. I'm the union organizer in this shop."

38

Immediately they wanted to know more about it.

"Well, to be frank with you we aren't so strong yet but we're building right along," Simons went on. "Our idea is to work on grievances just like yours. You know as well as I do that things aren't what they ought to be in this plant. The bosses do anything they please and we've got to take it. That's all going to change when the union comes in here."

The four fellows agreed to come to a meeting at Simons' home the next day. He had most of the other union men from the shop there to make an impression. At a second meeting the original four boys brought eleven others with them. Bob Travis thought the number was getting too big to be safe, so he called the next meeting in some fellow's basement. To disarm any spies that might have got in, the place was kept dark except for a single candle which added more romance than visibility. The men really went for the atmosphere of mystery.

Travis talked to them at length about their problems, about the speedup and the other conditions. Then he told them in concrete detail what had been done in his plant, Toledo-Chevrolet, and how. The men were deeply interested, especially in the story of the 1935 strike in Travis' plant. The "atmosphere" undoubtedly helped also. They listened as though hypnotized.

Shortly before and especially after the national elections union sentiment flamed up throughout the whole plant like fire before a wind. Roosevelt carried the state and city overwhelmingly and the auto workers who had resisted their bosses' attempts to pin sunflowers* on their overalls

*Insignia of Alf Landon of Kansas, President Roosevelt's opponent in 1936.

really began to feel their oats. General Motors and the other auto manufacturers had left themselves no out on the question of choice, a favorite maneuver during the campaign having been to accompany the announcement of the first Social Security pay deductions with a mournful note saying in substance: "It hurts us more than it does you."

"Manifestly," somberly intoned Lincoln Scafe, plant manager at Cleveland Fisher Body, "the heavy tax enacted on the company must have an adverse influence on what it might otherwise do in employee benefits of one form or another." And so the blame for continuing lower wages also was shouldered onto Roosevelt, whose vast responsibility evidently halted only at the soaring profits of the corporation, which were due to exceed $200,000,000 that year.

The lineup of forces in the campaign in Republican Michigan was unmistakable. Anti-progressive, anti-union elements were solidly behind the GOP candidate who on his visit to Detroit had a long and much-publicized afternoon with Henry Ford. Roosevelt, on the other hand, signalized his arrival in the motor capital by a trip through Hamtramck, the all-worker municipality within the borders of Detroit, then proceeding past wildly-cheering multitudes into the center of the city where he delivered one of the great militant speeches of his career.

Labor-baiting William Randolph Hearst and the arch-reactionary Liberty League, among whose leading donors stood the great auto barons, were also enthused proponents of Alf Landon while the Coughlin-sponsored candidacy of William Lemke was recognized for its palpable aim of drawing votes from the President—a crude intrigue which completed the auto workers' disillusionment with the radio priest. Nor could they help remembering revelations that spring of Black Legion identification with the Republican administrations in a number of important Michigan cities as well as the report that the sinister organization had counted no fewer than two hundred delegates at a convention of the Republican Party in Wayne (Detroit) County.

But the conditions under which the auto workers gave support to the Democratic ticket revealed a distinct and healthy departure from the past. The union had undoubtedly made the difference, together with what had been learned in the fiasco of NRA days. At that time, guileless and untried, the auto workers had waited for others (chiefly Roosevelt) to do what had to be done by themselves. The result was dismal failure and retrogression. But the sin of dependency had been largely cast off. And the sputtering action in a score of plants—of which the great sitdown was the culmination—that was touched off by the November elections gave testimony that the precious trait of self-reliance had been learned, that the stupendous electoral victory of Roosevelt was, for the auto workers, more than a mandate. It was the trumpet call to their own resurgence.

And Flint was no exception. There were seven stoppages at Fisher One in one week. Some were occasioned by the company's wage "adjustments," others by the speedup. Everywhere in the plant the crews had been reduced while the speed of the line was maintained as before.

In some cases group and piece rates were cut as high as 40 percent. Moreover, the foremen refused to show the men their time sheets since they were indulging in the practice of juggling production figures, deducting from one group to make up a "deficiency" in another. On one day the trim shop quit an hour early—just walked off their jobs as a protest. "Speedup and no money," they growled in disgust. In another department the workers struck for an extra man. The plant manager slowed their line from 50 to 45 jobs. Another group got a 20 percent restoration on a wage cut.

It was largely a spontaneous movement onto which the union had not yet securely attached itself. I happened to be in Flint at the time getting out the first issue of the *Flint Auto Worker*. Travis and I visited Bud Simons at 2 in the morning following his shift. Simons was almost weeping with eagerness to get going.

"Honest to God, Bob," he said, "you've got to let me pull a strike before one pops somewhere that we won't be able to control!"

"You think they're as ready as that?" Travis asked, trying to conceal his own excitement.

"Ready?" Simons cried, his voice pitched high with impatience. "They're like a pregnant woman in her tenth month!"

While they were talking a sudden glare from a car's headlights struck the drawn window blinds. The lights flashed on and off several times. Travis went up to the window and pulled one of the blinds slightly aside and peeked out.

"That's the Black Legion," Simons explained matter-of-factly. "They think there's a meeting here tonight."

I realized suddenly the reason for the ancient deer rifle

that stood in a corner of the room which for a moment I had regarded as slightly exhibitionistic.

"Sometimes they get out and come closer to the house and start whining," Simons continued. "They make the most godawful noises. I swear I'm going to take a potshot at them one of these nights."

"They may be company stooges," Travis said, "just trying to scare you off. The management knows what you're up to. For the time being that's your best protection. They figure they'll be able to keep tab on whatever happens to be stirring by watching you."

While driving back to the hotel Travis picked a worker up who was waiting for a bus near the Fisher plant. He was a young chap but looked all done in.

"Working overtime?" Travis asked him.

"Yup."

"How is it?"

"Terrible."

"Speedup, huh?"

"That's it."

"I never worked in a plant," I said, "what's it like?"

"I don't know," the young man searched for words, "you just get to feeling so poohed out you don't know if you're sick or exhausted or just plain disgusted."

"What you fellows need is a union," Travis said as the chap got out at his little hut near the Buick plant at the other end of town.

"You said it!" he replied with deep conviction.

The little encounter gave me the lead for my paper. The Speedup. Everyone I spoke to in Flint had much the same story to tell. One didn't hear nearly as much complaint about wages. It was always the speedup, the horrible speedup. Flint workers had a peculiar grey, jaundiced color which long rest after the exhausting day's work did not erase. Even on Sunday when they wore their best and walked in the open one felt that one was in a city of tuberculars. It was the speedup that organized Flint, as it was the one element in the life of all the workers that found a common basis of resentment. Wives who feared the intervention of the union vented their execration on the speedup which left their husbands trembling and exhausted after their work and narrowed the life of the family to the mere acts of physical continuance.

One of our young members from Buick, Gene Richards, described the tortures of the speedup system for the *Atlantic Monthly*. He told how the men would suddenly set up a frightful aboriginal howling which would spread throughout the entire plant before letting up—as the feeling of physical and spiritual outrage sought an outlet. Frequent swearing also brought a measure of relief as would other excesses, such as the discussion of sexual activities in minutest detail. And the laughter of the workers leaving the plant at the end of each day—"sincere but weary"—was the sign of their resumption of the dignity of human beings. But Richards could not remember where he had parked his car—"the morning was so long ago."

Yet the speedup was an industrial unreality, a purely subjective thing to the General Motors plant managers whose schedules were adapted perforce to the figures of the corporation's central planning department through a system of inter-plant competition. Human endurance simply could not be brought into these calculations except as some vague ceiling which might yet be stretched outward upon necessity. This refusal to recognize reality found expression in incredible rationalizations, a typical example of which is given by the following quotation from *Saf-T Fax*, the company paper of the Delco-Remy (GM) plant of Anderson, Indiana:

If when the day ends, your work leaves you totally exhausted, something is wrong. Perhaps you have had insufficient rest the night before, or it may be eye-strain. It may be a bad working posture that can be corrected by a slight change in the way you carry yourself. It may be that you don't select a nourishing lunch. Whatever it is, find the cause and try to remove it.

Travis realized that Simons was right, the time was getting ripe. The moment was approaching when the spark would have to be set to the tinder. He laid the groundwork for action by setting up a system of key men in each of the departments where the union had members—about forty in all. These men he instructed on how to act in case of surprise developments, how they were to come together at a given spot in the plant, reach a quick decision and take appropriate steps. He gave each of the men a "volunteer organizer's" card with the international seal and the signature of the officers on it.

"Boys," he said solemnly, "the whole future of the Flint workers depends on you. In fact I can truthfully say that the fate of the auto workers throughout the country rests on your shoulders. I know you're not going to let them down. Whatever happens stick together. Don't leave the shop under any circumstances. And remember—*nobody gets fired.*"

The first union-led sitdown took place three days later. Though use of the sitdown is now illegal, it was not so at the time and in fact its "rediscovery" in 1936 entered greatly into the auto union's plans and strategies and eventual triumphs. The tactic had already been tried successfully in a strike at the Bendix, South Bend, plant, which had established the basic advantages of the technic for the auto industry and especially for employer-ridden cities, like those of Michigan, where official violence had almost invariably accompanied strike action.

The widespread use of the sitdown strike during the winter of 1936-1937 opened a violent discussion concerning its legality. Opponents castigated it as a revolutionary act, as unlawful seizure of property, a step precedent to direct expropriation. The workers countered this claim with the argument of their property interest in their jobs, which the U. S. Industrial Commission of 1915 had found a "concept worthy of attention." Meanwhile, they were painfully concerned at all times to disprove any socially radical motives by meticulously caring for the property which they temporarily occupied and by repeatedly offering to leave it if the company involved pledged not to operate during negotiations. The auto union sought to raise the question of legality to a moral issue by arguing that the sitdown was meant merely to balance the extraordinary advantage in bargaining enjoyed by the employers, a situation which the Wagner Labor Act had sought to correct. However, this law had been persistently contravened by the industrialists, forcing the union to other action. Congress eventually adopted a measure outlawing the sitdown. But the act was unnecessary. For once the asserted aim of the new strike technic—the institution of sincere bargaining relations in the great mass production industries—had been attained, its use was largely abandoned.

Three days after Travis' meeting with the union's volunteer organizers, a situation such as he had anticipated arose. The day before the supervision had removed one worker from a group of "bow-men."* Two of the men were brothers, typical farm boys from mid-state, named Perkins. Another was a little Italian-American, full of guts. None of them were in the union but they had been reading about the Bendix strike so they simply stopped working. The foreman and the superintendent came over and begged them to get back to work, they were holding up the line. A long discussion took place over the increased production required due to the removal of the one man.

"The day crew is doing it, why can't you?" the superintendent asked. It was perhaps the billionth time this argument had been repeated in an industrial plant.

They sat gabbing that way till there was a job-gap of twenty jobs. And then the workers got a little disturbed to see it. It made them nervous to be responsible for such disorder on the production line. Finally they agreed to go back to work, to continue putting out for that night. But tomorrow they'd talk to the day shift fellows about it! Before they got back to work, however, the whole department had become interested in the argument. At shift-end the excitement overflowed. Everybody talked about the sitdown of the "bow-men." So that's what a sitdown was! Nothing to it, really! The men felt awfully pleased about it somehow.

*The "bow" is a supporting angle-iron that is welded across the top of the roof structure of the auto body.

47

When the two Perkins boys came to work the next evening they found their cards missing from the rack. In their places were tell-tale notices: "Report to the employment office." They went and sure enough there was their money waiting for them. But the union had anticipated this contingency. The committee had talked the situation over with Travis the night before, after the end of the shift. It was decided that this would be an excellent opportunity to come out into the open. If anyone was victimized over the little stoppage the entire "body-in-white"* department must be closed down.

When the two brothers showed Simons and the other committee members their red cards the latter ran up to the department and spread the word:

"The Perkins boys were fired! Nobody starts working!"

The whistle blew. Every man in the department stood at his station, a deep, significant tenseness in him. The foreman pushed the button and the skeleton bodies, already partly assembled when they got to this point, began to rumble forward. But no one lifted a hand. All eyes were turned to Simons who stood out in the aisle by himself.

The bosses ran about like mad.

"Whatsamatter? Whatsamatter? Get to work!" they shouted.

But the men acted as though they never heard them. One or two of them couldn't stand the tension. Habit was deep in them and it was like physical agony for them to see the bodies pass untouched. They grabbed their tools and chased after them. "Rat! Rat!" the men growled without moving and the others came to their senses.

*Where the main welding and soldering work of the assembly process takes place.

48

The superintendent stopped by the "bow-men."

"You're to blame for this!" he snarled.

"So what if we are?" little Joe Urban, the Italian, cried, overflowing with pride. "You ain't running your line, are you?"

That was altogether too much. The superintendent grabbed Joe and started for the office with him. The two went down along the entire line, while the men stood rigid as though awaiting the word of command. It was like that because they were organized but their organization only went that far and no further. What now?

Simons, a torch-solderer, was almost at the end of the line. He too was momentarily held in vise by the superintendent's overt act of authority. The latter had dragged Joe Urban past him when he finally found presence of mind to call out:

"Hey, Teefee, where you going?"

It was spoken in just an ordinary conversational tone and the other was taken so aback he answered the really impertinent question,

"I'm taking him to the office to have a little talk with him." Then suddenly he realized and got mad. "Say, I think I'll take you along too!"

That was his mistake.

"No you won't!" Simons said calmly.

"Oh yes I will!" and he took hold of his shirt.

Simons yanked himself loose.

And suddenly at this simple act of insurgence Teefee realized his danger. He seemed to become acutely conscious of the long line of silent men and felt the threat of their potential strength. They had been transformed into something he had never known before and over which he no longer had any command. He let loose of Simons and started off again with Joe Urban, hastening his pace. Simons yelled:

"Come on, fellows, don't let them fire little Joe!"

About a dozen boys shot out of the line and started after Teefee. The superintendent dropped Joe like a hot poker and deer-footed it for the door. The men returned to their places and all stood waiting. Now what? The next move was the company's. The moment tingled with expectancy.

Teefee returned shortly, accompanied by Bill Lynch, the assistant plant manager. Lynch was a friendly sort of person and was liked by the men. He went straight to Simons.

"I hear we've got trouble here," he said in a chatty way. "What are we going to do about it?"

"I think we'll get a committee together and go in and see Parker," Simons replied.

Lynch agreed. So Simons began picking the solid men out as had been prearranged. The foreman tried to smuggle in a couple of company-minded individuals, so Simons chose a group of no less than eighteen to make sure that the scrappers would outnumber the others. Walt Moore went with him but Joe Devitt remained behind to see that the bosses didn't try any monkeyshines. The others headed for the office where Evan Parker, the plant manager, greeted them as smooth as silk.

"You can smoke if you want to, boys," he said as he bid them to take the available chairs. "Well, what seems to be the trouble here? We ought to be able to settle this thing."

"Mr. Parker, it's the speedup the boys are complaining

about," Simons said, taking the lead. "It's absolutely beyond human endurance. And now we've organized ourselves into a union. It's the union you're talking to right now, Mr. Parker."

"Why that's perfectly all right, boys," Parker said affably. "Whatever a man does outside the plant is his own business."

The men were almost bowled over by this manner. They had never known Parker as anything but a tough cold tomato with an army sergeant's style. He was clearly trying to play to the weaker boys on the committee and began asking them leading questions. Simons or Walt Moore would try to break in and answer for them.

"Now I didn't ask you," Parker would say, "you can talk when it's your turn!" In this way he sought to split the committee up into so many individuals. Simons realized he had to put an end to that quickly.

"We might as well quit talking right now, Mr. Parker," he said, putting on a tough act. "Those men have got to go back and that's all there is to it!"

"That's what you say," Parker snapped back.

"No, that's what the men say. You can go out and see for yourself. Nobody is going to work until that happens."

Parker knew that was true. Joe Devitt and several other good men who had been left behind were seeing to that. The plant manager seemed to soften again. All right, he said, he'd agree to take the two men back if he found their attitude was okay.

"Who's to judge that?" Simons asked.

"I will, of course!"

"Uh-uh!" Simons smiled and shook his head.

The thing bogged down again. Finally Parker said the Perkins brothers could return unconditionally on Monday. This was Friday night and they'd already gone home so there was no point holding up thousands of men until they could be found and brought back. To make this arrangement final he agreed that the workers in the department would get paid for the time lost in the stoppage. But Simons held fast to the original demand. Who knew what might happen till Monday? The Perkins fellows would have to be back on the line that night or the entire incident might turn out a flop.

"They go back tonight," he insisted.

Parker was fit to be tied. What was this? Never before in his life had he seen anything like it!

"Those boys have left!" he shouted. "It might take hours to get them back. Are you going to keep the lines tied up all that time?"

"We'll see what the men say," Simons replied, realizing that a little rank and file backing would not be out of the way. The committee rose and started back for the shop.

As they entered a zealous foreman preceded them, hollering: "Everybody back to work!" The men dashed for their places.

Simons jumped onto a bench.

"Wait a minute!" he shouted. The men crowded around him. He waited till they were all there and then told them in full detail of the discussion in the office. Courage visibly mounted into the men's faces as they heard of the unwavering manner in which their committee had acted in the dread presence itself.

"What are we going to do, fellows," Simons asked, "take

the company's word and go back to work or wait till the Perkins boys are right there at their jobs?"

"Bring them back first!" Walt Moore and Joe Devitt began yelling and the whole crowd took up the cry.

Simons seized the psychological moment to make it official.

"As many's in favor of bringing the Perkins boys back before we go to work, say Aye!" There was a roar in answer. "Opposed, Nay!" Only a few timid voices sounded —those of the company men and the foremen who had been circulating among the workers trying to influence them to go back to work. Simons turned to them.

"There you are," he said.

One of the foremen had taken out pencil and paper and after the vote he went around recording names. "You want to go to work?" he asked each of the men. Finally he came to one chap who stuck his chin out and said loudly: "Emphatically not!" which made the rest of the boys laugh and settled the issue.

Mr. Parker got the news and decided to terminate the matter as swiftly as possible. He contacted the police and asked them to bring the Perkins boys in. One was at home but the other had gone out with his girl. The police shortwaved his license number to all scout cars. The local radio station cut into its program several times to announce that the brothers were wanted back at the plant. Such fame would probably never again come to these humble workers. By chance the second boy caught the announcement over the radio in his car and came to the plant all bewildered. When told what had happened the unappreciative chap refused to go to work until he had driven his girl home and changed his clothes! And a thousand men waited another half hour while the meticulous fellow was getting out of his Sunday duds.

When the two brothers came back into the shop at last, accompanied by the committee, the workers let out a deafening cheer that could be heard in the most distant reaches of the quarter-mile-long plant. There had never been anything quite like this happen in Flint before. The workers didn't have to be told to know the immense significance of their victory. Simons called the Perkins boys up on the impromptu platform. They were too shy to even stammer their thanks.

"You glad to get back?" Simons coached them.

"You bet!"

"Who did it for you?"

"You boys did."

Simons then gave a little talk though carefully refraining from mentioning the union.

"Fellows," he said amid a sudden silence, "you've seen what you can get by sticking together. All I want you to do is remember that. Now let's get to work."

The men got the double meaning of his last words and from that moment the barriers were down at Fisher Body No. 1. Organization shot out from "body-in-white" to the other departments—into paint, trim, assembly, press-and-metal; even the girls in "cut-and-sew" began heeding the call.

And more. The news of the Fisher One sitdown spread through the entire city. The Fisher One boys began bringing friends into the union from Fisher Two, Buick and Chevrolet. The response at Fisher Two was especially good. In one afternoon alone Travis signed up fifty workers in a beer hall near that plant. Shortly after, he rented a store across Fisher One from a union sympathizer and the first open meeting was announced. There was an overflow crowd. Mortimer came back for the meeting, accompanied by Adolph Germer of the CIO. Dick Frankensteen came up also to bring the greetings of the Detroit workers and to tell of equally exciting things occurring in the motor capitol, the Midland Steel sitdown strike having just begun. As the workers stood outside the open door of the jammed hall, craning their necks for a look, while the applause crashed out repeatedly, there was no one any longer that could doubt that the union had come to Fisher One.

And in fact the management itself was seemingly prepared to admit this fact. It began to bargain regularly with the union committee. Numerous grievances were corrected, wage raises and speed reductions won. At the same time the stewards system was being perfected inside the plant and union buttons began to sprout like dandelions everywhere.

3

Rooting Out the Fifth Column

STRATEGICALLY it was not improper for the Fisher One plant to take the lead in the union drive. The body plants were especially vulnerable to organization attempts as the size and cumbersomeness of the car bodies made storing of them in anticipation of strikes almost impossible. But there was danger in any one of the city's plants forging too far ahead of the others. For if trouble came the workers at that plant might be isolated from the rest, divorced from their help and sympathy.

The great concentration of auto workers in Flint was not at the body plants but at Chevrolet and Buick which employed 14,000 and 16,000 men respectively—the largest of all General Motors' 60-odd factories. Actually the word "factory" hardly applied to these mammoth units as each was an aggregation of plants, a sort of factory-city. Certainly no union could be regarded as permanently established in Flint until Chevrolet and Buick were "cracked." But these plants continued to be rather slow in getting under way though conditions, particularly at Chevrolet, were easily as bad as at the pace-making Fisher One plant.

Plant No. 4 of the great Chevrolet combine was one of nine factories, a unit destined to play a most significant role in the final phases of the strike. Here the engines were made for all Chevrolets produced in the country—over a million a year. Four thousand men on each of two shifts were employed in this plant which actually consisted of one enormous room several stories high where the workers in common sight of all toiled at a wonderful *continuum* of machines and conveyors.

But conditions in this plant were hardly consistent with its admirable product. Located in a deep hollow beside the Flint River the factory was always damp and muggy. In the summer the heat was insufferable and in the winter the cold air would penetrate through the cracked walls. Hot water registers roasted the men that worked near them while those at a distance half froze to death. With no ventilation to speak of, often a fog of smoke, of grinding dust or exhaust from the motor test department pervaded the plant. The toilets were kept in filthy condition and at low temperature to discourage workers from overstaying their relief time. Relief men were scarce. Obsolete and wornout machinery and insufficient room increased the strain and danger of work. Accidents were frequent as a result while improper attention given cuts and injuries caused numerous infections and other complications. The plant was nicknamed the "Hell-Hole" by the workers as a tribute to its notoriously bad working conditions which the *Flint Auto Worker* never tired flaying.

Arnold Lenz, plant manager of Chevrolet, responded with gusto to the opening of the union drive in his plant, firing a number of men for "solicitation on company premises" and other familiar excuses. He wasn't going to be caught with his pants down like Evan Parker at Fisher One. No sir! Lenz was a disciplinarian of the old German school, cold, ruthless and efficient. In 1936 when admiration for Adolph Hitler's methods was being openly expressed by many American industrialists Arnold Lenz did not have to disguise his penchant that way. He would even give the works council (company union) representatives the benefit of this preference and regale them with stories of his early anti-union background.

In Germany, he would narrate, he had worked as a young man in a foundry which was solidly organized. The other men asked him to join the union but he refused. From pleas and arguments they turned to threats—but still he remained firm. And one day as though by accident one of his fellow workers poured some molten metal on his legs. He was badly burned—but after recovering and returning to work, did he join the union? Certainly not!

Bob Travis asked Lenz for a conference to discuss the discharges of Chevrolet union members and was surprised to get a prompt reply setting the day and hour. Lenz wasn't one to miss out on a fight, verbal, or otherwise, as later events proved. He would take pleasure in telling the young snip off. And that was exactly what he did. Sure he fired those men, he admitted to Travis, but he had had good cause. There were rules in the plant and they had to be obeyed. No worker was going to get it into his head that he could make new rules just because he belonged to some union. General Motors ran its own plants and had no intention of turning them over to anybody else. So what would Mr. Travis do about it, please?

"Nothing—just now," the union man replied between clenched teeth. "But don't think, Mr. Lenz, that you're going to be able to get away with this forever, defying the Wagner Act and discriminating against our members. You're going to have to deal with us one of these days and you can be sure we'll remember all these things."

"Young man," the German said, smiling condescendingly, "you seem to have a lot of piss and vinegar in your blood. But I guess I can handle you all right." And then to prove his constancy of purpose he told the union organizer his favorite story of the German plant he had worked in and the molten metal which had failed to change his mind.

Travis knew that there was danger of blighting intimidation to the union drive at Chevrolet as a result of the discharges. There was, moreover, the possibility that if such steps of the company continued the workers in the affected departments might be provoked to wildcat strike action which because of the weakness of the union could have very harmful results. For Arnold Lenz would know how to step down with Prussianesque brutality to crush such demonstrations.

Nevertheless, despite the union's warnings against premature action, several spontaneous stoppages occurred in the Chevrolet factory. One such strike took place toward the middle of December in Plant No. 6 when Joseph Meoak who had recently been selected as a union shop steward was ordered transferred to another job. Such transfers were usually antecedent to a discharge—they isolated the offender from his supporting rank and file and served as a final warning to him to quickly mend his ways.

However, Meoak's buddies wouldn't permit his transfer. They quit work and folded their arms, letting it be known that they would not resume until they had been assured that Meoak would remain with them. And then Lenz' disciplined supervision got into action. The plant police came running from all parts of the factory. They seized Meoak and gave him the bum's rush out of the plant. As the other workers still refused to go back to their jobs the assistant plant manager began making discharge slips out for every last one of them. And the plant police stood at hand ready to carry out his orders. The inexperienced men looked at each other in indecision; then hanging their heads and swallowing hard they went back to their machines.

An anomalous sequel to this occurrence indicated the thoroughness of Lenz' anti-union methods. The company union representative in the afflicted department was called into the front office after the matter was settled, put on the pan and fired. This individual was not a member of the union, was not even sympathetic to it but the finger of guilt was pointed at him for having "done nothing to prevent the sitdown!" He appealed personally to Lenz to have his punishment countermanded but Lenz told him that the Detroit office of the corporation was opposed to reinstating discharged men since it had been its experience that such individuals normally became sources of labor trouble!

Bob Travis was hard put to it for means to counteract these anti-union moves. He called on the international for more help and several additional organizers were sent up. First to arrive was Roy Reuther, a brother of Walter. He was soon joined by Bill Cody and Ralph Dale of the

Milwaukee Seaman Body plant, by John Bartee and Les Towner from Studebaker in South Bend and others.

The three Reuther brothers are a rather unique phenomenon in American labor history. Trained to the work of labor organization by a father who was for years head of the AFL central labor council in Wheeling, West Virginia, they told how, when they were youngsters, old Reuther would set them on a soapbox in a park on Sundays and make them practice public speaking. This early background, supplemented by other schooling, stood them in good stead when they became active in the UAW.

The energetic nature of the brothers seemed to multiply their numbers even beyond the exceptional three. It was very confusing to newspaper reporters and others who often mixed their names up, giving a sense of their being in all places at all times. A humorous example of this occurred during the Kelsey-Hayes strike in Detroit when Walter was in the company office with Dick Frankensteen, discussing terms for a possible settlement. Suddenly a sound truck outside began blasting away, giving the union negotiators "support." It was Vic Reuther. Then someone slapped a *Flint Auto Worker* on the plant manager's desk. It had a picture of brother Roy on the front page.

"My God!" the executive exclaimed, looking at Walter. "How many more of you are there?"

Travis set Roy Reuther and Bill Cody to work on the Chevrolet unit. Then something plopped into his hands which he figured he could use as a temporary diversion: the exposure of two stoolpigeons in the Chevrolet plant. It was merely a question of stalling for time as the deadline for the national General Motors strike was rapidly approaching. Then of course all such individual troubles as the Chevrolet firings would be swept up in the greater current.

Since auto workers were everywhere aware that there were spies amongst them it did not discourage them to learn that one of these had been unearthed. On the contrary it gave them an increased feeling of confidence in their union, a sense of cleanliness and added strength. But in the case of the Chevrolet stoolpigeons there was the extra feature that the spies were caught just at the time when the workers were experiencing some examples of their insidious handiwork. Bob Travis calculated that the exposures would furnish at least a partial compensation for the discharges and thus act to counter-balance the fear and discouragement that might otherwise have seized the Chevrolet workers.

The names of the two spies had been made available to the union by agents of the LaFollette Committee. The work of these men that summer and autumn, particularly of Charles Kramer, Harold Cranefield and Benjamin Allen, proved an enormous boon to the union campaign. With the help of many union members, dozens of spies were turned up in the various plants of Michigan during the crucial period before the great auto strikes. The most spectacular case was that of James Howe in Detroit, who was chief steward and leading union recruiter inside the Midland Steel factory. On the eve of the strike at that plant, in November 1936, Secretary-Treasurer George Addes found Howe's name listed in a footnote on the galley sheets of a LaFollette report. He turned the information over to John Anderson, organizer of the Midland local, who isolated the spy and led these workers to the first significant victory of the eventful season in Michigan.

The Chevrolet spies, Dick Adlen and John Stott, were both leaders of the old union group which had sabotaged Mortimer's early organization efforts. Another Chevrolet stoolpigeon, a Pinkerton man, "Frenchy" Dubuc, had been caught by a fluke but he was being saved by the LaFollette Committee for other purposes. The Committee's investigators had impounded records of the Pinkerton office in Detroit and among them had found a report involving the Flint local, a copy of which was turned over to Travis. Travis didn't at the moment realize that it was Dubuc who had written the report, though he half suspected that the wily French-Canadian was a spy. The clue appeared in the following sentence of the report:

I try [sic] to locate Dubuc but I was told that he was out late last night and left early this morning for Birch Run to move his mother back to Flint and therefore could not talk to him.

Actually this was Dubuc talking about himself in the third person, a familiar camouflage which the Pinks had taught him to use. After reading the tell-tale sentence to him, Travis looked at him with a queer sort of intensity.

"Frenchy," he asked incisively, "did your wife ever tell you who it was who visited your home that day?"

Though his heart was in panic, Dubuc's beefy, dark face was stolid. His lids contracted until mere slits of his eyes showed through them. He shook his head.

"Okay," Travis went on, "I want you to be sure to ask her when you get home. Let me know right away. It's important, you understand?"

Dubuc felt that he was surely trapped. He couldn't exactly understand what Travis' game was but he concluded fantastically that the union leader must be working for the UAW inside the detective agency in a sort of counter-espionage capacity. He made up his mind in a desperate moment. He hurried over to the Dresden Hotel and threw himself on the mercy of Charles Kramer, the LaFollette investigator.

This did not end Dubuc's career as a spy, however. For several months he acted as a sort of special agent for the LaFollette men and when the Pinkerton agency was brought before the committee at its February 1937 hearings in Washington, Dubuc's testimony proved more than embarrassing to its officials who, desirous of sparing their most bountiful client, General Motors, had testified that the corporation had months before severed all connections with them.

A very simple expedient had been successful in smoking out the two men whom the union was now planning to expose. Knowing that the reports of operatives to their district offices in Detroit were being filed by telephone since the investigation had started, the LaFollette agents decided to look into this matter. They learned that the receiving numbers of all long-distance calls were recorded on the phone bills and accordingly went down to the phone company offices in Flint and subpenaed the duplicate bills of a number of suspected individuals. In the cases of both Adlen and Stott they found a number of the Corporations Auxiliary in Detroit listed several times. Pinkerton had been more shrewd, forbidding its spies the use of their home phones to make reports.

Of the two Chevrolet spies, Dick Adlen was an old type

disrupter but John Stott was a different kind of stoolpigeon, posing as a stanch progressive and hobnobbing with the "Reds." Among Stott's many union functions was the chairmanship of the welfare committee and as he went around visiting sick members he would pour a little subtle poison into their ears about the union organizers.

Bob Travis planned to make the most dramatic use possible of the union's tipoff against Stott and Adlen. The occasion he chose was the first open meeting of the Chevrolet division of the local, which was scheduled for the day after Christmas. Much hard work had been done in preparing for this meeting and the turnout proved gratifying considering the recent firings, about 150 chancing exposure and discrimination by attending. The spirit was excellent. One of Joseph Meoak's buddies tore the cover off, speaking out his own name and everything.

"I don't give a damn what happens to me!" he cried. "I'm working in Plant 6 and I tell you it's terrible. If we don't organize, what's going to happen to us?"

In reply to the wild charges of communism which were already being hurled at the CIO, another worker said: "I don't think there are any Communists here, at least I don't know of any. But every man knows the conditions we're working under in Chevrolet."

One member proposed strike action immediately and suggested that each steward be given a whistle and the next discharge or transfer that took place the steward in question would blow his whistle and the whole plant would go down.

"Let's not run away with ourselves, fellows," Bob Travis said. "We could close the plant down today" (he was exaggerating a little) "but the time isn't right yet. If General Motors wants a fight, don't worry, they're going to get it. But we'll pick the time and place and not them. In the first place we wanted you boys to get your Christmas bonus. That's going to come in handy now, in case.... You see where the Atlanta and Kansas City boys didn't get theirs.* All we're asking is that you fellows hold your ranks and complete the work of organizing your plant. We'll see to it that the men who got fired won't be in want."

The men could see the logic of this position. One old chap delivered a little sermon about the Good Samaritan and "the man in the ditch." The union organizers he likened to the former and the workers to the latter. His listeners—most of them church-goers—nodded at what seemed to them an apposite figure. Another member expanded further in the spirit of the holiday season, saying:

"We've got to work together for a better civilization. We've got to have unity and brotherhood. What was yesterday? Why is Christ so great? Because He was for brotherhood. I tell you, if we're working against the things this union stands for we're tearing down the Temple of God."

Ed Geiger of the Buick unit then spoke, pledging support to the Chevrolet group. Though one of the old AFL crowd, Geiger had dissociated himself from their disruptive tactics and become a tireless union advocate at his factory. He was followed by Walt Moore of Fisher One who told of the exciting things going on in that plant. Moore's story of how the Fisher One committee had contacted the plant manager and demanded that he intervene with Arnold Lenz to get the fired Chevrolet workers rein-

*They had gone on strike before the holiday.

66

stated brought a great cheer from the audience. And indeed, such solidarity among the men of the different factories was a thrilling new thing in Flint.

At the end of the meeting Bob Travis took the platform and instructed the guard to lock the door.

"Brother Reuther, will you come forward?" he said solemnly.

Roy Reuther stepped up on the platform and began to lay the foundations for the exposure of the spies with careful oratory. He was a "great mouthpiece," as the workers put it admiringly. Only John Stott was present. Dick Adlen had evidently gotten wind of our plan and had stayed away from the meeting, a very unusual procedure for him. Reuther deferred the actual naming of Stott until he had given him a chance to confess voluntarily. In this way he hoped to put other suspects on the spot whom Travis and I meanwhile kept under microscopic scrutiny.

"I'm going to count ten," he said at last, "and if that brother, pardon me, if that rat doesn't step forward I'll put the finger on him...."

The hall had been in wild confusion after the announcement of the presence of the stoolpigeon. But as Reuther began his slow counting the men became dead silent and watched his arm as though it were tolling the count of doom. After the "ten" there was a heavy pause and the men turned in their seats and looked about. But Stott sat motionless, revealing only a slight tenseness that would not have been visible to one who did not suspect him.

"Well, we gave him his chance," Reuther said with finality. "We wanted to be fair to him. We wanted to see if he had one speck of manhood left. Now I'm going to tell you who this rat is. But first let me tell you what he did. He was in a position to get the lists of all union members to the company. Oh yes! This rat had an important union post. He had the trust of his fellow workers. He was even very militant in his talk but that was only to conceal his treachery. It's this man that we've got to thank for the discharges that Arnold Lenz has put across. It's this man who is taking the bread out of the mouths of the fired men's children just so Corporations Auxiliary will pay him his lousy sixty dollars a month! I don't blame him for not wanting to come out here and admit his guilt. But I'll give him one more chance. Stand up! We know who you are. Tell your fellow workers: 'Yes, I admit it. I sold you out. I betrayed you for thirty filthy pieces of silver!...'"

The men couldn't take any more. They rose to their feet, shouting:

"Who is he? What's his name?"

Reuther tried to calm them.

"We don't want any physical violence, brothers," he cried. "That's not the union way."

"Name him!" they yelled.

Finally Reuther got free from the compulsion of his oratory. He pointed his finger dramatically and said:

"John Stott, stand up!"

Stott rose and walked briskly to the front and standing squarely beneath Reuther said to him:

"You're a goddam liar!"

Several men rushed toward him and one of them got hold of his coat but we tore him loose. Travis shouted a warning and the men slowly resumed their seats. Stott cleared his throat meanwhile and repeated:

"It's a lie. Prove it."

One was forced to admire the brazen calmness of the fellow. He could have no idea of the method that had been used to trap him and consequently was merely stalling, hoping that the union would not be able to produce any real evidence. Unfortunately we could not tell about the subpenaed phone bills since the LaFollette men had not yet exhausted that procedure and had asked that it be kept secret. Travis stepped forward and said:

"Never mind! We've got the proof all right, you dirty rat! And so has the United States Senate in Washington. You'll be answerable to them on January 11 when you'll be made to testify in the Capitol chained to a G-man—you and your buddies, Arnold Lenz and Floyd Corcoran."*

I had arranged for a photographer who came in and took several front and side views of Stott—"just like a convict" —who characteristically crossed his eyes when the bulb flashed, seeking an incongruous disguise. A committee then conducted him home to impound his records (he was secretary of the Chevrolet unit) as well as to guard him from possible attack by some irate unionist. The meeting ended in a blaze of enthusiasm.

*Chevrolet personnel director.

4

Strategy and the Rank and File

THE Chevrolet discharges were quite possibly part of a complex company scheme to precipitate premature strikes in plants where the union was weak or in strategically unimportant ones where the halting of production could not harm the corporation but could do much damage to the union. What course Arnold Lenz would take, for instance, in case of an attempted strike was illustrated in the little stoppage over Joseph Meoak's transfer.

More obvious was the evidence of company provocation in two other early strikes, at Atlanta and Kansas City. The danger of these walkouts—despite the fact that the locals in both cases were strong and the strikes remained firm—lay in the possibility of their embroiling the entire situation before the union was ready for the struggle on a national scale. If they had been allowed to force the issue, they might easily have resulted in swift calamity.

Fred Pieper, the leader of the Atlanta local, was responsible for bringing on the first strike in this plant early in November. As the result of a twenty percent cut in rates for the new model there was much dissatisfaction prevalent here. Nevertheless, overall strategy called for great restraint in the situation since the union was still very weak at the time in the important centers and the Atlanta plant was hardly significant enough to take the lead in the expected struggle. Yet Pieper was suddenly burning with impatience. One day he instructed his members to wear their union buttons to work—heretofore stringently prohibited by the corporation—and if there was any trouble from the management the men were simply to walk out of the plant.

"If every General Motors plant in the country isn't struck within a week and twenty-four hours," Pieper blustered, "you can take me out and horsewhip me!"

A small group of the union members took his harebrained advice and wore their buttons to work on the designated morning. The management was obviously all set for the event. Some company union representatives from the trim department complained that the union buttons constituted intimidation against non-union men and the plant manager accordingly gave the offenders their walking papers. The other workers in the department shut the line down in protest and the strike was on.

It was given a prompt and full authorization by President Homer Martin who wired all General Motors locals to "stand by for notification from the international union concerning action to be taken." The order, evidently presaging a call for a national strike, came as a thunderbolt to the other general officers who had not been consulted in the matter at all. Then inflammatory releases began to emanate out of Atlanta which quoted long-distance phone assurances from Martin to the local strike committee that the date for the national strike was to be definitely set. And all this time Martin was nowhere to be found.

All of a sudden calls came pouring into the office from newspapers all over the country. What were the details about this "deadline" Martin had announced for the following Monday? Frank Winn, the union's publicity director, insisted that the reports were false but several papers maintained that they had obtained the dope from Martin himself. Then several GM locals in different cities contacted the office and announced that Martin had ordered them to get ready to strike "on Monday." What the hell was this all about? they demanded angrily. Why hadn't they been notified sooner?

All of us at Detroit headquarters ran around bordering on insanity. No one knew where to reach Martin. Several times we got a tip but each time he had left the place indicated and gone on somewhere else. Finally Vice-President Ed Hall caught up with him in Kansas City.

"You dumb son-of-a-bitch!" he roared into the phone. "You get your ass back here by tonight or that'll be the last trip you'll ever take!"

Martin returned, very much chastened but denying everything. No one accused him of anything but over-zealousness at the time, perhaps of a desire to pull off a big *coup* and put his name in the headlines. He was always thinking in terms of political advantage and his pitiful lack of understanding of the union's broader problems developed a tendency in others to excuse the most irresponsible actions in him. He was after all the president of the union—it was best to keep his eccentricities quiet. He had already become notorious among newspapermen, however, for his wild statements. After getting hurt several times by running into subsequent denials, they always made sure to check first with Frank Winn or other officers of the union before using anything that Martin would give them.

When the international executive board was called into session soon after, the business about the national General Motors strike started all over again as Martin lined up his supporters to vote for the strike to begin immediately. The maneuver was facilitated by the fact that the general officers, except for the chairman, had no vote on the board. For two days the sane element battled to prevent this disastrous step. When a decision could no longer be held off, Dick Frankensteen was rushed out of the Midland Steel negotiations and down to union headquarters to cast his ballot. Martin himself characteristically walked out of the meeting before the vote was taken, relinquishing his gavel to Ed Hall. Frankensteen's ballot made the count six-to-six and Hall threw the deciding vote for further delay.

"Well, that's that!" he said in his unequivocating manner. "Next order of business."

Other dangerous trends, fraught with meaning for the future, showed themselves at this board session. The Martin adherents aired the idea at secret caucuses of pulling the UAW away from the CIO and making peace with the AFL. Since in the event of a strike the only support to be expected would be from the industrial unions, such a proposal was nothing short of treachery. The opposing group on the board, led by Walter Reuther and Dick Frankensteen, got wind of this plot and smoked it out by moving a reaffirmation of loyalty to the CIO which the others could not openly combat. And Adolph Germer, a CIO representative who had been assigned to the UAW but had been more and more elbowed out of participation in the union's planning by Martin, was "cordially invited" to attend all important sessions thereafter.

The constructive board group proposed a careful procedure in the crisis, the basis of which was to stall for time until the unions in Flint and Cleveland were ready to take the lead. George Addes pointed out by reference to per capita payments that Delmond Garst, despite all his shouting, could show only 25 members in his St. Louis plant whereas factories in Detroit, Pontiac and Lansing did not have as many as that. Bob Travis was called down from Flint and reported that he needed another month at least before he could get things really moving.

Meanwhile arrangements were made to contact General Motors relative to the Atlanta situation. However, the corporation denied authority in the matter, insisting that it would have to be handled by the Atlanta plant management on the spot. Yet when Ed Hall flew down to the Georgia city, the company officials there shifted the buck right back again. The union had to satisfy itself for the time with issuing angry fulminations while taking steps to intensify its General Motors efforts everywhere.

Several weeks later the Kansas City strike occurred when a leading unionist, Roy Davis, was fired for leaping over the conveyor line to go to the toilet. This act though a technical violation of a company rule was habitual in the plant and was in fact actuated—the toilet being 300 yards distant by the long way—by another company rule limiting relief time to three minutes and by a third forbidding running inside the plant! The union committee asked that the discriminatory action against Davis be rescinded but as the management refused the strike was called.*

By this time it was clear that the corporation intended picking time and place for its battle with the union as well as to set the issues on as trivial a basis as possible. The UAW leaders, perceiving this danger, went to Washington and after conferring with CIO chiefs, John Lewis and Philip Murray, issued the formal announcement of the union's intention to seek collective bargaining privileges with General Motors.

"We are hoping there will be no necessity for a strike," Lewis said. "That will be up to General Motors."

The corporation's response came promptly enough, although indirectly. On December 18th in opening the new Indianapolis plant William Knudsen took occasion to make slanting references to the union's preparatory moves. Announcing that the corporation had no desire "to discourage organization of any sort as long as it is done on legal and constructive lines," he added: "I think collective bargaining is here to stay but I do think collective bargaining

*Here, too, action might have been delayed to fit into the broader union program. But this was Homer Martin's own local and he was certainly not the one to give preference to strategic over immediate considerations. Hearings before the LaFollette Committee later substantiated fully the impression of the time that company provocation was planfully at work here when Edward S. Clark, leading Pinkerton official, inadvertently let drop the damaging admission of having received an order from General Motors to get evidence on Davis concerning violation of the safety rule! Clark then got the wind up, refusing further details, and had a row with Senator LaFollette for prompting another Pinkerton witness who was called on the same matter. The Senator could not have known the peculiar significance of the case or he might have forced the Pinkerton men to startling revelations.

75

ought to take place before a shutdown rather than after." It sounded almost like an invitation or so the union was pleased to interpret it. CIO Director John Brophy was immediately dispatched to Detroit where he helped to draw up the UAW's official request for a conference which was then hastened to the corporation.

No one expected anything positive to come out of such a conference. To assume that the Wall Street group that controlled General Motors would make any basic change in its attitude toward collective bargaining without a major struggle would have been like losing consciousness of all the bitter facts of history and of the auto workers' experience over more than three years. It never even occurred to anyone that we were not in for a good fight.

Nevertheless the parley was asked for and for the following reasons. First, to seize the initiative in the anticipated struggle. Next, in order that the union might meet an ultimate authority and learn from it exactly where it stood. And finally, to offer to put into operation the law of the land sanctioning collective bargaining which the big industrialists had thus far flagrantly disregarded. This statutory basis of the UAW's request was shrewdly emphasized as it put the union in the position of championing the New Deal against its law-defying enemies and thus identified its cause with the huge electoral mandate of November.

And indeed the union's case was impressive enough. Not only had the corporation circumvented and violated the provisions of the Wagner Act but in a number of instances where the union had sought redress before the National Labor Relations Board, General Motors had gone into the courts and obtained orders restraining that body from functioning. Thus the case of the auto workers entered the greater struggle against judicial usurpation which at this point in the nation's history had again assumed a leading position in the dialectics of progress versus reaction.*

The union's letter asking for the meeting listed the auto workers' chief grievances and proposed that these be the basis of discussion in the projected conference; viz—speedup, discrimination, job insecurity and the "abuses of the present piece-work system of pay." In anticipation of the corporation's traditional response concerning autonomy of each individual plant in the settlement of such grievances reference was made to the union's repeated rebuffs at the hands of plant managers (as for instance most recently in Atlanta). Yet at the secret conference that soon followed between union and corporation this was the entire substance of the latter's position. The corporation had no authority, Knudsen said, all questions involved must be settled locally.

The union replied that this position was counter to all the known facts of corporate policy and control, let alone common sense. Every local committee that had bargained with General Motors managements had had the repeated experience of seeing its demands or the management's concessions checked, amended or overruled by the central

*Was it mere chance that shortly after the General Motors strike and the great unionizing impulse that it released, the Supreme Court should have finally reached its long-delayed judgment on the constitutionality of the Wagner Labor Act? This decision, reversing a trend of adverse votes on New Deal legislation, might have averted the GM strike if it had come sooner though it is hard to think that even a judicial order would have restrained the autocratic corporation without the sanction of the union behind it.

office. However, the corporation head held to his position. The meeting ended exactly at the point where it had begun.

The union then requested a second, "general," conference which would take up only issues that were "national in scope" and which would hence be "determined by the policy of the General Motors Corp." Minor questions could be left to the local managements and plant committees. A sort of implied ultimatum tagged the new request:

> We feel that it is quite evident that you have either misunderstood the purpose and intent of our first letter, or you have deliberately evaded the issues involved. But let me [Martin] insist that whether there is a misunderstanding or evasion the issues are real and should be met without further delay or equivocation on your part.

And there the official sparring halted and the initiative was taken over by the rank and file.

The union's strategy held that the chief burden of the strike must be borne by Flint's Fisher One and by Cleveland-Fisher with the former taking the lead. These two plants were the major body manufacturing units of the corporation—"mother plants," according to GM terminology—being responsible for the fabrication of the greater portion of Chevrolet and other body parts which were then shipped in so-called "knock-down" form to the assembly plants throughout the country. All the stampings for the national Chevy production were turned out in Cleveland. Fisher One on the other hand manufactured irreplaceable parts for Buick, Oldsmobile, Pontiac and Cadillac. In particular the great dies and enormous presses needed to stamp out the mammoth simplified units of the new "turret top" bodies were concentrated in the Cleveland and Flint body plants. Possibly three-fourths or more of the corporation's production were consequently dependent on these two plants; an interlocking arrangement that was not unusual, moreover, in the highly specialized auto industry and especially among the leading corporations. There were perhaps a dozen other plants equally crucial to General Motors but in only the two designated was the union strong enough to halt production.

The entire blueprint of the union's organizing schedule depended upon this type of careful selection for its forces were terribly limited and the power it opposed so commanding. It was a similar process of weighing and considering that had dictated the choice of General Motors for the great test. The bristling defenses of Ford had thus far stood proof against the UAW's organizing attacks. Union advances at Chrysler, on the other hand, had forced the best relations with any of the "Big Three"*—a fact that was sedulously publicized by us, with intended detriment to General Motors, of course, and which came back to plague us when the Chrysler Corporation was the chief antagonist. Accordingly, General Motors presented the most logical option for the union's first major challenge.

The strategy of "divide and conquer," though unavoidable, was highly precarious, however, in that it depended for success upon the silent collaboration of the other two major companies besides the one which the union had engaged. But if the great corporations refused to be isolated in this manner and joined for concerted action against the union—and attempts to that end were made even at this

---

*General Motors, Chrysler and Ford accounted for four out of every five cars produced.

early stage—the most ingenious plans might not prevail. Fortunately, experience that season was not favorable to a united front of the auto manufacturers. For company strategists could not accept success of the UAW as a permanent thing and meanwhile each group evidently thought that the union, weak as it was, could be indirectly manipulated to the detriment of its competitors.

In the Midland Steel strike in November, for example, Ford had sought to stiffen the attitude of the management against the union, aiming at prolonging the strike to the disadvantage of Chrysler, the chief purchaser of Midland products. When the Kelsey-Hayes sitdown occurred the following month the squeeze play was reversed and the River Rouge insurgent—with his supply of wheels and brakes tied up—was now on the sweating end. Ford production suffered an almost complete eclipse before that company was able to force a settlement, pretty much along union lines, including an epoch-making seventy-five cent guaranteed minimum wage for all Kelsey workers. Union negotiators Walter Reuther and Dick Frankensteen in giving an account later of the Kelsey discussions referred figuratively to the one vacant chair in the conference room —this was where the despotic spirit of the elder Ford had sat.

A problem of an entirely different nature was that raised by the threatened glass shortage resulting from a nationwide flat glass workers' strike which had now been in progress for some weeks. The union strategists feared that if General Motors' supply of glass would run out before the auto strike was called and if the auto workers were thus forced out of employment due to a distant, extraneous cause the effect might be to antagonize them against the union. In any case, it would be exceedingly unlikely that they could be brought out again that season, even though in their own behalf. The union checked carefully with its members in the GM stockrooms at the different plants and conferred with the glass union heads who estimated the stocks in the corporation's plants as not exceeding a one-month supply.

This would indicate that the date of action could not be too long put off. For the purpose of further strengthening the union's position two months would not be too much time but the dangers of so indefinite a postponement were too great. The deadline was tentatively set for immediately following the holidays. The fact that Frank Murphy, whom auto workers' votes had elected over his Republican opponent, would then be in the gubernatorial seat at Lansing, did not go unnoticed by UAW strategists. The only question remaining was this—if Fisher One led off, could Cleveland-Fisher be depended upon to follow suit? If not, the corporation would be able to continue rolling its great money-maker, Chevrolet, off the lines in its widely scattered assembly plants and the strike would lose half its effectiveness.

There had been some recent union successes at the Cleveland factory, some rumblings and stirrings, but nothing to compare with the exciting developments at Fisher One. Cleveland-Fisher had taken the lead in 1934, organizationally speaking, and again in 1935. As a result the workers in this plant had suffered heavy reprisals, two thousand of them having been laid off, victims of the corporation's policy of decentralizing away from the union "hot spots."

It was felt, consequently, that this plant would not be in a position to risk taking the rap again, not at least until some other group would start off. However, even the best of union generals are apt to underestimate at times the temper of their rank and file. This certainly was true of the UAW leaders in respect to the Cleveland plant.

These workers took strategy into their own hands when on December 28th a surprise sitdown in one department swiftly spread through the entire factory. The local union men hardly knew what to do with the strike. They, too, like almost everyone else had expected Flint to take the lead. Louis Spisak, the president of the Cleveland group, was frantic. Finally he got in touch with Mortimer by phone. Mortimer and I were with Bob Travis in his hotel room in Flint when the call came in. Mortimer put his hand over the phone. He was wearing a smile as big as his face.

"Cleveland-Fisher is on strike," he said. "They're sitting in."

Travis and I began to dance around in the tiny room. Then suddenly we got anxious and hung over the phone.

"Tell him not to settle till you get there! Tell him to sit tight and agree to nothing!"

Mortimer nodded his head.

"Okay, Louie, I'll come right down. Don't worry, everything will be all right. You'll get all the support you need. If they try to put the heat on tell them you have no authority to act, tell them the situation has been taken over by the national office. You can tell them I'm coming down to take charge."

Mortimer heaved a big sigh after hanging up.

"Boy, there's a weak sister! It looks like the mayor and all the city fathers are after him to settle the strike. The company knows what's up all right. When Atlanta or Kansas City strikes, you can't even see the plant manager, but Cleveland—that's different!"

We packed Mortimer into his car.

"Don't forget, Mort," we repeated excitedly. "*No settlement without a national agreement!*"

"Okay, okay," Mortimer said imperturbably as he drove off.

And thus was born the strike's first slogan.

The new season had opened in Cleveland as everywhere else in General Motors plants with widespread wage-slashing, coming in the form of piecework "adjustments." These grievances broke out into a number of short stoppages during the month of December. Finally after much delay a conference between the management and the union committee was scheduled for the morning of December 28th. But at the last moment the company postponed the meeting until the afternoon. It seemed so slight a thing—a matter of a few hours. But to the workers who carried the memory of years of accumulated grievances the seemingly insignificant final delay had the effect of a last straw. A grievance of the strongly organized quarter panel department was to have come under discussion. When these fellows heard of the postponement they said: "To hell with this stalling," and yanked the power off. The steel stock, metal assembly and trim departments followed suit in rapid succession and in a few minutes the whole plant was dead.

The strike started at 1 p. m. and in less than two hours Mayor Harold Burton (now U. S. Supreme Court Justice) had arranged a conference between the management and Spisak at the city hall. Plant manager Lincoln Scafe, displaying an immense eagerness to reach a quick settlement, announced hopefully that the strike was merely "local in origin and will be settled in conference between employees and management." How well he knew what the score was! Spisak weakly agreed to the mayor's plan calling for evacuation of the plant by the sitdowners, resumption of work and immediate opening of negotiations. But when he conveyed the proposal to Paul Miley, steward of the quarter panel department and now the sitdown leader, the latter flatly turned it down. Miley called the heads of other departments into conference. Charley Beckman, "Beany" De Vito, Jerry Strauss and the rest all backed him up.

"Tell Louie to get in touch with Mortimer," they said. "Tell him to call Mort here to take things over."

When Mortimer arrived on the "Mercury" from Detroit, the reporters were waiting for him at the station. They told him of Mayor Burton's plan and asked him for comment.

"That's out!" he replied firmly. "The union will demand that the Cleveland dispute be settled on a national basis."

And that put the seal on the thing. Following a huge and enthusiastic outdoors meeting at the plant with the sitdowners occupying places at the windows, the local executive board went into session with Mortimer and approved his recommendation that the local dispute be merged in the national situation.

Lincoln Scafe complained pathetically that the union committee had "run out" on him.* Mayor Burton said he was "still willing to meet" whenever the union desired to do so. But ace mediator James Dewey who had been hastily called into Cleveland left soon after, describing the situation as hopelessly deadlocked.

The die was cast. The union had taken the bull by the horns. The great and long-awaited General Motors strike was finally under way. Now it was up to Fisher One in Flint to follow through.

*Soon after the big strike ended, Scafe was fired by General Motors, reportedly for having provoked the situation which played so patly into the union's plans.

85

5

"Protect Your Jobs!"

Wɪᴛʜ the Cleveland plant struck the union's strategy problems were very much simplified. A further lucky "break," coming this time also on a silver platter from the company, facilitated the confirmation of the second main feature of the strike plan. On the evening of December 30th, or only two days following the beginning of the Cleveland strike, Bob Travis received a phone call from "Chink" Ananich, one of the Fisher One boys. "Chink" was working on the swing shift and had slipped out of the plant to make his important announcement.

"They're moving dies out, Bob!" he said excitedly.

"You sure?"

"Yeah! The boys in the press room working near the doors by the railroad dock say they got crank press dies on some trucks and they're loading a flock of freight cars."

Travis made his mind up instantaneously.

"Okay! They're asking for it!" he said almost gayly. "Tell the boys stewards' meeting at lunch time. Bring everybody down."

There is hardly anything about which a unionist is more

sensitive than on the subject of the "runaway shop." It is one of the oldest of tactics used against organization efforts. In Travis' own experience, besides, the memory was fresh of how General Motors had slipped two-thirds of the jobs right from under his co-workers at Toledo-Chevrolet in revenge for the defeat it had sustained in May 1935. Present always to his mind were the confusion and suffering and despair that this act had caused, and the picture of fathers of families coming to the union office and pleading that the organization do something to get their jobs back. Those who were still working felt as though they were taking the bread out of the others' mouths. The role played by Travis in the Flint strike and by many volunteers who later came up from his local to engage in it was directly traceable to this tragic experience and to the desire of the victims to pay off the responsible corporation in the coin of union solidarity.

After "Chink" Ananich hung up Travis called the Fisher One union office.

"Put the flicker on," he told the girl.

There was a big red 200-watt bulb over the front of the office which was right across from the plant. The boys near the windows inside the factory had instructions to give a look over every so often. If the flicker was on that meant something was up and that there would be a meeting. At 8 p. m. the workers streamed out of the plant for "lunch hour." In four minutes the union hall was filled with an excited crowd of men. The report of the moving of the dies had evidently spread everywhere by this time. Everybody's mind seemed made up before even a word was spoken. Travis got right down to brass tacks.

"Boys, we'll make this snappy," he said. "I understand there's something happening over there on the press room dock."

"That's right," one of the men called out, "they're taking dies out of the press room. They got four or five cars lined up there."

The men from the die room substantiated this.

"Well, what are we going to do about it?" Travis asked, looking slowly about the room.

There was a cold sort of pause. A chap raised his hand and stood up.

"Well, them's our jobs," he said quietly. "We want them left right here in Flint."

"That's right!" several others exclaimed.

"Boys," Travis said, still holding himself back, "I'm not going to tell you what you ought to do. That ought to be plain enough to you if you want to protect your jobs. In my plant in Toledo, General Motors walked off with 1,500 jobs a year ago and in Cleveland the Fisher Body boys struck just Monday to save theirs. What do you want to do?"

"Shut her down! Shut the goddam plant!"

The cry was taken up by the whole room till it was nothing but one big shout.

"Okay, fellows, that's what I wanted to hear you say. Now the important thing to remember from here on out is—discipline. You can't have too much of it in a strike, especially at the beginning. Roy and I will come in after you've got the plant down and help you get everything organized. Bud and the rest of the committee will be in charge. You'll have to enlarge the committee so as to get representation on it from all departments. Remember, absolutely no liquor. And tell the girls in cut-and-sew to go home and come around to the Pengelly headquarters tomorrow morning. We'll have plenty of work for them to do. Okay, good luck!"

"Everybody stays in till the warning whistle!" I yelled from the door.

"That's right," Travis said. "We don't want any stooges tipping the company off ahead of time."

The men stood still facing the door. It was like trying to chain a natural force. They couldn't hold back and began crowding forward. Then suddenly they broke through the door and made a race for the plant gates, running in every direction toward the quarter-mile building front which bordered the main highway from Detroit.

We waited outside, anxiously watching the windows. The starting whistle blew. We listened intently. There was no responsive throb. Was it right? we asked ourselves, looking at each other. Had they pulled it off?

"Here's where the fight begins," Travis said between tight lips as we stamped nervously on the cold pavement.

But there was no sign of any untoward activity inside the plant. Several minutes passed. Then suddenly a third-floor window was flung open and there was "Chink" Ananich waving his arms.

"Hooray, Bob! She's ours!"

Then other windows went up and smiling workers gathered about them.

"Was there any trouble?" we shouted.

"Naw!"

A little later the girls came out, wearing overalls and

working caps. And there was a straggling male here and there. But the vast majority of the three thousand men remained voluntarily inside the plant that first night.

After leaving the union hall one group of men had rushed right back to the railroad dock to stop the movement of dies. A superintendent interceded, arguing that only one die was being shipped out and that to Lansing for repairs. This was the story the company later took up officially. "Oh, yeah," the men said, "then what do they need all these freight cars for?" The company had evidently meant to start with small dies that stamped out panel moldings and similar small parts. These dies alone would have required months to replace. Then the bigger dies would have followed, evidently during the night layoff.

A locomotive backed up to the dock to hook on to the cars.

"There's a strike on!" the men yelled to the engineer.

"Okay!" he replied and he waved to the brakeman to never mind and trotted off again.

The job of organizing the sitdown was tremendous, particularly since the great majority of the workers had had no experience with unions or with the discipline required in such crises. Many joined up only on that first night while the sudden calling of the strike had eliminated the possibility of even the most elementary preparations. The situation was pretty chaotic the first few days as a result.

One of the early steps was to confine the sitdown to one building, the north unit, as it was called, and to merely subject the south unit and press shop to a constant patrol. This cut the defense needs. Getting the men assigned to their tasks and functioning regularly presented many difficulties. The strike committee had not yet completely established its authority and there were accordingly some resistance and friction at first together with a certain tendency to anarchy of action. But the men very quickly learned the importance of leadership and even proposed on their own measures endowing the strike committee with special powers.

At first the foremen were not excluded from the plant. They were even allowed to mingle with the men until some funny things began to happen. They would be caught urging workers to leave or even eavesdropping on the strike meetings. Finally they were told to go. On New Year's Eve when discipline almost completely broke down in the plant, the foremen sought to take advantage of the circumstance. They smuggled liquor inside and passed it around stealthily. Also they brought two prostitutes in and several of the strikers got "burnt" that night. According to the flexible rules in vogue in the beginning as to obtaining leave almost everybody had some "good reason" to go out that night, though actually bent on celebrating. The strike committee counted noses at one point and found fewer than a hundred men in the entire plant. And several of the gates had been left unguarded.*

*The passing of the old year while inside the plant made more serious sitdowners thoughtful about the strange enterprise in which they were engaged. Francis O'Rourke at Fisher Two, a devout, middle-aged man, memorialized the situation thus in his strike diary: "There it is, twelve o'clock, whistles, cheers, 1937. Peace on Earth. Why must men in the world's most perfect democracy have to take such steps to survive?... May our Heavenly Father watch over, protect us from harm and speed our settlement so we may return to our families. I ask in Jesus' name—may His will be done."

The committee immediately ordered all further leaves to be halted and called union headquarters for reinforcements. An attack by the police or company guards at this time might have resulted in a rout of the strikers. Perhaps the only thing that saved the strike during this period of disorganization was the revolutionary newness of the sitdown tactic which undoubtedly proved far more confusing to the company than to the union, rendering impotent the traditional strikebreaking technics.

Early one morning during this initial period the plant police, who were still allowed inside, were changing shifts. Most of the strikers were asleep but as the squad marched down the long aisle one of the men suddenly woke and in his still dazed state, seeing uniforms and swinging clubs and guns, began shouting: "Police! Attack! Police!" In all stages of undress the sitdowners came tearing from their beds, pantless, shoeless, but each with a club or homemade billy in his hand. The plant guards halted and backed up against the wall where they stood, wide-eyed and trembling, until the half-sleeping strikers could come to their senses.

The strike committee and other leaders toiled ceaselessly during these first days as the secretary's, Harry Van Nocker's, strike journal witnesses in such items as the following:

"M. M. and S. that Walt Moore be put to bed. Carried."

"Decision: Brother Bully be relieved from all further duties in kitchen until such a time as sufficient rest qualifies him for further duties."

Yet these early difficulties were not merely a result of the lack of discipline in the men or the newness of the tasks but were also a gauge of the complexity of the life and functions of the sitdown. It constituted a complete social unit in which the chief administrative body was the committee of seventeen whose decisions were subject to the daily checkup of the membership meetings. These meetings were like the townhall gatherings of a basic democratic society. The entire life of the sitdown came into review here and most of its ideas and decisions originated on the spot.

While functioning on one or more of the many strike committees all the men were likewise divided into social groups of fifteen, each headed by a steward or "captain." Usually these squads consisted of men who worked together in the shop. They set up house in some cozy corner of the plant and lived family-style for the duration of the strike. This camaraderie proved one of the most precious experiences of the men and greatly enhanced their feelings of coherence. They hated to give it up when the strike ended. As one fellow later put it:

"The first three days after the strike before the plant reopened were the lonesomest of my life."

Everyone had to work, naturally, putting in six hours' strike duty a day, three hours on and nine off. This would be picket duty at the gates, outside patrol, health and sanitary inspection, kitchen police, etc. The kitchen was open day and night, serving coffee and sandwiches at all times to supplement the three warm meals which were prepared outside under the supervision of my wife, Dorothy Kraus, and Max Gazan, a former chef of the swanky Detroit Athletic Club, both of whom had already had experience in the methods of supplying mass food needs during the Midland

Steel and other Detroit sitdowns. Life was geared on a 24-hour-a-day schedule to accomodate the varied habits of the men, half of whom were adapted to "afternoon" work.

Cleanliness was highly stressed because of its close relationship to morale. Regular hours were set aside for bathing and the slogan was: "A shower every day." Men who went to bed dirty were haled before the kangaroo court and sentenced to scrub the bath-house. Beds and "living quarters" were inspected daily by the sanitation committee. Three o'clock each afternoon was set aside for "clean-up time." A crane whistle hooked into an airline would give the signal and all windows in the plant would be opened, no matter what the temperature was outside.

Then all the men would gather at one end of the plant and start down to the other end in functional waves. First a group picking up refuse. Then a group moving things into place. And finally the sweeping squad, each sweeper being accompanied by a helper with a pail and shovel who would gather up the refuse. This was dumped into the refuse truck on the rear dock and carried off by the plant maintenance crew which worked throughout the strike. However, on one occasion the committee had to put pressure on the city health department to force the company to continue this service. On the other hand the management furnished the brooms for the cleanup squads and on agreement of the union to keep toilets clean, supplied tissue and paper towels all during the sitdown.

In the beginning the men slept in the bodies that were held captive by the strike. But these were found to be too cramping after a while. Also many of the strikers objected that such use would ruin the expensive upholstery although only a few of the bodies along the line had reached this late stage when the conveyor had been halted. These cars displayed signs reading "Hotel Astor," "Mills Hotel," etc. One bed mounted on a portable body-truck enabled its occupant to move whenever the urge seized him for a change of scenery. The truck superstructure was draped with curtains and on the floor beside the bed lay sheepskins that were normally used for body polishing, making a soft, luxurious rug. In recognition of this voluptuous splendor a card hanging on the curtain was marked: "Papa Sloan." The majority of the men slept in more humble comfort, building their beds from wadding that went into car cushions, having first laid out some back seat springs on the ground. A "Quiet Zone" was reserved in the rear of the plant on the second floor where absolute silence was preserved and guarded through twenty-four hours.

The strike committee and the so-called "special patrol" had sleeping quarters that were set apart because of the constant come-and-go among them. The "special patrol," which was headed by Pete Kennedy, slept only by the forty-wink method as it made its rounds once every hour, day and night. The tour took about thirty-five minutes. This was the hardest working group of the strike. Only the most trusted men had been designated for it. It was the eyes and ears of the sitdown, chasing down all rumors and suspicious occurrences. No one ever knew what the route of the "patrol" would be from time to time. It was changed repeatedly and often the group would double back on its tracks in case someone had tried to slip around it.

The strikers insisted meticulously on the observation of all plant rules concerning maintenance and safety. In the paint department, for example, there was a ventilator that had to be kept running to carry off the fumes that gathered from evaporation of the paint in stock. The proper committee saw to it that the motor running the ventilator was regularly supplied with gas. The union likewise asked the company to remove a thousand acetylene torches and gauges from the shop to prevent the strikers from playing around with them, possibly starting a fire or getting hurt. It also asked that the heat patrolman be kept on the beat, particularly to check the heat in the paint ovens which couldn't be shut off without discontinuing heat in the entire building. Guards circulated constantly in the dormitories looking for live cigaret butts in the hands of inadvertent sleepers.

The strictest measures were aimed at the importation or consumption of liquor. Everybody was searched at the entrance. If a bottle was found it was confiscated and publicly poured down a sewer. Some liquor got in nevertheless. If a man was caught drunk he was warned; a second time, the same; but a third violation brought permanent expulsion from active participation in the strike.

The care of property and ethical concern expressed by the strikers were dictated by their stern insistence upon the legality of their entire procedure. And considering the vastness of their undertaking and the imperfectness of the agencies which they could put to work, the success of these efforts was certainly extraordinary, as was attested by numerous reporters and other impartial witnesses, including Lieutenant-Governor Leo G. Nowicki, whom UAW organizer Stanley Novak (now state senator) gave a Cook's tour through the plant. Rather than demonstrating any swashbuckling freedom with the company property that was temporarily under their wardship, they bent over backwards to disprove the revolutionary motives with which inspired propaganda sought to endow them. One day the strikers were shocked to find several finished bodies marked by deep file scratches. The comment of Bud Simons at a strike meeting was typical:

"That was done by a stoolpigeon because who else would do such a disgusting thing?"

A number of women workers at Fisher One heeded Bob Travis' call and came down to union headquarters at the Pengelly building the morning after the strike started. But not so Pat Wiseman who had wanted to sit in like the men and was angered at the discrimination of being ordered out. Heck, for six years she had done men's work in the plant, most of the time as a striper when she had carried the heavy apparatus on her hips like any man, working near the baking furnaces where even those "superior males" had sometimes toppled over in a faint. Feminine? Pat knew it was all hokum but one day she got the few other girls who were strong enough to do this work to try some of that sentiment stuff on the superintendent. Every time he passed nearby they would start weeping— tears came easy amid the heat and fumes and pain of excessive physical exertion—but it took a long time before the superintendent's heart was touched.

Pat, whose deep voice was eventually to command as much respect as that of any male in the union's councils, spurned such womanish work as kitchen duty during the strike. If she couldn't sit in she'd picket outside and she never missed a day. Once a male companion on the token line which was maintained throughout the strike asked her jokingly what she expected to get out of it, a union job?

"I never see a woman take such a lead before," he said.

"I'll tell you why I'm doing it," Pat snapped back, her nostrils flaring. "You're getting fifteen dollars a week more than I am for the same number of hours and I'll be damned if I don't work as hard as you do!"

Other Fisher One women, including many wives of strikers, accepted assignments in the kitchen without complaint. Donna Devitt, Hazel Simons and a few others had union backgrounds to go by. But many more could look back only at church or social activities, the Ladies' Aid and sewing clubs. It was often difficult to make the transition to the new type of organization where responsibility was so much greater, where so much more depended on one's efforts.

Bessie Taylor, whose husband, Lawrence, worked at Fisher One, and their friends the Brubakers and the Parrishes had all become interested in the union at the same time. Taylor himself had long been union conscious, having worked as a youth in the mines of Indiana. After coming to Flint he judged the General Motors city as "the scabbiest hole in the country" and for years he talked of leaving it. But where to? When he stayed in the plant that first night, his wife came down the following morning to see what it was all about.

Bessie asked if he couldn't come home that night at least since it was New Year's Eve and they had invited some friends.

"No," Lawrence replied firmly. "Tell them to accept my hospitality but that I have some important work on." He smiled. "You can tell them to save one toast for me."

The forbearance was like a symbol of a new existence, in which immediate pleasure must give way to the demands of loyalty and self-sacrifice. But it was the goal that made such relinquishment meaningful. Lawrence Taylor foresaw a time of dignity and self-respect under the aegis of the union.

"Honey," he would tell his wife, "when I walk out of this factory it'll be through the front door."

And Bessie Taylor, fully agreeing, took her place among those working for the prideful vision.

The sitdown, coming suddenly, often disrupted family plans of long standing and a deep adjustment had sometimes to be made before adherence to the struggle was asserted. Such was the case of Lottie and Jim Krank.

Lottie Krank, mother of seven, had worked with her husband at Fisher One. The Kranks had lost two homes in Flint, the last in 1930. They swore they'd never buy again. But when things started on the upturn after the depression, the compelling desire to own the roof over their heads made them forget their resolution and though their place was in a pretty rundown condition they began to pay on it.

Lottie got a job to help. She operated a power machine in the sewing room where the girls were terribly sped up and averaged only sixty cents an hour. When the sitdown started her husband came into her department to tell her he was staying in and Lottie's forelady promptly ushered her out by the rear exit. All that night Lottie tossed in bed thinking about the strike. She wasn't a union member herself and she was worried about their jobs and about losing their house by missing out on the payments. She went down to the plant the following day and asked her husband to come home with her. They had some talking to do. Krank told his steward he'd be back and left. All afternoon husband and wife discussed this thing, until suppertime. It was no argument. Not once did they raise their voices. It was just that Lottie didn't want to be rushed into anything. They'd always worked out their problems together. Finally she stood up.

"Let's go down to the union hall," she said. Her husband looked at her. "I want to sign up."

And Lottie became one of the most active women in the strike.

The Pengelly building, union headquarters—soon known simply as "Pengelly"—the center of the strike's outside organization, gave the appearance of utter chaos to the outside observer because of the manifold activities that occupied its every corner during all hours of the day and night. The hall was more than a mere strike headquarters. It quickly became the very navel of existence for thousands of Flint workers and their families. The quarters were pitiful enough in appearance. They occupied the third floor of the tottering, decrepit building that stank from mold and age. The interior had not been repaired or painted for decades. The stairs creaked warningly under the heavy tread of the workers and at times of big meetings a perilous bulge in the rotten flooring of the hall was noticeable. When it rained, water leaked from the roof and a dozen pails had to be distributed to catch the drippings.

The division of labor between the inside and outside phases of the strike gave the latter such functions as preparation of food, publicity, welfare and relief, pickets and defense, union growth. For properly feeding the sitdowners at a minimum cost we had the experience of the Detroit strikes to go by, though the Flint kitchen soon developed a magnitude all its own. In the beginning, 500 to 1,000 sitdowners were fed three hot meals a day but as the strike deepened this figure mounted steadily, with more and more outsiders requiring to be fed. During the last two weeks several thousand people were at least in part dependent on the union kitchen.

The food committee was fortunate in obtaining for its headquarters a restaurant right across the street from the plant.

"I used to work in that factory," Ray Cook, its owner, told my wife, "and I know what those men are up against."

The union insisted on paying the rent and other expenses of the store, but Ray Cook would take no other remuneration in turning his entire facilities over to the committee. Much additional equipment had to be bought, nevertheless. Eventually the mammoth strike commissary included 24 roasting pans, a new army range, six 30-gallon stock pots and 20 huge kettles for transporting food. One regular day's consumption attained these gargantuan figures: 500 pounds of meat, 100 pounds of potatoes, 300 loaves of bread, 100 pounds of coffee, 200 pounds of sugar, 30 gallons of fresh milk, 4 cases of evaporated milk. The job of preparing and distributing this food took in close to 200 people.

A typical day's menu included:

Breakfast—eggs, coffee, bread, fruit, cereal.

Lunch—soup, roast beef, vegetables, bread, butter, dessert, drinks.

Supper—kippered herring, potato salad, bread, drinks, dessert or fruit.

Whole crates of oranges, apples and grapefruit were kept in stock inside the plants. Meals were carefully balanced and the greatest precautions against dysentery and other similar disorders were taken. The food was carefully guarded in transport by a large squad, a legitimate concern since the Pinkerton agency later admitted that one of its stoolpigeons served on this committee. Transportation was put in the hands of the city's bus drivers who, out of gratitude for the UAW's support for their own strike which had been outlawed by their parent body, did yeoman service in behalf of the auto workers' sitdown.

Despite the hugeness of the feeding problem, peculiarities of taste and habit were not neglected where they could be satisfied without too much expenditure of time or effort. On Fridays fish or spaghetti or baked beans were substituted for meat in deference to Catholic sitdowners. On one occasion an unavoidable oversight caused a disquieting incident. A meal of stewed beef kidneys had been returned to the kitchen half uneaten. In Detroit the strikers, chiefly of foreign birth or extraction, had found such food quite delectable but a larger number of the Flint men were of southern origin and they were not very partial to beef altogether. Gazan and my wife went into the plant to find out what was wrong and they were told quite bluntly:

"It's bad enough to have to eat the flesh of the critters, let alone the insides!"

Adjustments were made accordingly.

Several hundred cars were made available to the union by their owners for use in the strike's many transportation requirements. The sound equipment and cars were always preciously guarded, day and night. The distribution of the *Flint Auto Worker* also required an army of willing workers. When all the plants in the city closed, the problem of continuing to reach the workers by our only available means of communication necessitated a house-to-house distribution of the paper.

The union early became the center of pleasure as well as work for thousands of strikers. Nothing more than the manner in which they and their families flocked to headquarters demonstrated the true character of the strike as a social upheaval. If it were only for the way the workers came to sit and chat with their fellows, discussing the momentous events of which they were the center and chief actors, the union had already given them something deeply significant which they had not had before.

For the men in the plants, the long days and nights of the six-week vigil grew very heavy at times, making pastime a major function of the strike. The basement cafeteria was the center of social life. Here three ping-pong tables were going all the time. Cards and checkers were played everywhere in the plant and the strikers did some boxing and wrestling and played football outside. Every "family" group had its radio and there were magazines and books in abundance. Throughout the strike, Merlin Bishop and Eugene Fay of the union's education department taught classes in the history of the labor movement and parliamentary procedure. The kangaroo court also gave much opportunity for funning, especially after the issuance of the inevitable injunction brought disillusionment as to judicial infallibility.

There was one homespun game that was very popular. A mob of men would gather around in a ring and someone would call a fellow's name. He'd have to sing, whistle, do a jig or tell a story. Once Bud Simons, the strike chairman, was chosen and as he'd done athletic dancing in his youth he surprised the boys with a Cossack dance and got a big hand. But thereafter Bert Harris, the former Black Legionnaire, went around whispering darkly that that proved Simons was a Communist.

The hour before strike meeting every evening was devoted to entertainment, sometimes with outside talent as when Maxie Gealer, manager of the Rialto theatre in town, sent over a tap dancer or a singing team. The union-conscious "Contemporary Theatre" of Detroit put on a group of labor plays for the men and got a big hand. But best of all the strikers liked their own hillbilly orchestra which broadcast its nightly programs over the loudspeaker for the benefit of the many outsiders who gathered each evening to listen. The hopeful spirit of the strike was expressed by the orchestra's sprightly "theme song," which had been adapted on the first night of the strike to the music of the well-known southern folksong, "The Martins and the Coys."

THE FISHER STRIKE

> Gather round me and I'll tell you all a story,
> Of the Fisher Body Factory Number One:
> When the dies they started moving,
> The union men they had a meeting,
> To decide right then and there what must be done.

Chorus

These four-thousand union boys,
Oh, they sure made lots of noise,
They decided then and there to shut down tight.
In the office they got snooty,
So we started picket duty,
Now the Fisher Body shop is on a strike.

*　　*　　*

Now this strike it started one bright Wednesday evening,
When they loaded up a box car full of dies;
When the union boys they stopped them
And the railroad workers backed them,
The officials in the office were surprised.

Now they really started out to strike in earnest.
They took possession of the gates and buildings too.
They placed a guard in either clockhouse
Just to keep the non-union men out,
And they took the keys and locked the gates up too.

Now you think that this union strike is ended,
And they'll all go back to work just as before.
But the day shift men are "cuties,"
They relieve the night shift duties,
And we carry on this strike just as before.

And so it was—with spirit, with ingenuity and firmness
—the Fisher workers prepared to "carry on" their strange
and crucial strike.

6

Counter-Attack

WITH the strike taking strong root in Cleveland and Flint —a sitdown closed the small Fisher Two plant at the other end of the latter city on the same day that the Fisher One strike began—its national momentum picked up with spectacular swiftness. Atlanta and Kansas City were still out. On December 31st a sitdown occurred at the important Guide Lamp plant in Anderson, Indiana. On that day also the union struck at Norwood, Ohio, the men walking out of the plant. Buick and Chevrolet assembly lines in Flint meanwhile closed immediately as a result of the Fisher One and Two sitdowns.

The immediate effects of these strikes and shutdowns were widely felt as the corporation issued "stop orders" to all feeders. Steel workers in Youngstown and rubber workers in Akron were among the first victims of this measure. The corporation also announced the early closing of other key divisions—Delco-Remy, AC Sparkplug, Pontiac Motors, Oldsmobile—estimating that a total of 135,000 of its 275,000 employees would be affected in the first week of the strike. On January 4th, Toledo-Chevrolet was struck and the enormous Ternstedt plant in Detroit began to curtail production. The workers of Janesville-Fisher Body and Chevrolet sat down on January 5th and those at the Cadillac plant in Detroit followed suit two days later. The union's strike omnibus went through its orderly, relentless course.

In describing this first period of the great strike, Homer Martin illustrated his knack at turning a phrase.

"When will you call a general strike?" a reporter asked him.

"This strike is getting more general all the time," he replied.

But the corporation's counter-attack wasn't long in getting under way. The strike was no more than three days old when General Motors lawyers entered the circuit court of Genesee County and in drumhead justice style, without show cause hearing or previous notification to the union, secured an injunction. The writ obtained not only ordered the Flint strikers to leave the plants but also forbade them from picketing them after they got out. Indeed this was in keeping with all legal precedent in the state since even "peaceful picketing" had been repeatedly and categorically banned by the Michigan supreme court which in 1922 had declared the books closed on the entire issue. Any picketing that had taken place subsequent to this ruling had been in bold defiance of law and had been forced therefore to defend itself literally by a mass display of power.

Sheriff Tom Wolcott entered the two Fisher plants to read the injunction to the strikers. Old Tom was a cartoonist's image of the typical sheriff: enormously paunchy, battered slouch hat, unlit cigar stub in mouth-corner, and the rest. But the former butcher was really not a bad fellow and thoroughly hated his assignment, which was the first of its kind for him. Politically, Wolcott was a Democrat, having swept the one-time Republican county in November by close to a three to one plurality, and while no radical he was certainly closer to the New Deal outlook of Governor Frank Murphy than any other local official. It was a detail that later proved of fateful importance to the strikers who had helped elect him.

When Old Tom came to Fisher One the men were all practiced up to receive him. They acted very nonchalant and as if his presence in the plant were quite the ordinary thing, though many of them were scared enough. The sheriff was escorted to the second floor where the strike meetings were held. He mounted the platform, puffing and perspiring, and the men gathered around and looked up innocently at him.

"Is Bud Simons here?" the sheriff began.

"Naw, he's gone out to church." (It was Saturday.)

"Is Harry Van Nocker in the crowd?"

"He went home, his old lady's giving birth."

"Is Walter Moore here?"

"He's gone fishing."

"Is Jay Green here?"

"Where's Jay? Hey, Green! That's funny. He was just here a minute ago. He musta gone to the john or something...."

And then they began shooting questions at him.

"How much you weigh, sheriff?"

"Hey, sheriff, my cousin got a ticket—can you fix it for him?"

Old Tom began to read the order but his trembling hands shook the pages so he couldn't keep his eyes on the print. His voice which was normally a sort of confused nasal mumble was hardly audible.

"Speak up!" the men shouted, made brave by Old Tom's pathetic exhibition. "What the hell's the matter with you, you scared or something?"

It finally got so bad that he had to stop altogether. He folded the papers and put them away and the strikers began singing "Solidarity."

"Well, boys," the sheriff said when they'd finished singing, "I read this to you and it means you got to get out. I'll give you half an hour to clear out of here. If you don't come out peacefully other means will be used to force you out."

But all the while he was quivering as though he had the ague and the sweat streamed down his immense face and neck.

That afternoon the sheriff tried to get service on the international officers who were in Flint in connection with a nationwide General Motors conference. The issuance of the injunction was announced at the meeting and a resolution was adopted with cheers calling for resistance to it and for preservation of "the right to strike and picket by spreading the present strike to every General Motors plant if necessary." At that moment seven of the locals represented at the conference were already on strike. The general nature of the struggle was signalized in an eight point program of demands dealing with "certain fundamental policies" which, it was emphasized, unquestionably fell under corporate jurisdiction:

1. A national conference between the UAW and GM.
2. Abolition of all piece work systems of pay.
3. Six-hour day and thirty-hour week; time and one-half for work above these.
4. Minimum wage "commensurate with an American standard of living."
5. Reinstatement of all employees "unjustly discharged."
6. Straight seniority.
7. Speed of production to be mutually determined by each plant management and shop committee.
8. Recognition of the UAW as sole bargaining agent for General Motors employees.

A board of strategy consisting of the international officers and representatives of the CIO was empowered by the conference to conduct the negotiations with the corporation though final ratification of any agreement was reserved for a further conference. The board of strategy was also given complete power to direct the strike, a measure secretly aimed at any possible irresponsibility of Martin whose conduct up to this point, however, had been exemplary.

The sheriff came up to Pengelly hall bearing his writs while the mass meeting that followed the conference was on. He was turned back at the door with the information that the meeting was "closed" to all but union members. "I'd like to see Mr. Martin," he remarked modestly. But Martin was at the moment in the throes of oratory, tearing the selfsame injunction apart with brilliant sallies.

"Forty years ago it was illegal even to call a strike," he asserted. "It was illegal to walk on a picket line. In my opinion Mr. Sloan would make it illegal today if he could do so. This is certainly in keeping with the all inclusive injunction which the General Motors corporation just got from their judge here in Flint.

"Legality? It was General Motors that fired hundreds of men because of their union affiliations—a violation of the law. It was General Motors that spent thousands of dollars for labor spies to spy upon union men and destroy labor unions. It was General Motors that piled up all kinds of armaments for the purpose of warring against men who went on legitimate strike. We ask if General Motors is sincere. If so, we say: what about your gas and other weapons of war? Will you destroy them or keep them for strike breakers to use on picket lines?"

The sheriff was conducted into one of the side offices where CIO representative Adolph Germer held him in conversation until the meeting had broken up; Martin, George Addes and the other officers had been led out down a fire escape and were well on their way to Detroit.

But the question of the injunction could not be permanently evaded in such fashion. Larry Davidow, a Detroit attorney hired by Martin, was sent up to Flint to confer with the union leaders. While there, he happened to sit in on a preliminary meeting of some church and professional people who had expressed interest in organizing a citizens' committee on civil rights. The lawyer was questioned about the injunction. Davidow exhibited a painful inferiority complex in the presence of the churchmen. One of the ministers, a tall, ascetic-looking individual with a stiff wing collar, seemed especially to trouble the lawyer as he went into some of the legal technicalities surrounding the court order.

"And what does the union intend doing about it?" the minister disregarded the circumlocution, raising his thick white eyebrows.

Davidow smiled weakly and crushed his folded hands between his knees. "That I wouldn't be in a position to say," he replied, the only answer, as a lawyer, he could give, unless he were to assume a greater authority over the union's affairs than he had.

"Well," the man of the cloth exclaimed, "if there is not the completest candor on all sides here I shall have to withdraw immediately from this conference!"

He rose stiffly, put on his hat and stalked from the room.

We looked at each other for a few moments until Rev. R. L. Atkins, the superintendent of the Flint district of the Methodist Episcopal church, broke into a hearty laugh. This churchman proved to be of entirely different caliber from his temperamental colleague and did much to arouse sentiment against the use of violence during the strike.

On the injunction, Davidow's private views were to us very disquieting. The next step, he explained, would be for the judge to issue a bench warrant against the strikers and their leaders charging them with contempt for disregarding the writ.

"What do we do then?" Travis asked suspiciously. There had been a statement in the press quoting Martin as saying that if the law required the strikers to leave the plants they would just simply have to do so. Travis wondered if Davidow was responsible for that position.

"There's nothing you can do. You'll have to obey the order," the lawyer replied. "Otherwise the sheriff can deputize an army of a thousand men if necessary to take the plants over."

"You mean just walk out of the plants and hand the strike to General Motors on a silver platter!" the strike leader exclaimed. "I'll be damned if I will do that! You won't get me to tell those workers to expose themselves to violence and bloodshed just because GM happens to own the courts of Genesee County."

However, Davidow's advice was not final on the matter. Lee Pressman, the CIO's chief counsel, and Maurice Sugar, a well-known Detroit labor lawyer, had set to exploring other possibilities out of the dilemma. Was there, Pressman asked, a state law in Michigan governing the eligibility of judges to try cases in which they were personally interested? Yes, Sugar replied, there was such a provision. He got an assistant to check the statute books for the exact wording. It was contained in section 13888 of the code:

No judge in any court shall sit as such in any case or proceeding in which he is a party or in which he is interested.

Well, Pressman said, maybe it was far-fetched, but what if the old geezer who had issued that *ex parte* injunction was a General Motors stockholder? Of course it didn't seem likely that the big-time GM lawyers would have slipped up on that one but still it was worth looking into.

A phone call to an associate in New York sent him hastening to the General Motors building with a request for the corporation's list of stockholders, A to D. The result was far more exciting than the attorneys could have hoped for. Not only was Judge Edward D. Black of Genesee County a General Motors stockholder, he actually owned 3,365 shares of the stock which according to the current market quotation were worth $219,900!

The union blasted this damaging discovery before the public eye. The injunction, it argued, citing precedents, was without legal force and would be so regarded. Pressing the point for all it was worth, it petitioned the Michigan house of representatives to institute immediate impeachment proceedings against the judge for seeking to contravene the law. The dramatic sally created a furor the reverberations of which were heard for months afterwards. Questioned in Flint, Judge Black admitted ownership of the stock though he professed ignorance of the statute in question. He would discuss it with the union attorneys, he said, when they brought the charge into court—meaning his own!

"I am not worried about this," he said with hollow bravado, "it sounds like communist talk to me." And he had a most judicious afterthought in condonation of his action: "I pay taxes in Genesee County too. But no one criticizes me when I sit in a case which involves the county."

Nevertheless, the injunction procedure was knocked into a cocked hat. General Motors denied previous knowledge of Judge Black's ownership of its stock but though it immediately announced transference of its suit to Judge Paul V. Gadola's court the bad odor of the first fiasco forced it to delay pressing the case for almost three weeks. It was a brilliant victory for the union.

But the injunction was not the only move projected by the corporation. During the first days of the strike, City Manager Jim Barringer had called a secret meeting of all General Motors works council (company union) representatives whom the plant managers regarded as "safe."

Here the city official outlined an entirely prepared plan for a "back-to-work" campaign. The plan was duly approved and soon after launched amid a fanfare of publicity under the title of "The Flint Alliance—for the Security of Our Jobs, Our Homes, and Our Community."

The foundation for this movement had been laid by GM chief Alfred P. Sloan in a letter addressed to all General Motors employees. Sloan's message overflowed with paternalistic concern for their trials, due to "action beyond your control and that of your company." This, moreover, at a time when General Motors' products were in great and increasing demand, assuring "plenty of jobs, with generous hours of employment, for some time to come." Wages also were higher than ever in the corporation's history.

The "real issue" in the strike, the GM president maintained, was two-fold: "Whether you have to have a union card to hold a job; will a labor organization run the plants of General Motors." Giving repeated assurances to the workers that their company would protect them from the rule of "labor union dictators," the corporation spokesman wiped out the basic platform of the UAW in five peremptory replies:

1. General Motors will not recognize any union as the sole bargaining agency for its workers....

2. Work in General Motors plants will continue to depend on ability and efficiency of the workers....This means that you do not have to pay tribute to anyone for the right to work.

3. General Motors will continue to pay the highest justifiable wages....

4. General Motors' standard work week will continue to be forty hours....[Until passage of the Walsh-Healey Act requiring

the 40-hour week for all work on government orders, the corporation had been equally adamant on the 48-hour week.]

5. Seniority rights will be observed under the rules laid down by the Automobile Labor Board.... [This agency, set up during the 1934 crisis, had quickly fallen under company domination and had been repudiated even by the obsequious AFL long ago.]

The task of organizing the "Alliance" was given to a friend of Barringer's, George Boysen, a former mayor of the city and an all-around political adventurer. For many years paymaster at the Buick Motor Company, Boysen was presently manager of a small manufacturing firm that didn't seem to be hitting the economic buck. All of which evidently gave him perfect authority to act as spokesman for Flint's 42,000 workers. The plan of the "Alliance" was modeled after the streamlined strikebreaking method that Pearl Bergoff had introduced during the 1936 Akron Goodyear strike. New times, new methods. The day of imported strikebreakers was past; each threatened locality could furnish its own. But the Flint plan was even a refinement on the Akron program.

Headquarters for the Flint Alliance were opened in the heart of the city. In a few hours thousands of members were reported. Membership was not confined to workers. Businessmen, storekeepers, housewives, even school children were registered to swell the lists. The city was inundated with little white cards and unionists invented a game that could be played with them. You signed yourself "Alfred Sloan" or "William Knudsen" and appended a little posy, like: "I own GM and its employees."

On the day following the setting-up of the Flint Alliance foremen, superintendents and company union representatives came into Buick, Chevrolet and AC with their pockets bulging with application cards. These they circulated openly through every department along with supplementary petitions expressing "loyalty" to the company, "satisfaction" with the conditions of work and "appreciation" for the "coöperative efforts" of the management. By a strange coincidence exactly similar petitions appeared at the same moment in Detroit, Cleveland, Baltimore and Buffalo. "We want to work!" was the underlying burden of them all.

Naked coercion was often used in obtaining signatures to the petitions. For example, Bob Thurlow, a works council representative at Chevrolet who had joined the union, refused to circulate them in his department.Only two of his co-workers signed, consequently, and the foreman called Thurlow aside.

"Bob," he said, "that petition has been brought back. We don't expect you to sign it but go ahead and read it."

Thurlow thought: "It won't hurt me to read it." So he went over to the general foreman's desk and folding his hands ostentatiously behind his back so that the other workers could see he wasn't signing anything he read the petition. Upon the foreman's further importuning him, however, he recited Rule No. 19 to him, Arnold Lenz's own rule which prohibited the circulation of any petition on company property. Men had been fired for violating this rule, he pointed out. The foreman was again forced to retreat. But on the following day, evidently under higher orders, he came back once more with the petition but before circulating it among the men he took Thurlow aside and said to him:

"Now, Bob, I don't want to fire you so I don't want you to do anything that will force me to. When I pass that petition around I don't want you to do or say anything about it. The company had a meeting last night and rescinded that order [Rule No. 19] about circulating petitions."

Under the circumstances Thurlow was forced to withdraw his objections to the procedure though he and two others refused to the end to put their names to the petitions.

However, such courageous action was necessarily isolated as even the union instructed its members to sign the "I-Love-My-Boss" petitions, as the workers derisively called them, as a measure of self-concealment unless they happened to be in some well-organized department. Nevertheless, there were cases of workers who steadfastly refused to do so in spite of all coercion. One union member at Buick, Frank Fitzgerald, actually pocketed a petition as it came to him and refused to return it despite threats of his foreman and a company guard. Fitzgerald insisted that he was going to turn it over to the "proper authorities." Another Buick man stubbornly insisted that he didn't understand the wording of the petition—just a dumb worker—so how could he sign it!

However, the result of the drive was a huge paper success for the company which promptly published astronomical figures of its workers who were allegedly opposed to the strike. But aside from this publicity a fundamental aim of the signature campaign was to commit the more reticent workers, those who were "sitting on the fence," who would possibly be responsive to a show of strength but who could not be expected to get actively into the fight, either on the one side or the other. The petitions served to draw this timid or backward yet numerically important group into the struggle through the enlistment of its proxy. The core idea of the process was the exaltation of the peace-loving, contented, "American" *majority* as against the violent, trouble-making, radical *minority*. It was always a "handful of misguided workers," under the domination of "outside agitators," who were depriving Flint's 10,000 employees of their livelihood. The cartoons displayed by the *IMA News*—the supposedly neuter sports and fraternal sheet which to combat the *Flint Auto Worker* suddenly blossomed into a news organ devoted to printing "items of fact"—always emphasized this viewpoint, showing a small group of fist-waving, frenzied men standing at the plant gates while an enormous mass of calm and silent workers approached slowly but inexorably toward them. This implied movement may have been mere wishful thinking but in any case it tipped the hand of the organizers of the anti-strike campaign who—like George Boysen—never failed to proclaim their purely peaceful motives.

"We merely wish an enrollment for its moral effect toward smothering the strike movement," the head of the Flint Alliance had announced, "restore peace in Flint and men and women to their jobs."

Yet even if there were not more immediate proof to the opposite effect soon available, secondary signs were abounding that in the minds of its originators the strike-quelling movement was a relentless emotional progression toward the realm of action. The first synthetic mental state was one of "gloom" at the "bleak prospect" of "hardship" and "distress" caused by the strike. The next was "anger" against the "labor dictators" who were to blame. Then the "intolerable situation" cried out for rectification. And soon enough the once despairing workers were transformed into a grim battalion of activists.

Despite the non-belligerent declarations of its founders, the Flint Alliance dropped the first hint of inevitable violence into the sitdown, a cue which the workers in the plants did not miss. Francis O'Rourke, the strike chronicler at Fisher Two, began writing into his diary at this time reports of haunting fears of attack.

Here it is evening again—evils always come in the night. Be on your guard at all times, men. Are the guards on each door? Watch the back of the shop. They could come across the railroad bridge and sneak up on us from the rear....

And everywhere, the strike's tension began to mount, imperceptibly.

Simultaneously with the launching of the back-to-work movement in Flint, similar things got underway in other General Motors centers. At Chevrolet Forge in Detroit local newspapers coöperated with company unionists in taking photos of a crowd of several thousand workers waiting outside the plant for their checks and ran them under eight-column spreads, describing the gathering as a protest meeting and the men as being in an "ugly mood." Other newspaper reports from Pontiac told of "loyal" workers evicting a group of men who attempted to start a sitdown in the Fisher Body plant there. The company unions in all plants were resuscitated to fig-leaf the end-the-strike movement and give the impression that the workers were "acting upon their own initiative" in circulating petitions and other material. Letters were sent to tens of thousands of workers by these "committees" who always had access to the addressographs and other company equipment of the various plants as well as the not inconsiderable funds needed to cover the printing and mailing costs.

And the attacks on the strike from other sources were likewise multiplied. A move in the U. S. Congress to incorporate unions and outlaw sympathetic strikes was reported as making swift headway. Catholic Bishop Gallagher of Detroit abominated the sitdown. "We're fearful that it's Soviet planning behind them," he averred. The newspapers began to treat the strike as a national calamity and clamored for presidential intervention. But the most effective blow was one that fell from a rather unexpected hand when eight AFL international unions under lead of Metal Trades chief John P. Frey protested to General Motors against its entering into any agreement that might interfere with their "legitimate" claims. Frey told AFL men in Cleveland to go back to work. "We have no quarrel with the Fisher Body Company," he said. Yet only the Bricklayers among all these unions claimed any actual membership in GM plants. Naturally, the corporation seized eagerly upon this intervention and sent effusive assurances that the auto union would never be granted sole bargaining rights in violation of other claims.

The auto union leaders huffed off this AFL treachery, satisfying themselves with the more important support of local Federation men who, because they were on the scene, were in a position to be of considerable help. The Flint AFL body backed the strike throughout. John Reid, secretary of the state federation, castigated the intervening AFL unions and Frank X. Martel, chief of the powerful

Detroit central labor body, reaffirmed his endorsement. To the workers themselves, sitting in the plants at Flint, the news of the craft union attack brought sneers and ridicule: What more could you expect from that goddam AFL? And they guffawed with immense enjoyment when they read the fine rapier-thrust of John Brophy's reply to the Metal Trades head.

"What Frey says," the CIO director asserted, "means no more than if it was said by the Shah of Persia."

Meanwhile repeated efforts of Governor Murphy and conciliator James Dewey to get the corporation and the union into conference met with stiff rebuffs from the former which maintained that to begin negotiations while the sitdowners were in possession of its plants would be tantamount to "condoning" their "illegal action." To the union's offer to leave the plants under pledge of the corporation to keep them closed until a settlement was effected and to refrain from moving machinery or equipment or from encouraging back-to-work movements General Motors replied that it would not bargain on the question of evacuation. On this point, it insisted, there must be unconditional compliance; when the plants had been returned the corporation was ready to begin negotiations "frankly and without prejudice" on such demands of the union as fell in the category of "corporate policy."

The first resort to force occurred on January 7th outside the Chevrolet factory, the circumstances being so chosen as to give the impression of a first boiling-over of rank-and-file resentment against the union. At the change of shifts a group of unionists were holding an outdoors meeting in front of the temporary union headquarters across the street from Plant No 9. A couple of amplifiers had been hooked up over the front of a tavern and a union organizer was addressing the small group of men who had gathered to listen.

Suddenly a knot of men, later identified as chiefly foremen and superintendents, came out of the plant yard, crossed the street and engaged the union group with their fists. In the melee Irvon Carter, an assistant superintendent, smashed the sound equipment with a hammer. It was not till after the damage was done that the police came. They escorted the company group back to the plant and then returned to arrest two of the union men, both of whom had been hurt in the fight. They were thrown into jail and held incommunicado while the "Beer Vault," the tavern that had rented space to the union, was closed as a warning to other small storekeepers in the neighborhood.

The whole thing was pure provocation and almost led to violence that evening when a protest demonstration was held outside police headquarters. The police refused to allow a union delegation to visit the prisoners so the demonstrators had to content themselves with shouting and singing their solidarity, hoping that they would be heard by the incarcerated men.

Suddenly Gil Clark, one of the old union clique which had given Mortimer so much trouble in his early organization efforts, and another chap who was unknown to any of us began calling on the demonstrators to storm the jail. We were just able to stop them when something queer began happening inside.

The cops had been watching from the second story. All

at once they drew the windows down and backed away from them. For some reason there seemed to be something ominous in this action. It had just begun to drizzle. Using that as an excuse, we lined the demonstrators up on the sidewalk and started them marching quickly back to Pengelly headquarters.

Just as the last unionists were filing away a squad of police with masks, heavy gas vests and gas guns* came running out of the building and rapidly deployed along the front lawn, prepared to attack. But noting the retreat of the union men, they halted indecisively. The officer in charge, Capt. Edwin H. Hughes, also hesitated, evidently taken by surprise. But he did not give the order to fire. The little provocation had just missed the mark. Yet the circumstances of the police demonstration made us feel on retrospect that recourse to violence on the part of the company or its agents was not far off.

*This regalia had probably been furnished by General Motors, according to LaFollette Committee reports. It was common practice in a number of cities for the administration to accept gifts of this sort from industrialists. As late as November 1936, GM had bought $5,000 worth of tear gas for use in the anticipated conflict, while training in its proper handling was given to company guards by State Police Commissioner Oscar J. Olander.

7

Battle of Bull's Run

THE CORPORATION needed violence. Far more than would have been true in a normal strike it had to produce a situation that would destroy the eminently peaceful and decent impression of the sitdown. Besides, such a procedure would have to involve the sitdowners themselves directly to have its full force. An attack? Clearly that was what was indicated.

No doubt the idea created some difficulties. After all, nothing of the sort had ever been attempted before. And the thought was not pleasant either that the workers on this occasion would be in such a secure position—for once equalizing the immense advantages of their opponents. An attack on the great Fisher One plant with its hundreds of defenders was out of the question. But in the city's other sitdown plant—Fisher Two—a Pinkerton spy who was among the original strikers had come out to report to the corporation that there were no more than a hundred men in occupation. This plant would be an easy objective.

The Fisher Two factory, located about two miles northwest of Fisher One, was actually a part of the great Chevrolet group. It was by no means a key plant, however—nothing like Fisher One, for example—for there were a dozen others like it assembling Chevrolet bodies in scattered places throughout the country. Hence to recapture this plant would mean little to the corporation in a practical way. But psychologically—it would mean much. And even if the attempt were unsuccessful the resulting violence would lay the basis for the calling of the National Guard.

That this was the primary purpose of the plan was later admitted by several officials who were directly or indirectly involved. City Commissioner Joseph Shears, for example, in an interview with the author quoted the authority of Capt. Caesar Scavarda, who was in charge of the state police in Flint, to this effect. The idea was to force Governor Murphy's hand by creating a situation that was ostensibly beyond local control. The governor would then have to declare martial law and suspend all union meetings and other activities. The strikers would thus be starved out and the plants repossessed at point of gun. The back-to-work movement would take care of the rest.

The project also called for the involvement of Sheriff Wolcott who as a Democrat and devotee of the governor would prove crucial to its fulfilment. However, the plotters realized that Old Tom would not knowingly play part in the conspiracy and would, therefore, have to be sucked in by artifice. Capt. Edwin Hughes of the city police, whom we recently met in his fighting togs outside police headquarters, was given this responsibility. In fact, Hughes, who was friendly with Wolcott, had been assigned by City Manager Jim Barringer, mastermind of the pro-company crowd, to keep in close contact with the old fellow from the beginning of the strike.

At noon on January 11th, 200 Flint businessmen met in the Adams Room of the Durant Hotel to talk over the the strike crisis. George Boysen, the head of the Flint Alliance, was the feted guest. "Flint is confronted by a movement that is vicious," he warned. "They have taken possession of the plants and the same thing is liable to happen in your business. If they once get Flint, if they succeed in making Flint helpless, then we're all through."

It was a sort of moral preparation for what was to follow later in the day. Immediately after the luncheon, City Manager Barringer and Harry Gault, a General Motors attorney, got together with a few carefully selected men. And simultaneously things began to happen at Fisher Two that led to the strike's most exciting evening.

First the union transporters carrying "dinner" to the Fisher Two men were stopped at the gate by the plant guards. It was the first time anything like this had occurred. Unlike the Fisher One sitdowners, the occupants of the smaller plant had allowed the company guards to remain in possession of not only all entrances but of the entire ground floor. They themselves occupied merely the second floor which meant that food and other supplies had thus far been delivered to them actually at the pleasure of the company.

And now suddenly the company no longer pleased. By shutting the gate it said virtually to the men: Get out or starve. Of course the men had no intention of getting out. The outside pickets got a 24-foot ladder, placed it along the side of the building and the food was run up that way.

It was only a momentary victory, however, for it was not in Barringer's "plan" that this problem should be solved so peacefully. Soon after, in fact, probably following hurried consultation with the city hall, the plant guards formed a flying wedge, overcame the small picket group defending the ladder and confiscated it.

Then other things began to happen. The plant heat was shut off. And next all traffic approaches to the factory were closed by the police while owners of parked cars within the immediate area were told to remove them. Thoroughly aroused by these moves, the union hastened all available pickets to the plant as well as the sound car which was directed unobserved right through the police cordon over a small unpaved road by a Chevrolet worker.

It was clear that the sitdowners must immediately gain possession of the gate. For in case of an attack if the police could get inside the plant their advantage would be enormous. Strike director Bob Travis himself hastened out to Fisher Two to supervise seizure of the main gate. Over the sound car's loudspeaker he encouraged the men to proceed.

Twenty Fisher Two men were selected, armed with plant-made billies, to do the job. When they began to descend the stairs, led by Bruce Manley and Hans Larsen, there was a tense stillness over everybody. Things thus far had been so orderly, so "coöperative"—it was regretful that this state of affairs should have to end. The rest of the men clustered around the stair-head listening. The exchange of words was brief.

"I want the key to the gate," the squad captain snapped.

"My orders are to give it to nobody," the chief of the company police replied.

"Well, we want that door opened," Manley said. "We've got to get food in here."

The men hesitated a moment. Then they took a firmer grip on their clubs and moved toward the gate.

"Get the hell out of there!" they warned and the guards sided away with alacrity. They disappeared before anyone could notice where they went. Actually they hurried to the ladies' restroom and locked themselves into it while their captain got to a phone and called police headquarters to report—in keeping with the blueprint—that the company guards had been "captured" and were being held prisoner by the strikers.

Meanwhile the sitdowners' special squad approached the locked doors at the gate, put their shoulders to them and pressed. There was a sound of ripping wood and the doors flew open. The men ran out and a great cheer went up from the pickets. This was answered by triumphant shouts from the boys upstairs who had crowded to the windows. Many came down. The sitdowners and pickets mingled joyously, shaking hands and pounding each other on the back as though a tremendous feat had been consummated. It was such a simple thing to have done and yet it meant much. To the Fisher Two boys this was the first freedom they had tasted in two weeks; it meant reestablishing vital contact with the outside world.

But while the strikers and their sympathizers were celebrating in this manner things were taking place at police headquarters. As soon as word was received that the Fisher Two men had "acted" in response to the shutting off of the food supply, Capt. Hughes immediately phoned Sheriff

Wolcott with the pre-arranged news that the strikers had "kidnapped" the company guards and that there was violence at the plant.

The sheriff hadn't the slightest notion of what was up. He and about ten deputies quickly donned their riot togs, got into their cars and drove to the plant. Old Tom felt sure he could re-establish peace by asking the pickets to disperse. On the road he was passed by several speeding police cars and before his own auto had a chance to turn around at the plant and park, he found himself in the midst of a confusion of activity.

One of the pickets had shouted suddenly:

"Here comes the police!"

And several squad cars, sirens screaming, headed from north and south on Chevrolet Avenue, came to shrieking stops in front of the plant. Instantly a dozen heavily caparisoned men looking like some sort of monstrous prehistoric beetles piled out of the cars and came running toward the main gate, pulling their gas helmets over their faces as they ran. Several gas grenades exploded in the picket line, forcing the picketers to break and dash for safety. At the first alarm, however, the insiders who had been mingling with them had scrambled back to the plant, slammed the doors shut and barred them. The police were there that moment. One of them smashed a pane and inserting his gas gun shot a shell inside.

Meanwhile the sound car had remained temporarily disregarded by the attackers as the riot squad opened the attack. Vic Reuther began shouting over the mike:

"Pickets, back to your posts! Men in the plant, get your fire hose going!"

The wind was from the north, causing the gas that was sent into the picket line to be blown directly back toward the cops—a lucky detail. The pickets themselves had gone but a short distance off, looking about for things to throw. They had been only temporarily discomfited by the gas attack. Moreover, there were a number of experienced union men among them—particularly some of Bob Travis' boys from Toledo; several from Norwood (suburb of Cincinnati); and a group of the scrappy unemployed organization that had been set up by the Fisher One friends and by Charley Killinger, an ex-Buick worker. With whatever they could find these men began to heave, running in closer all the time.

There had been some women and children among the pickets also. The women ran off to deposit their kids in a nearby restaurant and were soon back. Inside, meanwhile, the sitdowners had recovered quickly, unwinding a fire hose and dragging it toward the door. It was a little short but the strikers let fly anyway, blowing the cops back with the force of the stream. The men upstairs had another hose poked through a window and playing on the police outside while two-pound car door hinges began raining down. All this occurred within five minutes or less and now suddenly the officers, several of them drenched through and through, began to retreat unceremoniously toward the Flint River bridge out of range of the water and the hinges.

The sitdowners and pickets yelled in wild triumph. The men on the ground floor hauled out cases of empty milk and pop bottles for the pickets to use in case of another attack and the boys upstairs dumped quantities of hinges onto the sidewalk for them. Thus the second coming of the police found the plant's defenders completely prepared. The second assault group was several times larger than the first. These men were not masked and besides their clubs were merely armed with gas grenades which they sought to hurl through the upper windows with the object of forcing the sitdowners back from their vantage points. But the men inside would seize these with a gloved hand and quickly douse them in a pail of water which had been brought out for the purpose.

Very few of the police got very close to the building at all this time as they were met by a thick barrage of popular ammunition. They had not expected so quick a recovery or so violent a defense. Some of the boys inside had rushed up to the roof while others had crawled out on the top of the low south wing where they had a perfect throwing position. And the water poured from the fire hoses in a vindictive rushing flood.

The strikers once more shouted exultantly as the police took to their heels again, this time with the pickets close behind them. Several of the hard-pressed officers drew their pistols as they ran and discharged them indiscriminately into the ranks of their pursuers. The strikers began to fall. Those near them would stop to carry them back but the others kept on, swept forward by the emotion of battle. They came upon the sheriff's car with the sheriff and several deputies still in it. They seized hold of it, rocked it several times and then gave it a big heave and crashed it over on its side. The corpulent old fellow had all he could do to crawl, grunting and whewing, out of the auto but just as he had righted himself on the pavement a hinge came sailing and glanced his temple.

As the sheriff's car had crashed, its trunk flopped open, revealing a couple dozen tear gas bombs and a gun. These were carried into the plant and subsequently attained fame as a LaFollette Committee exhibit. Also "confiscated" from one of the stranded police cars was a patrolman's daily report sheet on the back of which the enterprising cop had recorded the license numbers of parked cars on the scene, probably for the purpose of establishing guilt in the mass "riot" charges, if not more serious, that could be anticipated.

In the retreat one officer was caught by some pickets who tore his gas mask and other equipment from him before releasing him. The luckless fellow ran for dear life when let go. The boys on the low south roof broke off the coping and threw it for better range as the police retreated farther and farther back. The rout was complete. The police stopped on the bridge about fifty yards south of the plant. Angered by their crushing repulse those in charge began to distribute rifles to the officers. But at this point the sheriff, though incensed at his own reception, interceded.

"There's going to be no shooting here!" he told Chief Wills. "I'm the leading law enforcement officer in the county during any trouble and those are my orders."

The guns were put back.

Nevertheless, soon after one of the men on the low roof suddenly grabbed his side and exclaimed:

"I've been shot."

The boys carried him inside, took his trousers down and sure enough there was the bullet wound in his hip. Then another chap came in—he'd been hit in the shoulder. And soon the bullets came peppering, splattering against the building and dinging through the windows. Some of this shooting came from the Chevrolet No. 2 side of the street, where police and guards could be seen behind the dark windows. One of Wolcott's own deputies, Clark Thompson, was shot in the right knee by a gunner firing from an upper window of this building, the target having been without doubt deliberately chosen to further embroil the sheriff.

The police did not attack again, contenting themselves with firing gas shells from the bridge down into the pickets' ranks and especially at the sound car around which a ring of defenders stood immovably. Vic Reuther, Bill Carney (of the United Rubber Workers) and other organizers had taken turns at the mike all through the fighting, shouting encouragement and directions to the pickets. Once a woman picket grabbed the mike and hysterically castigated the police: "Cowards! Cowards! Shooting unarmed and defenseless men!" Often the metallic voice coming over the loudspeaker sounded like an unintelligible garble in the noise and commotion but to the fighting men and women its mere presence was an extraordinary support. Though a large group of guards ringed the precious instrument, several times a gas bomb would lodge under the car and the fumes seeping through the floorboard would half-suffocate the inmates. But they never gave up their crucial posts.

Ambulances had meanwhile arrived and the wounded men were carried off. A report from Hurley Hospital where they were taken was later brought to the union to the effect that the emergency ward had been ordered cleared of occupants some time before the attack was started. Fourteen of our men had bullet wounds, mostly buckshot, while only one was critically hit, having received a pistol bullet in the abdomen while chasing the police. He was Earl De Long, a young bus driver, several more of whose colleagues had engaged courageously in the fighting. A dozen police and sheriff's deputies were also treated at the hospital for head and other body injuries, the results of well-aimed strikers' brickbats.

Bob Travis, who had alternated between shouting directions over the microphone and personally leading counter-attacks on the police, was among the union men carried off to Hurley Hospital, having received gas burns in the eyes from an exploding shell. At Hurley, after undergoing preliminary treatment, he was placed under arrest but slipped off by way of a rear stairway and exit. He returned to Fisher Two but left again when two state police contacted him with an imperative call from Governor Murphy.

The list of union wounded illustrated the breadth of support which the Fisher Two men had received. Aside from De Long, Fred Stevens, leader of the bus strikers, was likewise hit; also William Lightcap and Lee Nontell of Toledo and Tommy Hoskins of distant Norwood. Charley Hammer, who was wounded in the right arm and back, was from the Buick plant while George Huber, hit in the left arm, was from Chevrolet. Nevertheless, the larger number of victims, like Hans Larsen, Pete Pavlich and others, were from Fisher Two itself, as was George Scheer whose father, Claude, was also struck. The latter had come down to bring his son food when he heard of the plant being shut off and had remained to make the battle an all-family affair.

Large crowds of onlookers had witnessed the entire battle, standing somewhat beyond the clusters of police on both ends of the street. Despite rumors of a mobilization by the Flint Alliance none of these civilians engaged in the fighting on the side of the attackers. On the contrary, they were clearly sympathetic to the strikers and as those in the sound car directed a steady appeal to them to join the pickets many began coming over.

The police grew fearful of being caught between the several groups of watchers and pickets, particularly as the former began to express more and more openly their sympathy for the strikers. The officers sought to drive them off by shooting gas shells into their midst but the crowds merely jeered, spread out temporarily to allow the gas to thin out and then returned. One heroic policeman sent a shell crashing through the window of the restaurant near the north end of the plant where reporters and spectators had gathered to warm themselves.

At the other end of the factory, as the police slowly retreated up long Chevrolet hill which started at the Flint River bridge, they drove the spectators before them. About half-way up they halted and continued from this point to shoot down into the hollow at the sound car and pickets, now and then turning to explode a shell in the direction of the crowding onlookers. But through it all the voice of the sound car could be heard though several hundred yards away, alternately rising above the turmoil of the exploding guns and sounding like the very soul of courage:

The corporation has charged the sitdowners with disregard for property. But it is General Motors who tonight through their city police have destroyed property. All during these days the

Fisher Body workers have been sitting down peacefully, protecting their jobs; yes, and religiously guarding the machines at which they earn their livelihood. Not a scratch has marred a single object inside the plant until tonight when the police shot their gas and bullets into it in a cowardly attack upon these unarmed and peaceful men. What could they do but defend themselves as best they could? They must now fight not only for their jobs but for their very lives. Let General Motors be warned, however, the patience of these men is not inexhaustible. If there is further bloodshed here tonight we shall not be responsible for what the workers do in their rage! There are costly machines in that plant. Let the corporation and their thugs remember that!

The brave words coming out of the war-scarred hollow dramatized for the crowds of onlookers the workers' own sense of their struggle, their knowledge of the odds they were fighting against, their dangerous state of siege even in the midst of victory. An exploding shell shot down the street and its racket drowned the voice in the dark. The gas had clustered so thickly around the front of the plant that the pickets and the sound car could be seen only vaguely from the top of the hill, through the maze, resembling the insubstantial figures of a distant mirage. But suddenly the incredible voice would rise again, sounding as fresh and as firm and as courageous as ever:

You police who get your bread and butter from the workers, you are workers yourselves. You weren't hired by the citizens of Flint to foment violence but to preserve law and order. How do you like to shoot down unarmed men who are merely asking for what you yourselves regard as a decent American livelihood? Is that a crime? Will you be able to look into the eyes of the honest people of this community after tonight? We call upon you—do not again act as strikebreakers for General Motors. Go home to your families and let the Fisher Body workers continue their peaceful struggle for the right to live!

But the mood of the strikers and pickets at the plant had nothing of this urgent note. Everybody was in a wonderful uplift. Despite the many who had been wounded and the occasional gas shell that came zooming down the street all carried the intoxication of a great victory. A salamander with burning coals was roaring on the sidewalk and a group of singing pickets, including some women, was clustered about it. Suddenly the great searchlights on the Chevy side of the street down by the river flashed on and began making a slow arc. What was it—another attack? Everybody halted in his tracks and stood waiting.

"Pickets, on your guard!" the warning sounded through the loud-speaker.

But it turned out to be nothing. Perhaps it was the company that feared an attack from the union's side. Another time a queer enormous thing-on-wheels began to rumble down the hill toward the plant. What was that? To the pickets it looked like some monstrous new instrument of attack. They prepared to let sail their missiles. Then suddenly some torch flares on the truck burst into flame and the monstrosity could be recognized as the ambulating apparatus of a newsreel photographer. The pickets weren't sure whether or not to let him have their hinges anyhow when the sound car microphone gave the contrary command.

"Don't throw, boys," Vic Reuther's tireless voice intoned. "Let the world know the truth about General Motors and their thugs!"

The truck was allowed to draw near and the union warriors posed for the film man, raising their clubs and shouting fiercely, looking very wild and primitive indeed. It had been a great night for the news photographers, many of whom had shown real courage, mingling in the midst of the battle to get their shots. The strikers were only beginning to understand that it was after all a job to these men. Of course they made them show their Newspaper Guild cards but it was otherwise hard for the workers, and not only the workers, to get used to the newsmen's eager but unattached interest in the strike.

"God, what a fight!" I heard one photographer exclaim joyously to a colleague after taking a particularly good shot. "But isn't it just our luck it had to come at night!"

As things quieted down everybody got busy making preparations for an all-night vigil. It was considered certain that the police would attack again as soon as they had received a new supply of gas. Reporters told us that the Detroit and Saginaw departments had been contacted for this purpose. (Fortunately for the strikers, there was nothing available from these sources.) We built barricades in the street at both ends of the plant by shoving abandoned cars abreast each other. Meanwhile the cops looked on almost disinterestedly from up the hill. I had taken charge of this work when Gene Richards, another of the Buick boys who had engaged in the night's fighting, protested this use of other people's cars without their permission.

"I don't think that's right," he said. "After all, the owners might object."

"Object!" I shouted melodramatically. "Brother, this is war!"

Such incidents gave us many laughs on retrospect. Even on the scene, after the fighting had ceased, one would hear uproarious outbursts as the men told of ridiculous things done under the first impulses of terror. Joe Ditzel, Bob Travis' friend from Toledo-Chevrolet, had aimed his tear gas pencil at a cop who was approaching the sound car, pulled the lever—when plop—it exploded in his own face. He had held the darn thing the wrong way! Another time Les Towner, an organizer from South Bend, had taken the mike and in his excitement went off on an elaborate exposition of the aims and virtues of collective bargaining.

After the police had retreated, Jim Widmark, a Buick man, suddenly noticed his fiancée among the pickets. Eleanor had just arrived and Jim, taken by surprise, began upbraiding the girl for exposing herself to danger. She accepted the rebuke for a moment while the pickets listened solemnly. Suddenly Eleanor exploded:

"Good grief! Why shouldn't I be here? I'm no better than any of these other women!"

Widmark smiled, secretly proud, and walked away as the pickets broke into laughter.

The strikers modestly confessed a great initial fear when the fighting had begun. Then the intoxication of battle had caught them up and they had known no other impulse. Already some of the recent actions amazed them. There was "Chink" Ananich, for instance, who had come over from Fisher One. During the intensest fighting he had dropped from the roof to the top of the conveyor-bridge linking Fisher Two and Chevy 2 above the street and stood there with arms folded facing the police, a thrilling, if rather foolhardy, challenge.

The street in front of the plant looked like "No Man's Land." It was littered with broken glass, bottles, rocks, hinges. The water blown from the fire hoses had frozen over (the temperature ran around 16 degrees that night), forming a sheet of ice from sidewalk to sidewalk. A heavy aura of gas kept eyes tearing for hours after hostilities had ceased. Inside the plant the ground floor was covered by an inch-deep pool of water. The hose lay uncoiled ready for use. The strikers had taken over the cafeteria and were already setting up their kitchen there despite the heavy tincture of gas prevailing. The room adjoining was appropriated by the strike committee. Upstairs the strikers showed reporters and photographers around, pointing out bullet holes in the windows and walls and posing for pictures. Everyone went about heavily armed and weighted down with throwing material. The body conveyor over to Chevy 2 was being blocked off with an incomplete body which had been left stranded by the strike and by tons of assorted parts and plain scrap.

Around midnight we were told that the governor was sending the National Guard into Flint. The report was unsubstantiated but we took it up and announced it over the loudspeaker. The men cheered. Strange thing! But it was not the troops that the workers thought of, for troops in themselves could only mean danger to the strike. No, it was the arm of the governor that they saw in the militia, an arm that they trusted would be used to re-establish peace and halt the violence of General Motors' police whose attacks they felt had not yet ended.

The night grew steadily colder and the pickets and strike sympathizers began to fall away rapidly. The crowds in the street had finally dispersed and only a knot of police remained on the hill, stamping in the cold, waiting. A reconnaissance tour of the plant showed an alarmingly small number of men remaining. The upstairs was deserted; downstairs there was only a tiny group in the cafeteria keeping warm. Evidently many of the sitdowners had slipped home for the night, seizing the first opportunity in two weeks to do so. The next day they returned with a multiplied force but this night the plant that had been defended so gallantly was almost abandoned through overconfidence and neglect.

What if the new supplies of gas arrived and the police attacked again? There would be no holding them with our small number, we told ourselves panic-stricken. Roy and Vic Reuther and I talked these things over with a tired sort of desperation. It was 2:30 and still no word of the troops and no reporters around either to tell us what the latest developments were. We did not know that the governor had recently arrived in Flint and that the newsmen were with him at the Durant Hotel at that moment.

Then suddenly an insane, an unheard of thought came to us. Why not evacuate now, before the inevitable attack started and while still on the peak of victory? The plant wasn't worth the risks of holding it and losing it. The effect on the morale of the strike would be devastating if it should be taken from us. We even discussed the practical details of the evacuation. We could announce to the press beforehand that we were leaving voluntarily, line up our men and march out in triumph!

Fortunately, this aberration was short-lived, though for a few minutes it was considered on a plane of unreality.

Then it died, melting with horror the way those insane urges do that sometimes cross the mind.

Perhaps it was the sudden vision of the skimpy picket line at the blazing salamander, amazingly gay and light-spirited, that drove these defeatist thoughts off. There were not more than a dozen pickets left, including a couple of women, one of them Genora Johnson, the young wife of a Chevrolet worker who had become a leader in the auxiliary, but these were circling the fire almost jauntily, singing and telling jokes. Just now they were intoning songs of their own making and were all taken up with their creative endeavor. They would take some popular song and one would propose a line and another a second—and the collective effort kept them occupied and happy. They sang ("That Old Gang of Mine"):

> Not a cop down on the corner,
> It's a pretty certain sign
> Our union men are holding fast
> That old picket line.

> All the boys are singing strike songs,
> They forgot "Sweet Adeline."
> Those union men are holding fast
> That old picket line.

> There goes Jack, there goes Jim,
> Down the picket lane.
> Now and then we meet again,
> And boy, they're not too tame!

> Gee, we get a happy feeling
> When we hear those brave men chime:
> "Our union men are holding fast
> That good old picket line."

The executive offices of the plant were in the fore part of the building downstairs but had remained untouched through all the fighting except for one large window pane broken by a gas grenade. This part of the factory seemed fantastically luxurious amid the litter and confusion of the rest of the building. Of course the workers would not think of invading these sacred precincts but I felt less awe or delicacy than they and kept coming back here for liberal use of the plant manager's phone in seeking to reach Bob Travis. When he had left several hours earlier, he had promised to keep us informed. Thus far, however, we had not heard from him and Pengelly knew nothing of his whereabouts either.

Finally I got through to him at the Durant Hotel where he was waiting with Adolph Germer for the union's turn with the governor who had been in session with the city officials since his arrival at 1 a.m. Mayor Harold Bradshaw had made the official petition for the National Guard, arguing the inadequacy of local agencies to "maintain" law and order. "Further rioting and disturbances are threatened," the petition said with classic impersonality. The governor had not yet decided to call the troops or at least he said nothing of doing so to the union representatives when they finally got to him at 3 a.m. Travis talked frankly to Murphy.

"Fourteen workers were carried away from the plant on stretchers," he said. "One will be dead before morning, the doctors say. If one more worker is hurt there will be warfare on the streets of Flint."

While Travis and Germer were still with him, the governor called the sheriff back in. Old Tom seemed terribly broken up over the whole situation. He was puffing and wheezing with excitement and worry and explained how he had been taken by surprise that evening. He had driven right into a hornet's nest. It was all a terrible mistake, he insisted.

"General Motors didn't want it, Bob," he said. "It's those small businessmen, those self-starters."

After the labor men had departed the governor conferred with Edward Kemp, his legal adviser, and then issued the order for the National Guard to hold itself in readiness.

"The public authority in Michigan is stronger than either of the parties in the present controversy," the governor proclaimed. "Neither of them, by recourse to force and violence, will be permitted to add public terror to the existing economic demoralization."

At about 4 a.m. we were told of the governor's intended action when other organizers came finally to relieve us. Returning to the Pengelly building Vic Reuther and I discussed our recent insanity about evacuating the plant.

"Jesus, wouldn't it have been beautiful if we had gone through with it!"

Already it was hard to understand what had gotten into us.

8

General Motors Breaks a Truce

ON THE MORNING following the Fisher Two battle, the curious began to arrive early on the scene of the night's fighting. The radio and papers had had a Roman holiday over it and everybody wanted to get a look at the battleground.

Someone in the crowd that stood looking at an overturned police car began twisting on one of the parts and suddenly the entire swarm descended on the machine and with a strange frenzy—half anger, half cupidity—began stripping it. Everything went—tires and wheels and doors off their hinges and seats and lights and radiator. By noon it looked like a carcass that the crows had finished with and yet newcomers found something that could still be torn from it, some souvenir that would identify the owner with the amazing battle out of which the workers somehow had emerged victorious.

Before noon the workers began coming to union headquarters to sign up and pretty soon there was a double line at the dues windows, extending way out into the vestibule. This continued for several days, one detail which the city

manager's brain trust had undoubtedly failed to antici-
pate. Some were incensed by the police attack. Some were
thrilled by the workers' gallant fight and especially by the
victory. Still others who had been sitting on the fence
thought: "Well, now the strike is going to end and I'd better get in right from the start."

The case of Bessie and John Garrison was fairly typical.
They had been married in the fall, had taken some furniture on payments and set up a cozy nook. Bessie, no flap-
per, was a good housewife and the newlyweds figured if
nothing went wrong they'd be able to put a good foot forward that season. Things were just beginning to swing
into line when the strike came. Certain departments at
Buick began to close down and the couple knew John's
turn would soon come. Then what?

The foreman of the foundry where John worked took
him aside one day and asked him if he'd like to go on special guard duty after work. The company was putting on
several hundred "loyal" workers to be ready in case the
union started any trouble. John didn't exactly like the
idea but he had half a notion to accept the offer. He was
that sore. He and Bessie hated the union, hated the strike,
listened to the radio and read the *Flint Journal* and cursed
the "outside agitators." Then when Boysen started his
Flint Alliance, they spoke of going down together and
joining. But somehow they never did.

On the night of the fighting at Fisher Two they sat glued
to the radio, listening to the sensational reports. They
stayed up late, though both had to rise early to get John
to work. After John went to bed, Bessie and her sister
Dorothy took a run down to the plant and stood with the

crowds listening to the sound car and watching the pickets. They looked very brave and picturesque from the distance. The fighting was over. Next morning Bessie said to John:

"I'll drive you to work. I'd like to use the car today."

She let him off at the corner near his plant and though neither had said anything about it, they parted with the same thoughts—about the fight last night. The radio reports had been twisted and garbled and prevailingly antiunion but certain details had nevertheless come through that might catch the imagination of a worker. As John approached the entrance gate he suddenly remembered such a detail, a phrase that had stuck in his mind:

"And the police were forced to retreat."

He burst out laughing, as the image presented itself to him, of the cops running to beat the band with a shower of milk bottles and hinges flying after them!

Bessie hadn't told John where she was going, but she drove right out to Chevrolet Avenue. She wanted to see what the place looked like after the fight. She found a gang of sitdowners sweeping the street and sidewalks of the debris. She thought that was nice and orderly.

There was one woman among the handful of pickets at the salamander. Bessie approached her and started a conversation. She wanted to talk about the strike and the union and last night's battle but she was surprised to find that the woman was just then more concerned about a personal matter: how to get back home in time to get her children off to school. There hadn't been a union car down for some time; if she could only get to the Pengelly, they would give her transportation home.

Bessie offered to drive her to the hall, accepting an invitation to go up with her. Then she stayed on as people were beginning to gather and everyone seemed eager to talk, thrilled at the previous night's victory. No one asked her if she belonged. They introduced her around and before she knew it, it was after noon.

She went outside for a bite and then drove over to Fisher Two where a big outside meeting was planned. She was terribly impressed and returned to the hall with several auxiliary members. She really felt like one of them already. There was so much to talk about and learn. The time passed quickly and soon Bessie had to rush home to prepare John's supper.

When he arrived she was simply effervescing with her day. "Those poor people!" she kept saying, never thinking of herself as one of them. However, her horoscope had told her that on this day a great change was coming into her life. She asked John to take her down to the meeting that night. She didn't mention his joining the union because that might have been a little previous. She thought: Let him hear some of those young union organizers speak— that'd decide him. John tried to act stubborn, but he didn't have to be coaxed long about the meeting. Actually, that morning in the shop, he had looked up one of the union men and asked him for a card.

The National Guard did not arrive until early the following morning but that afternoon during the meeting outside Fisher Two an observation plane of the militia droned aloft. The workers looked up to it with friendliness. Ten thousand of them packed the hollow at the foot of the two hills where the battle had raged. Little bits of glass and rock were yet palpable beneath one's shoes on the street and sidewalks and the air still bore a slightly acrid tang.

Hundreds of men and women were here from Lansing, Detroit, Pontiac, Saginaw, Toledo, Cleveland, South Bend and Norwood and more were pouring into the city every hour to view the scene of auto labor's great victory. Already the papers had begun to scream about the "invasion" of Flint and Michigan by "outsiders" and state police stopped all Ohio cars on Telegraph Road bound for Flint, insultingly searching them for arms and taking the names of occupants before allowing them to proceed.

However, positive feelings everywhere predominated among the workers. At Fisher One the strikers expressed as much pride over the previous night's victory as if they themselves had been involved in it. As a matter of fact, many of them had sneaked off to join the battle while those remaining had gone through realistic drills in anticipation of the attack they were certain would come to their plant if the other were "taken." Bud Simons' duplicate order-book for the occasion is full of such commands:

"Prepare hose on second and third floors."

"Establish pickets in stairways."

"We want doors left open at powerhouse."

A close watch of the crucial powerhouse was maintained. By arrangement with the boiler men when the crane whistle blew at the first sign of attack the full force of water would be turned on. One of the hoses was attached to an air line with which it was meant to blow the gas away. Piles of hinges—the so-effective weapon of the Fisher Two defense—were distributed everywhere, the pins having been drawn between the two halves for better throwing. In the cafeteria beaver-board targets were set against the wall and the men practiced heaving the hinges at them to get their muscles accustomed to the unusual weight.

Yet despite all these grim preparations the men were in excellent spirit. Secretary Harry Van Nocker tells, for example, how on a tour of inspection he found one striker writing out a "dispossess notice" for a buddy who had occupied his bed for a little snooze.

Similar evidences of high morale were given by the men who had been wounded in the fighting and who had been taken straight from the hospital to jail. They were now being held incommunicado and were forced to sleep in cold cells with insufficient bedding and on mattresses which were laid on the floor. Their wounds had not been properly dressed and in several cases there was danger of infection. But the men revived their courage incessantly through singing of "Solidarity," whose eight-worded elementary but evocative refrain brought them a steady, heartening echo from the friendly hosts outside.

> Solidarity forever!
> Solidarity forever!
> Solidarity forever!
> For the union makes us strong!

"We sang it four thousand times a day," Charley Hammer later reported. "We sang it at midnight, at three in the morning or at any time it came into our heads."

A Detroit preacher, H. P. Marley, who finally won access to the prisoners after they had been in several days, saw a mystic parallel in this debonair and inconquerable singing spirit:

"Being a minister my mind went back to the account of a great apostle who sang in jail. These too had faith—a modern faith in the right of humanity to control its own destiny."

The pro-company crowd in Flint had spasms of sudden fear when Governor Murphy failed to declare a state of martial law in the city as 1,200 troops marched in and 1,800 more prepared to move. No troops were sent to the plants themselves, moreover; they were billeted at an abandoned schoolhouse in the heart of the city. When Murphy further stated that neither the National Guard nor the state police would be used to serve 1,200 John Doe warrants* issued by Prosecutor Joseph Joseph in connection with the Fisher Two "riot" the dismay of the would-be strike-busters knew no bounds.

But Murphy, seeing in the resounding defeat of the corporation at Fisher Two the possibility of a prompt termination of the crisis, refused any course that might wreck this chance. The militia were to be used only for their quelling effect on the over-heated situation, while the forces of peace could function. It was a perfect setup for forcing the opening of negotiations—"for the purpose of conferring together without condition or prejudice," as the governor diplomatically put it in his formal invitation to the two parties. Under the circumstances it was impossible for the corporation to refuse the request though it insisted that such compliance must be considered as "without sacrifice of principles"—whatever that meant.

*These warrants charged kidnapping (ostensibly of the plant police who had actually locked themselves in the ladies' toilet all night), malicious destruction of property while rioting, felonious assault and criminal syndicalism.

General Motors officials were strictly on the defensive over the Fisher Two happenings. In response to the widespread public resentment manifested against the attempt to starve and freeze out the sitdowners, they hastily expressed their regrets for the violence and bloodshed. But they contradictorily insisted that the fight had been entirely between the police and the strikers—the company had had absolutely nothing to do with it. The temperature reduction in the plant, Knudsen said, was due to the fact that it was in a "shutdown condition." But the company "never intended" to stop heat, light or water in the occupied factories and would not do so in the future. (On numerous occasions actually it had played with these services in both plants and later particularly these words of the company head were belied in action.)

"Let's discuss matters equitably across the table and settle them that way," Knudsen said hopefully. "I don't want anybody to get hurt." This peaceful note was perhaps at least personally sincere with him. Always essentially the industrial engineer rather than the financier-politician, Knudsen regarded with honest pain the blighting effect of the strike on General Motors production. He was eager to see the abnormal state of affairs ended and his plants all humming with efficient activity once more. It was this practical viewpoint that made Knudsen a more reasonable protagonist than the corporation's New York rulers. The union negotiators always felt that if left in his hands the strike would have been promptly settled. But Knudsen carried little weight among the controlling circle of the billion-dollar corporation. It was the fabulous du Pont family, owners of one-fourth of GM stock, and their supporting Wall Street coterie that had the final say-so over the fate of General Motors' 250,000 workers.

And for this group the strike was by no means over. Even if it was considered expedient for the corporation to assume a regretful and seemingly coöperative attitude for a few days until the bad odor of the Fisher Two events had subsided this would not in the least affect the anti-strike movement which was ostensibly independent of the company. In fact, this movement continued to develop at an accelerated pace despite the official contrition of the corporation.

The "loyalty" petitions still rained down from heaven while Governor Murphy's desk was piled higher and higher with protests, demands and threats. A Bay City "Alliance" was modelled after the Flint original and held a rabid meeting meant as a warning against the union's coming into that city. The Ternstedt (Detroit) post of the American Legion adopted a resolution calling the strike "a despicable attempt to force the rule of the minority upon the rights and freedom of the majority." The Chevrolet Forge company union leaders in Detroit with ostentatious solicitousness announced the setting up of committees to arrange for relief for their needy co-workers and to appeal to their creditors for extension of time.

And in the nation's Capitol, Congressman Clare Hoffman, arch-reactionary from Allegan, Michigan, in a speech before the House, castigated Murphy for having "supported mob rule with troops" while Rep. Fred L. Crawford, Saginaw Republican, intervened with Roosevelt in behalf of the "loyal" GM workers.

At this juncture John L. Lewis spoke out incisively. He

no doubt wished to warn the auto workers not to allow the offensive which they had seized to drop out of their hands and at the same time to let the corporation chiefs know that they might not escape from the full blame of causing union blood to flow by the utterance of a few, cheap, sanctimonious regrets. On the very eve of the conferences between union and corporation he issued a slashing attack on the latter, striking right and left with broadsword blows at every vulnerable spot.

A resolution was to be introduced into the U. S. Senate, Lewis said, calling for the investigation of the history of General Motors as a holding company and of the manner it had acquired independent motor corporations, "each time inflating the values and watering the stock." Also to be looked into were excessive salaries and bonuses and the "mulcting" of "the consuming public and the stockholders." Lewis said he would ask Congress to determine if the corporation's policies were ruled "by remote control, principally by the du Pont family, who made a thousand million dollars out of the World War, and why Sloan and Knudsen receive munificent salaries for being messenger boys." And as though this were not answer enough to the company's incessant "outside agitator" propaganda he added that Congress would be asked to discover to what extent General Motors policies were dictated by foreign holdings and what such dictation had to do "with the wages paid American labor and the speed of the General Motors assembly line!"

His statement bristled with the imperative: "We demand;" "We want;" etc. He announced that the CIO was likewise asking the LaFollette Committee to "summon"

Chief Wills of Flint whom he qualified as "formerly a hired thug for the copper companies of the Upper Peninsula of Michigan—a killer who has killed several men...." "We want an investigation of Judge Black...." Sure, the CIO had helped the UAW and what was more, it would continue to send "money and men into Michigan." "They [GM] wanted a test of power," he concluded with a dramatic, prideful gesture toward the battling auto workers. "We are giving it to them!"

But the union needed no such hint. Further strikes were called at the Fleetwood (Detroit) and St. Louis plants. Enforced closures of additional General Motors factories left only a small minority of the corporation's 60-odd yet in operation. As several of these were forced down by glass shortage Philip Murray entered into the glass strike negotiations in order to effect a speedy settlement so that lack of glass might not slow up Ford and Chrysler production and thus endanger the union's utilization of the competitive situation among the "Big Three" to its own advantage.

The conferees meeting in the executive offices at Lansing included for the union, Martin, Mortimer and Brophy; and for the corporation, Knudsen, flanked by the Wall Street heavies: John Thomas Smith, GM's general counsel, and Donaldson Brown, member of the corporation's finance committee and a du Pont son-in-law. The union's position was unchanged. It merely wanted written assurances that the evacuation of the plants which the corporation demanded as a prerequisite for any negotiations would not be used as the basis of an intensified back-to-work move. Union spokesmen unofficially suggested that the best solution would be for the governor to put the National Guard around the plants, order the sitdowners out and lock up the factories until a settlement was reached.

"That's how they do it in Wisconsin!" Ed Hall boasted as the strategy board sat kibitzing with reporters all night on the hard floor of the corridor outside the executive suite. Present at Lansing for consultative purposes, besides the UAW officers, was a whole galaxy of CIO leaders: Allan Haywood, Len De Caux, Adolph Germer and Leo Krzycki of the Amalgamated Clothing Workers. The conferees had gone into session at 11 a.m. on Thursday, January 14th, and at 3 a.m. the following morning, Murphy, looking grey with exhaustion, came out to announce in his sometimes rococo manner:

"We have arrived at a peace."

"This administration is concerned with human rights and with property rights also," he added.

The union had agreed to evacuate all occupied plants not later than the following Monday morning, when the actual negotiations were to begin, upon reciprocal pledge of the corporation that during a period of fifteen days it would not remove "any dies, tools, machinery, material (except for export trade), or equipment from any of the plants on strike..." nor "endeavor to resume operation in any such plants" for that period.

The truce terms were by no means popular. Told of them, one of the Fisher Two strikers commented: "That's no settlement. I don't see no sense in the boys moving out if that's all we got." Of course there was some gratification in the fact that GM had been forced to back down and sign *something* with the union, but it was thin gruel.

Bob Travis and the other organizers in Flint didn't like the thing at all. Our whole organization of the strike had been built around the occupation of the plants; the shift to the outside would be like disarming ourselves. General Motors on the other hand was bound to gain by the change since it knew so much better how to fight that kind of a strike and it had a powerful, smoothly-geared back-to-work machine already in motion.

Fifteen days constituted a terribly short breathing period, besides. It would mean hardly any pressure at all on the company. For General Motors could meanwhile get its other plants going to build up banks in preparation for the complete reopening. Each successive day by the mere fact of its passage would ease it of more of this constraint while the union would be under a greater and greater pressure to come to terms as the end of the truce neared. It was clear that the union would have to stab for a quick settlement, taking its chances on a partial victory. But our hearts misgave as we thought of the odds and we were angry that the Lansing negotiators had not taken us more into their confidence.

It would be nothing more than natural that those at the front would be more sensitive to the other side's actual intentions than those engaged in the business of negotiating where painful smiles are multiplied in the hope of stimulating the possibilities of peace. We on the other hand saw gathering about us in the very face of the truce the increasing signs and atmosphere of war.

Though the charges against the fourteen wounded men who had been held following the Fisher Two battle were dropped, Prosecutor Joseph Joseph announced his intention of pushing "to the limit" the case against the seven leaders who, he alleged, had incited the riot by their "frenzied appeals." Summary arrests were forestalled only by the promise of union attorney Maurice Sugar that the men would give themselves up voluntarily for arraignment. Les Towner, Bill Carney and B. J. Widick, who had been in Flint only temporarily, left the state; but Bob Travis, Roy and Vic Reuther and I were forced to undergo the indignity of being mugged and fingerprinted as common criminals

Joseph also turned over 300 John Doe felony warrants to the sheriff and city and state police with the order that they be served immediately, forcing Murphy, who naturally wanted no vexatious interference with the conferences, to intercede once again to prevent such action.

The union nevertheless proceeded to go through with its part of the agreement to evacuate the plants. Guide Lamp in Anderson was emptied first. However, when the strikers sought to establish a picket line outside the plant to implement the "truce" an army of city police and deputized foremen fell upon the pickets, dispersing them and tearing their shanties down. The city after all hadn't signed the agreement! And General Motors on its side disclaimed responsibility for the civic authorities of Anderson who "clearly acted as they had a right to do."

Despite this additional hint of bad faith, the union still continued with its program of clearing the struck plants. Heading the parade as the men left the Cadillac and Fleetwood plants on the Westside of Detroit (within a couple of miles of River Rouge), Homer Martin, Walter Reuther and Dick Frankensteen marched beneath a banner reading: "Today GM—Tomorrow Ford."

This early heralding of an expanding union program gave the grim poker-face of Dearborn restless moments. Heavy wired doors reaching to the top of all entrance passageways were constructed during the General Motors strike at the big Ford plant. Barbed wire was strung on the fences surrounding the entire grounds while a system of tear gas that could be released by an electric push-button was installed inside the plant. All workers entering the grounds were frisked for leaflets.

Shortly after the Cadillac evacuation a number of workers from this plant received wires to report to work "Monday"—another violation of the terms of the "truce." The union grew really concerned but still did not decide to renege on its end of the bargain.

Arrangements had been made for a mammoth celebration at the Flint evacuation which was to take place on Sunday afternoon. It had been a difficult task to convince the sitdowners into accepting the "truce." There was danger of a widespread demoralization which the more responsible rank and file leaders sought to evade through united pledges of going out as a body to complete the work of organization in all plants of the city under the slogan: "The bigger the union the better the contract." The "truce" must be regarded as merely "the first skirmish in the tremendous battle," the union decided.

"The fight is not done," resolved the Fisher One men, setting their jaws. "We are going out to win and we will win. The nineteen days here proved that all men will be on duty at all times and will accept assignments. Nothing can stop us."

At the two plants a big roast chicken dinner with all

"fixins" was fed record groups as hundreds of additional men went into the plants the night before to share the honor of marching out with the boys. There was some resentment about this but the spirit of solidarity prevailed. "We hold no animosity toward these men," the Fisher One strikers officially decided, "who just came in for the chicken dinner and the glory."

In the morning the shop was given a thorough cleaning. Belongings were packed into bundles and things were restored to their places. Hearts were heavy and only the sight and taste of the magnificent feed brought the men's minds back to the positive things.

The women in the kitchen had outdone themselves. The men lingered at their meal. Already they were talking about their experiences during the sitdown as though it were long past. There was more than an hour yet before the evacuation but the people were beginning to gather outside. The strikers were to parade to the busses that would carry them to Fisher Two for the big demonstration, but they felt a little self-conscious in anticipation of the cheers they would get as they left the plant. For what?

Everybody at headquarters was likewise in the dumps. Bill Lawrence, a UP reporter, approached me breezily in the Pengelly vestibule. "Where's Bob?" he asked.

For no reason I lost my temper.*

"Can't you ever give a guy some peace!" I exclaimed.

"But I've got something important," he insisted.

*I'm afraid I did not give the reporters and other news-dispensers in Flint the attention their work and influence merited. Fortunately, our staff was early augmented by the arrival of Carl Haessler, a talented and resourceful labor publicity man, who proved extremely popular with the representatives of the fourth estate.

There was something about the way he said it and looked at me. I took him through a side door into Travis' office.

"Here's a statement Boysen is issuing tonight," he said, handing Travis the sheet. "I was nosing around their office and I saw it on the desk so I picked it up and read it. Williamson* said he hadn't intended letting anyone see it until after the evacuations but since I already knew about it he said I could have a copy but to keep it quiet until tonight. You might give me something on it in advance, though there isn't a hell of a lot to it from what I can make out."

Travis read the short statement. Calmly he rose to his feet, though his heart was thumping.

"Listen, Bill, just wait here a minute, will you?" And he stepped into the adjoining room with the mimeographed sheet and got the long-distance operator on the phone. There was some delay in getting Martin. He was finally reached at the Cass Tech auditorium in Detroit where a "victory" celebration meeting was being held.

"Homer," he said, "I just got hold of something important. It's a publicity release that Boysen's giving out tonight. Knudsen's agreed to meet with the Flint Alliance on Tuesday."

He read the release to him. But Martin's voice came back very cool.

"I don't think that means anything, Bob. What's the difference if they do have their meeting—it can't have any real effect. I think you ought to go right ahead with your plans."

*Floyd Williamson, representative of the New York agency that handled General Motors publicity during the strike.

162

Travis was in no mood to argue. He replied sharply: "Like hell I will!" and hung up. Then he picked the receiver up again and asked the operator to get him John Brophy at the same number. Since the beginning of the strike the CIO director had never left Martin's side, fearful of some outbreak of irresponsibility. His constancy had become a kidding point among reporters. When Brophy heard Travis' news he hurried back to the platform.

"We've got to see the governor right away," he told Martin. "This changes the whole picture."

The background of Boysen's little release now assumed special significance. Several exchanges between him and Knudsen had been made public all during the preliminary GM-UAW conferences in which the Flint Alliance head demanded assurances that those he represented would not be "overlooked" when the actual negotiations began.

Though Knudsen responded sympathetically he was careful to avoid any specific pledge on the subject and in fact in one letter punctiliously explained that the nonstrikers would not be represented in the negotiations in any way. This was clearly to set the union off the scent for the plant evacuations had not yet been completed. But on Sunday Boysen in a final note came to the point of what the whole series had been leading up to:

We earnestly request an appointment with you at 9 o'clock Tuesday morning, if possible, for a committee of twelve members of the Flint Alliance on which will be representatives of the vast majority of workmen of each of your Flint plants. The purpose of this meeting will be to discuss collective bargaining as it affects the great majority of your employees.

And Knudsen's reply, contained in the sheet the reporter

had brought and which was to have been withheld from release until just after the Fisher One and Two plants had been repossessed, had this damaging sentence which had been palpably waiting since the beginning and which revealed the dishonorable objective of the interlude:

We shall notify you as soon as possible as to a time and place for a meeting.

Thus with one cynical stroke would the corporation render its negotiations with the union utterly worthless before they had even begun. What a pretty picture that would make—the union committee with the corporation in one room of the General Motors building and the Flint Alliance committee and the corporation in another!

But even if the corporation refrained from granting the Alliance an immediate conference—which was very unlikely—the effect of the mere agreement to meet with it was to prejudice the union's chief demand, that for sole collective bargaining, in advance; to present it with an accomplished fact on the subject; "to remove from negotiations a point on which the corporation had agreed to negotiate," as the union's official explanation put it. But the slip-up of a high-paid New York public relations man and a reporter's news-scent together with the strike leader's alertness had nipped the disgraceful scheme.

After talking to Brophy, Travis had sped a "runner" out to Fisher One with a note for Wyndham Mortimer who was to have directed the evacuation proceedings. A special meeting was called immediately inside and the double-cross was put squarely on to General Motors. When Mortimer proposed that the evacuation be called off the men cheered.

"Yeah, man, that's the stuff! We stuck it out this long, let's stick till we win!"

Ten minutes after the time scheduled for the evacuation Mortimer announced the change of plans to the 5,000 people outside who had been standing for an hour in a steady drizzle. The strikers' wives were there and kids and infants in arms. Bud Simons kissed his wife symbolically for the photographers and clambered back into the plant. The boys lined up along the open windows, shouting to beat the band. A dummy labeled "GM Stoolpigeon" was lowered from an upper window and beaten and torn to shreds. The White Motor band of Cleveland, brought by Ed Stubbc to lead the parade from the plant, played the national anthem.

There was an even bigger meeting at Fisher Two following this one. Vic Reuther spoke over the mike: "This is the same voice that spoke to you Monday night. I think we should christen this square for posterity. We will call it Bull's Run for it was here that we put the bulls on the run."

Nelson Wooley, one of the wounded fellows, was called on to tell how it felt to get shot. With charming, modest literalness he explained:

"You don't feel anything for about twenty-four hours and then it begins to get sore."

Francis O'Rourke, more introspective than most of his fellows at this plant, did not share their enthusiasm about the new development. His diary recorded his shock, coloring what he felt was a general impression:

Here comes the band. Music, laughter. What is that announcement? We have been double crossed? We are not going to leave the plants? Gee! I feel dizzy....Discouraged men. Heartsick men. Men who had planned to go home, but who have decided to stay for our own interest. Again the long march from the front of the shop to the back of the shop. Back and forth until we are tired and then to bed. Now I lay me down to sleep....

But the overflow meeting at Pengelly that evening was as joyous as if the victorious end of the strike were being celebrated. Professor R. M. Lovett spoke as a "GM stockholder." "I came here to look over my property," he said mock-pontifically. "I was glad to see the way the boys were taking care of things but I noticed some bullet holes. They told me how police shot in and injured my property...."

Everybody was in a wonderful mood. It seemed that on this evening the strike and the union had suddenly attained full maturity. One could no longer imagine that these people would ever be able to live without the union again. It had become the very center of their existence. The men seldom came alone to the hall; they brought their entire families with them. And they never seemed to tire of hearing the new gospel from the lips of the union leaders. To many of us the spoken message of unionism had grown tiresome through infinite repetition. But it was nothing short of the evangel to these workers who had never been privileged to hear anything like it and yet to whose hearts the words expressed a close and familiar language.

The Flint Alliance incident was, to be sure, a splendid lesson in applied unionism, giving sharp focus to the demand of the UAW for sole bargaining rights, as Homer Martin now explained in a scintillating speech:

It is impossible to have more than one collective bargaining agency determining wages and working conditions of employees in the same group. One part of an assembly line cannot be on a six-hour day while an adjoining part of the line, or a scattering of workers along the line, is on an eight-hour day. There is no feasible method of collective bargaining other than through unified representation. That being true, to say the corporation will not recognize any union as the sole bargaining agency is in fact to say: "We refuse to bargain with our employees altogether."

Martin that night showed his genius for protean transformations. Forgetting how he had only that afternoon been ready to fall into General Motors' trap with wide-open eyes, he now assailed the corporation's breach of faith in the most fiery terms. After the meeting, Bill Lawrence, the UP reporter, got his reward for the tip-off by being given a half-hour's jump over the other reporters on the union's decision to make the postponement in the evacuation—which had thus far been given out as only tentative—permanent. But actually the scoop was the union's and General Motors was left holding the bag.

When it was too late Boysen offered to efface himself in a move that was as plainly company-inspired as was his first intervention. But the union replied that such a withdrawal was now meaningless if, through it, the corporation hoped to get the union to evacuate the plants. This would not now be done "for any reason." "By the same magic that General Motors waved the Flint Alliance out of the picture it can wave it back into the picture." It was still prepared to negotiate in the manner that had been agreed upon, it insisted, but on Monday morning when the union representatives went to the General Motors building they were merely handed a statement to the effect that negotiations could not proceed until the two Fisher plants had been vacated. And the situation went back to scratch.

9

Violent Crescendo

THE BATTLE was on again. The strike had not yet completed its third week but the feeling on all hands was that it was now in for a tough and stormy period. The union's strategy board discussed plans for making available a huge war chest for the increasing needs of the strike. More organizers would be put on everywhere though there were already a hundred on the rolls, three times the number of a month before. Time for a daily radio broadcast was purchased in Detroit.* A request for financial aid was drawn up by Secretary-Treasurer Addes and sent throughout the land, eventually bringing tens of thousands of dollars.†

---

*However, officials of the station termed one of the first speeches "controversial" and cancelled the contract.

†The total immediate cost of the strike in Flint ran considerably under $50,000. Though the sum was remarkably low for so huge an enterprise, the handling of these thousands of dollars proved a matter of deep concern to strike director Bob Travis. Travis insisted on making all payments above one dollar by check, giving his office assistants, Lou Scott and Olga Richards, nightmares of scrupulosity. This care proved fortunate in the sequel, however, when Homer Martin, in launching his factional campaign a few weeks after the strike, raised wild charges about thousands of dollars of strike funds being unaccounted for. A formal audit cleared the strike director completely of the accusation, actually showing an excess of $52.20 instead of the claimed shortage.

While funds came mainly from other unions, fraternal orders, churches and individuals were among those giving. Anonymous gifts of as high as $100 were received at international headquarters.

But meanwhile the new union was hard pressed for funds. The CIO had concentrated most of its resources on the steel industry which, despite our persistent pleadings and predictions, had been given priority over the auto industry as the first open shop citadel to be stormed. The auto workers took that little matter into their own hands. However, the result was that there was little money left to spare them in their crisis. And conscientious George Addes lost weight and sleep worrying about the situation.

Food for the sitdowners had to be improved as the ordeal drew out and scores more of the outsiders were fed every day. The union also began to give relief to emergency cases during their "waiting time"—two or three dollars, a half-ton of coal—this item alone averaging $300 a day. The bad effects of the protracted economic dislocation among small merchants were to some extent counteracted by the union's habit of distributing its purchases of food and supplies as widely as possible, always accompanied by a little prepared speech delivered by the union women to the storekeepers as to how the struggle of the auto workers concerned their welfare also.

And yet it was only a drop compared to the immense problem. In January alone losses in wages in Flint totaled over $4,500,000. Business was prostrated as a result, experiencing an average slump of 50 percent or more. Rents remained largely unpaid. Retail trade in all but the necessities was spiralling downward and even sales of foodstuffs and milk were beginning to "drop sharply." Wholesalers cut off all credits to grocers and other retailers who in turn were forced to halt the workers' accounts. Banks were refusing loans. Automobile and other sales agencies received cancel orders in clusters. The probate court reported an almost complete halt in alimony payments. And the county relief rolls mounted from 2,500 to 7,800.

This was pretty much the background picture after the breakdown of the shortlived "truce." It was a situation in which the anti-strike movement could increasingly flourish. The corporation could be depended upon to utilize the favorable opportunity.

The union had up to this point neglected the work of enlisting local support for the strike among the non-workingclass elements of the city. On a national scale more had been done, particularly under the auspices of the Detroit Civil Rights Federation, a broadly assembled organization which had been formed two years earlier in a successful campaign against repressive state legislation. A large number of noted authors, educators and other public figures were induced to lend their names in support of "civil rights" for the auto workers. But little of this goodwill was reflected in Flint where the feeling of dependency upon the beneficence of General Motors was such, that only in rare instances did professional people show any open sympathy.

Fear also played its part and there was good reason as shown in the cases of five pro-union teachers who were refused renewal of their contracts at the end of the school year. On the other hand teachers who browbeat their pupils for wearing their fathers' union button to school—

several such cases were brought to our attention—did so with impunity. High school students were asked to write essays on the criminal wrongs and dangers of the sitdown strike, with the palpable intention of causing a rift in family loyalties. Even physicians proved partisan. When later, a flu epidemic swept through the city, a number of them when called refused to attend several Fisher One sitdowners whom it was thought better not to move. Forgetting their Hippocratic oath, they found excuses or even openly stated their objections: "Not those out-of-town mugs!" Several doctors and other professionals were known to be active in the Flint Alliance.

There was more friendliness to the strikers shown by small business people, though as the strike dragged on such sympathy was put to a strain. A disadvantage was the intangible element in the union's chief demand: "recognition." A request for a definite wage increase would have gained wider support in a community where prosperity was rigidly geared to the workers' pay envelope. There were certainly not many cases like the one reported to us of a grocer who receipted the substantial bill of an active striker, saying: "Here's your wages, now we're both satisfied."

The union's welfare committee which was headed by one of Arnold Lenz's Chevrolet victims, Walter Reed, pressed the county agency for speedier handling of needy cases. Documentary evidence of anti-union bias on the part of Victor S. Woodward, welfare administrator, had been printed by the *Flint Auto Worker* before the strike—bringing agitated official demurrers—so that the union felt justified in asking for a change during the emergency. Governor

Murphy responded by sending in the state welfare chief, liberal Dr. William Haber, to take over the Flint office, while announcing that need alone would determine the giving of aid. The union's request that the intake staff be increased was agreed to and the waiting period cut to four days. The new administration met throughout the strike with the UAW committee and allowed its representatives, wearing large badges, to be stationed in the welfare offices to assist members and others in need of advice.

The union also intensified its recruiting work. Membership had picked up considerably during the strike but it was still inadequate at Buick, AC Sparkplug and even Chevrolet, though this last plant had shown the best recent growth. A hundred volunteers under Charley Killinger manned the organizing committee with Art Case, Lou Baraty, Ed Geiger, Henry Clark, John McGill and other future leaders of the vast Buick factory circulating workers of their plant, while women (Irene Mitchell, Laura Heyward, Rose Webber, Nellie Besson) were among the best missionaries at the AC plant where the female sex predominated. A tall drawly southerner, Gib Rose, began to attract notice for union salesmanship among his Chevrolet co-workers, accounting for a hundred new members before he and the other Chevy men were recalled to work.

The campaign was conducted house-to-house. Each volunteer was assigned a zone and from morning till night he knocked on doors, dropped into beer gardens, talked to workers wherever they could be found. The experiences of the campaigners gave us an excellent gauge of the popular mind in regard to the strike—the sentiment of both workers and non-workers was surprisingly sympathetic.

The success of the drive may have had something to do with the reopening of the Buick and Chevrolet plants which the company had closed voluntarily early in the strike. Certain it is that when the union thereupon merely shifted its activities to the factories themselves, this created as much excitement in the management as it did in the men. Hundreds of armed "loyal workers" in each plant were excused from other duties and many were kept inside overnight. The company police were bolstered by men hired directly from the city police force.

At Buick and AC violence flared several times as company guards attacked the sound car, that feared and hated symbol. And long after the strike two members of the city's detective squad testified under oath that City Manager Barringer had plotted with them to use the union's spreading organization tactics as a blind to kill Bob Travis, Roy and Vic Reuther and myself by manufacturing an incident outside the Buick plant. But how he expected to get all four of us there at one time was never made clear.*

The scene shifted momentarily to Washington where the principals in the great struggle were called by Secretary of Labor Frances Perkins. President Roosevelt continued to remain strictly aloof from the proceedings—he was busy ostensibly with his inaugural speech—and John Lewis was displeased. He felt that the Labor Secretary could not command the proper respect of the Wall Street men and had a notion that they would refuse to meet with him.

He was right. Perkins made the request of Alfred P.

*One of the detectives claimed Barringer had even provided him with an unlisted gun for the contemplated act.

Sloan but he turned it down flat. Unilateral conferences began with the Secretary speaking first to one group and then to the other, and getting nowhere fast. Lewis felt it was clearly time for the President to speak. This was no occasion for politic considerations (it was said by some that Roosevelt had given the AFL definite assurances that he would do nothing to aid the CIO in its crisis). The fate of millions of people hung in the balance. The existence of the CIO—labor's greatest hope—was at stake. "This is no time for neutrality or pussyfooting," was the way the blunt labor leader put it and he issued a statement that was designed to force Roosevelt out into the open:

This strike is going to be fought to a successful conclusion. No half-baked compromise is going to allow General Motors to doublecross us again. We are willing to hold immediate conferences with both sides holding their arms—that is, with the men remaining in the plants....We have advised the Administration that the economic royalists of General Motors—the du Ponts and Sloans and others—contributed their money and used their energy to drive the President of the United States out of the White House. The Administration asked labor to help it repel this attack. Labor gave its help. The same economic royalists now have their fangs in labor, and the workers expect the Administration in every reasonable and legal way to support the auto workers in their fight with the same rapacious enemy....

Here at last was the break the press had been waiting for. "Dictator" Lewis had spoken, demanding the payment of who-knew-what secret election pledge given for the $500,000 that the miners had poured into the Democratic campaign coffers. Editorial opposition to the strike had been almost universal heretofore, to be sure, but it had been forced to hold itself within bounds out of consider-

174

ation for the amazing popularity of the strikers' cause. A Gallup poll made public about this time gave an almost even split between those favoring the "John L. Lewis group of employees" and sympathizers of the "employers."

But President Roosevelt refused to be smoked out and, in a one-sentence statement, he rebuked the CIO leader:

Of course, in the interests of peace there come moments when statements, conversations and headlines are not in order.

This gave the General Motors bigwigs the chance they thought they wanted. Sloan-Thomas-Brown puffed their cheeks, tilted their noses and strutted magnificently off the scene. Now the world could see what they had been up against! They had recently "proven" with exhaustive figures what a tiny minority the union actually constituted in the plants. This made Lewis' arrogance all the more reprehensible. Now, they indicated, the corporation would proceed to carry out its independent course and hinted at resumption of injunctive proceedings. Meanwhile, straining the role of benevolent daddy to the breaking point, the corporation announced a plan of reopening as many of the unstruck plants as was possible to "alleviate distress."

The GM leaders likewise demanded that the back-to-work sentiment be put to an election test, though contradictorily refusing to accept the majority principle in such a vote for collective bargaining purposes. They had no intention of letting the Wagner Labor Act slip in the back door that way.

Lewis replied to the universal storm of attack.

"I do not believe," he said with fine scorn, "as some

have suggested, that the President intended to rebuke the working people of America who are his friends and who are only attempting to secure the rights guaranteed by the Constitution and under the public policy declared by Congress and under the Norris-LaGuardia Act...."

But he was more disturbed than appeared on the surface, partly revealing his concern when speaking to the auto leaders who had meanwhile hastened to Washington.

"Perkins thinks I'm responsible for the continuation of the strike," he told them. "She thinks you fellows would be willing to settle but that I'm the one that's keeping you steamed up."

"Well, we can quickly disabuse her mind of that delusion," Mortimer said. "It's the workers in those plants that are conducting this strike."

The statement was not mere rhetoric. Though the strikers watched these distant goings-on with interest, and while they applauded the aggressive words of Lewis and the other leaders, they had the strong conviction that this was all somehow window dressing and that the battle would in the last analysis have to be won by themselves. It was a spirit of independence and even intransigence born of struggle which the auto workers have never lost and which, as things turned out, it was indeed fortunate that they had acquired so early.

There can be no question of the anger that Lewis' action stirred in the Administration. Roosevelt objected to being drawn into the affair not only for personal-political reasons but also because he was anxious not to dim Murphy's star by his intercession. Perhaps, also, he was holding himself in reserve for the really ultimate moment.

And, meanwhile, Secretary Perkins was very resentful of the slur which Lewis, long inexcusably prejudiced on the subject of the lady Labor Department head, had cast on her mediatory capabilities.

She announced that she was contemplating a virtual demand that Sloan and Lewis get together and "lay their cards on the table." The formal request for such a meeting was soon issued. The union immediately acknowledged it—it was exactly what Lewis had wanted, rebuke or no rebuke, for he was merely interested in getting the corporation to open negotiations without requiring any self-defeating concessions by the union.

But now the company did an amazing thing—it turned the Secretary's mandate down. "The question of the evacuation of the plants unlawfully held is not, in our view, an issue to be further negotiated," Sloan wrote Perkins. "We will bargain on the proposals set forth in the union's letter of January 4th as soon as our plants are evacuated and not before."

It was sheer insanity. Lewis' intervention had been a bluff but nonetheless constructive attempt to force the beginning of negotiations through an appeal to presidential prestige. But the corporation's action in turning down the Administration's statutory (by virtue of the Act of 1913 setting up the office of Secretary of Labor) request meant that the entire onus of blame for the continued crisis was shifted to its shoulders. In one stroke it had lost all the publicity advantage it had gained through Lewis' demand and Roosevelt's rebuke. However, negotiations were the last thing the corporation wanted at this moment. It had other thoughts in mind.

And now the President sought to restore the delicate balance he was maintaining. Again calling the press and again allowing himself to be directly quoted he said:

I told them [the corporation] that I was not only disappointed in the refusal of Mr. Sloan to come down here, but I regarded it as a very unfortunate decision on his part.

Nevertheless, the corporation proceeded with the execution of its plan to reopen unstruck plants and thus restore jobs to thousands of its employees. The fact was that many of the plants had originally been shut down prematurely, not only to guard against the possible spread of the strike but also to heighten the impression of the catastrophic effects resulting from the action of the supposedly small minority of union workers.

Actually, many of these plants and particularly a number of those producing parts might have continued for some time building up badly needed banks of inventory; as a few in fact had done, remaining in operation long after finished bodies had ceased coming off the lines. So now to the corporation's normal beneficent role of giving jobs to its workers (and not primarily of making profits) was added that of "making work" under supposedly purely sacrificial conditions. The simple procedure of reopening the plants was thus enveloped in a lofty moral haze sanctioned by a holy law—dating from the Magna Carta, it was said—which a spokesman proclaimed in a break during a broadcast of the General Motors symphony orchestra:

"A universal principle—an age-old principle—an eternal principle—is the right to work."

There was only one danger in the "made-work" plan—

the possibility of further strikes being called in the plants that were opened. A strike in either Chevrolet or Buick in Flint for example would be a terrible blow to the corporation. However, following certain rash statements of several of the organizers on the subject Bob Travis hastened to give assurances that the union would not interfere with the reopening of these plants. But he warned against any discriminatory actions of the management. The logic of his viewpoint was that as long as General Motors production was crippled the fewer workers that suffered loss of work the better, particularly since back-to-work propaganda would be most effective among those who had been forced out of work while not themselves directly involved in the strike.

The Flint city authorities seized eagerly on Travis' assurances, inviting the union to a conference where they could be made official. The meeting was held in Prosecutor Joseph's office. Roy Reuther and I accompanied Travis while Joseph assembled Chief Wills, Sheriff Wolcott and Mayor Harold Bradshaw.

The absence of City Manager Barringer was significant since he was generally recognized as the key personality in the situation. But this uncompromising individual had evidently balked at the sort of informal recognition of the union that such a conference constituted. The others on the other hand seemed very pacific and eager to reach an agreement that would circumscribe the hostilities. They gave the impression of being overwhelmed by the strike.

Travis started off by telling Joseph that he felt that the former had called the wrong people if he was concerned about "avoiding trouble."

"Your man is Boysen if you really are sincere in what you say."

To illustrate what he meant he opened the Flint Alliance dodger that had been distributed the day before and read from it:

Every worker and citizen of Flint is invited to hear the legal rights of men who want to work explained at a mass meeting in the IMA Auditorium, Tuesday afternoon at 2:30 o'clock. They also will be asked to vote as to whether they want direct and forceful action taken to ensure that the rights to which they are entitled shall be given them.

"So you see," Travis said, "the only person who's threatening force and violence isn't here."

A pained, embarrassed look passed over Joseph's face. Then Bradshaw had a bright thought which did not at all sound spontaneous.

"I'll tell you what, why don't we call George and ask him to come down here?"

Joseph and the others greeted the suggestion enthusiastically.

"I'm sure he'd be glad to come," Joseph said as he seized the phone on his desk. Boysen agreed readily enough and we chatted amiably while waiting for him. Reuther engaged in an academic discussion with the grey-haired chief —the "killer who had killed several men" (Lewis)—who gave evidence of an almost childish mentality.

"Unions are opposed to violence," Reuther was saying, "because in the long run they're bound to be defeated by superior force."

"Well, you ought to get that sound car off the streets then," the chief said, making an ungainly effort to be pleasant. "You can't imagine how that gets people all riled up."

The others nodded anxious assent as Travis and Reuther and I parried significant looks.

"That's made more trouble than any other thing in this strike!" Bradshaw commented fervidly.

We had a flash of the truly profound significance to the workers' cause of the new tactics and instruments that were used in the strike. For once these appeared to be superior to those of their opponents who gave the impression of being helpless and disarmed by the fact that the workers had refused to fight with the traditional weapons.

The sound car particularly attained nightmarish proportions to the authorities and company agents everywhere whose repeated attacks upon it almost partook of a religious fervor—as though this instrument were a new god or idol that must be destroyed. In Detroit during this period two union sound cars were blown up. In Anderson the union car was seized by police. Another was immediately obtained: "They all sound alike, chief." In Indiana and Michigan, city after city quickly passed "anti-noise" ordinances as though in hope of exorcizing the monster in advance.

Travis assumed a hypocritical modesty:

"We're just a bunch of workers. We do the best we can. The other side has all the power and means of propaganda...."

"Never mind!" Chief Wills blurted out. "You've got real leaders. If we had one man like any of you boys outside Fisher Two that night, there'd have been a different story to tell!"

The others showed displeasure at the chief's candor and

the way Joseph cut him short made us think of what news-papermen had told us about old Wills, that he was nothing but a noncom office boy in the entire situation. For two years Barringer had been practically running his department.

When Boysen arrived, the others suddenly became all a-flutter.

"Sit down, George," Joseph urged obsequiously.

"No, I'll stand!"

Contempt was written all over his long, narrow face.

"Well, here's what we were talking about, George," Joseph began. "Chevrolet is opening tomorrow morning and we wanted to make sure that there won't be any trouble when the boys go back to work. We figure the city's had enough bad publicity for some time to come. Now these men have given us their pledge that nothing's going to happen outside the Chevrolet plant tomorrow...."

Boysen, a tall, leanish man, leered at Joseph as he spoke, without deigning to acknowledge his words by so much as a nod.

"Wait a second, Mr. Joseph," Roy Reuther broke in. "We have a question we'd like to ask Mr. Boysen. We think it's up to him to tell this group here whether the Flint Alliance is planning any violence."

Boysen looked out through a window and said in an abstracted, sneering manner:

"We've stated a thousand times that the Flint Alliance planned only to use legal means to get the men back to work."

"Well, how do you account for this statement in that case?" Reuther continued, slapping the dodger, and he began to read from it when Boysen gave the empty chair in front of him a violent shove.

"I don't have to be here!" he shouted. "I don't know these..." he motioned to us and seemed to hold some obscene word on his tongue. "To hell with this! The whole lot of you can go to the devil!"

He swung his arm, glared at us for a moment, then turned on his heel and slammed out of the room. The three of us and the city officials exchanged surprised glances. Then we rose to leave. It was evident that authority was no longer in this room.

The company's campaign of violence broke out simultaneously on several fronts. In Detroit, the scene was the Cadillac plant where a hundred of Commissioner Heinie Pickert's riot squad men went into action against the pickets (the sitdowners having left this plant as a result of the "truce"), splitting open several heads, including that of one woman.

The union's reply was to put a mass picket line outside the plant with Walter Reuther calling on the already famed Dodge "flying squad" to help. This aggregation which totaled several thousand volunteers had originated during an early strike threat at the Dodge plant and had become steeled by action during the Midland, Kelsey-Hayes and other strikes in the Detroit area. More recently it had engaged in a violent battle outside one of the plants of the Briggs Company when the union decided to close it following the discharge of several hundred UAW men. The unionists were reinstated. The Dodge group gave eloquent testimony of the phenomenal solidarity shown by the auto workers everywhere during this exciting period. Its members were on daily call and leaders Oliver Hamel, Mike Dragon and others would keep in touch with the union office while at work to see if and where they would be needed after the quitting whistle.

Simultaneously with the Cadillac violence, the union underwent a fiendish attack in Anderson, Indiana. Leaders here were members of the "Citizens' League for Employment Security," a counterpart of the Flint Alliance, which was made up chiefly of plant foremen, backwoods Rotarians and small-time politicians, and was openly supported by the city officials and police. When smashing the line at the Guide Lamp plant the plant manager himself assumed the heroic role. Mounting on a car top and waving an American flag, he shouted to the foremen and assorted mobsters:

"It's nights like this that a city shows what's in it!"

The mob next moved to union headquarters and in the presence of the police, swarmed in and demolished the place, throwing typewriters out of windows, ripping up all records and smashing the furniture. And all that night and during the next days organized terror strode through the city. Gangs would travel from house to house of known union members, ordering them out of town. Men and women were beaten. A number of workers deserted their homes the first night, leaving furniture and all.

When the third blow of company-inspired violence was struck at Saginaw—organizationally a suburb of Flint— the union decided that it was time to bestir itself. Joe Ditzel and several other organizers, mainly members of the United Mine Workers, were in nearby Bay City making arrangements for a mass meeting when they were attacked in broad daylight by a large group of company men. They got back to Saginaw only under police escort with the "vigilantes" following close behind.

In Saginaw the latter joined a larger mob. The organizers sought refuge inside the Bancroft Hotel but were attacked in the lobby and badly beaten while the police looked on benignly.

Finally the organizers were forced into an easily identifiable Yellow Cab and with several police cars before and behind them were rushed out of the city at a clip of sixty miles an hour. A large group of vigilante cars followed.

Inside the Flint city limits a grey sedan was parked with engine running, waiting for the arrival of the motorcade. It allowed the leading police car to pass, then as the Yellow Cab approached, it swerved suddenly straight toward it, sideswiping it off the road and right into a telephone pole.

The job was expertly done. The sedan, itself untouched, swung back on the road and disappeared to the north. The police car that was following the taxi and which had witnessed the entire maneuver made no attempt to stop it. Nor did the several cars led by Sheriff Wolcott which had met the escort at the outskirts of the city. The identity of the grey sedan or of its occupants was never known. The organizers in the Yellow Cab narrowly escaped with their lives though all were badly injured, three of them requiring several months of hospitalization.

The Flint strikers were tremendously aroused over this incident. Bob Travis announced that the Saginaw meeting which had been planned would now be held at all costs.

Details were worked out for a mass march on Saginaw of thousands of Flint men and women. A special guard would be left at the two Fisher plants to discourage an attack during the absence of these union supporters. The strike leaders felt that the critical point of the strike had been reached and that the union could look for an increasing onslaught by the company forces unless it took determined steps to defend itself.

It was plain that the company's entire campaign was merely a buildup for action in Flint. The Flint Alliance had already mustered the necessary forces for such action. At the January 26th meeting which had packed IMA Hall it was evident that the program of "moral mobilization" was approaching that extreme state where talk was to be transferred into deeds. And now came the corporation's formal suit for a new injunction, serving further notice of the oncoming assault which would have the added sanction of being directed against men who had been declared outside the law.

The legal phase of the corporation's all-out attack took the form of an amended bill of complaint and motion for injunction. It was filed in the court of Judge Paul V. Gadola, a tory stalwart whose personal holdings had evidently been carefully checked to avoid a repetition of the Black fiasco. The injunction asked for was "mandatory" and would if issued compel immediate evacuation of the plants. The company had gone through the technical procedure of offering to pay off the strikers in full so as to terminate their employment and thus to divest them of even the slight legal claim to occupation of the plants that had been made for them on the basis of their so-called "property right in their jobs."

If the unlawful seizure of the plants continued, the bill contended, the result would be "loss of the plaintiff's business and the diversion thereof to plaintiff's competitors" —and eventually, bankruptcy. The former result in any case seemed in fair way to being realized as the past few weeks' production figures would indicate. From the beginning of the strike, Ford's weekly output had steadily mounted from 16,360 to 28,325 units; Chrysler's from 20,550 to 25,350; while General Motors had skidded from 31,830 to a pitiful 6,100.

By asking also for the prohibition of outside picketing after the plants had been cleared the corporation once more revealed that its primary concern with the sitdown was its great effectiveness as a strike weapon and that all the palaver about property rights had been so much camouflage.

This fact was brought even more forcefully home in the simultaneous suit for injunction that had been filed in Cleveland. Here the accusation of an "unlawful combination and conspiracy to seize possession" had to be squared with the fact that the sitdowners had left the plant after only three days of occupancy. But this was accomplished by the argument that the "dispossession" of the company's property had been "continued by mass picketing from outside the plant." The company had, to be sure, with the aid of the city police unsuccessfully attempted on several occasions to break through the solid union phalanx. So now with an excess of delicacy it asked not for the complete outlawing of the pickets but merely for their restriction to two at each of the six plant gates.

Judge Gadola promptly issued a show-cause order and

set the hearings on the injunction for Monday, February 1st. This was a real surprise—the union was going to be given the right to speak before having judgment passed upon it! Yet Sheriff Wolcott without seeming cause or excuse—unless the case were to be considered decided before it had opened—expressed his readiness to eject the strikers upon command of the court.

10

Union Wit versus Company Force

To STRIKE DIRECTOR Bob Travis and his aides the moment cried out for a counter-offensive to the corporation's accelerated drive. The March-to-Saginaw had been countermanded by international headquarters. All arrangements for the demonstration had been completed when the order came cancelling it. This was done at the request of Governor Murphy, we were told.

We were incensed. During the Saginaw incident several attempts had been made to reach the governor for a request for state police protection, but all unavailing. We felt that his action at this time was tantamount to forcing us to disarm while allowing the company attack to go forward with impunity. If he was afraid of violence, we argued, then why couldn't he have sent a body of the state militia up to Saginaw on the day of the meeting as we had requested?

Travis realized that the union action would have to be something really spectacular—nothing second-rate would do under the circumstances. Ever since the beginning of the strike he had considered the possibility of "pulling"

Chevrolet. This plant, and particularly its motor-assembly division (Chevrolet No. 4) which made engines for a million cars a year, was generally considered to be the most important single unit in the General Motors framework.

Of course such a move was not necessitated from the standpoint of keeping the corporation's production crippled—this had long since been accomplished. But the contemplated action was regarded according to different motives. We felt that the strike was inevitably weakening because of its static condition which seemed to indicate that the union had long since demonstrated its major strength. This impression was accentuated by the reopening of the unstruck plants, a program that had been carried out in apparent defiance of the union's desire or power to resist it.

A successful strike in the corporation's prize unit would, therefore, not only shatter this impression of union weakness but would also reveal a continuing fatal vulnerability on the part of the company. It would, moreover, tear the situation from the sham center of the partisan courts back to the immediate arena of struggle where the workers had a more equal chance. And it would render the anticipated injunction, which would not cover Chevrolet, practically innocuous because of the occupation of the new and more important plant.

Travis had studied the Chevrolet plant from every angle since coming to Flint. Many times in the early days he had circled it in his little Willys-Overland "puddle-jumper," pausing at different points to contemplate its gigantic layout. The complex with its nine great factories and power plant sprawled over eighty acres through which the Flint

River bent and curved its way. From high Bluff Street you could look down on the magnificent industrial prospect and hear the mingled thunder of its stupendous productive processes. Or you might stand at the crest of Chevrolet hill at the change of shifts and watch the sudden turmoil of humanity burst from the plants—over 7,000 workers, with an equal number entering.

And for the moment the thought that this strange, unchained and elemental force would one day be a conscious, collective body of union men was utterly untenable.

And now the time had come for the test and Bob Travis did a curious thing. He decided to consult the auguries. Ever since "Frenchy" Dubuc had confessed himself a Pinkerton spy one of us was always present when he made his long-distance phone calls to his superior, Arthur Pugmire. We'd outline for him what he was to say beforehand and thus kept him in hand until he was to testify at the hearings scheduled by the LaFollette Committee. On the day the Chevrolet plant reopened Travis said to "Frenchy":

"I guess I'll go down to the booth with you today."

"What do you want me to tell Pugmire, Bob?" Dubuc asked, anxious to please.

"Well, let's see," Travis appeared to be thinking something up. "Oh tell him I was asking about Chevy 4, about the docks and entrances, the heat and light feeders and the underground approaches. Also, if you can get a boat up the Flint River to the plant. Make it sound like I was really interested."

"Frenchy" followed his instructions but got bawled out for his pains. "That guy Travis is kidding you," Pugmire told him. "He knows goddam well the union couldn't take

Chevy 4. He's just trying to pull your leg. You sure he isn't getting wise to you?"

The Pink chief's reaction was encouraging. Evidently the task of "capturing" Chevy 4 would be considered impossible. The company could be caught off balance if the strike could be launched swiftly and with ingenuity. The chief hazard would of course be the company guards. The workers reported that a veritable army was in control of the plant since the reopening, all provided with new clubs and many with guns. What chance would the union group, inexperienced, none too big yet, have against this mustering? With Ed Cronk, Howard Foster and Kermit Johnson, three Chevy workers, Travis retired to his Dresden Hotel room, with stringent orders not to be disturbed, to discuss these questions of strength and weakness and to work out a plan, if possible, of outwitting the Chevrolet guards.

The three men Travis had chosen were all in their early twenties. Johnson and Foster were of the intellectual type while Ed Cronk resembled nothing more than a big farm boy. And that was what he was. Many Flint workers had maintained a partial tie to the land through cultivating extensive vegetable gardens adjacent to their homes* while some lived miles out of the city limits where they could rent or buy a few acres and in off hours raise chickens, a cow or two and plant their rows of corn. During the sit-down, aside from concern about food and coal for their families, a frequent worry of the strikers was "keeping the hens fed."

*This was before the war turned even inveterate city-dwellers into tillers of the soil.

Ed Cronk had one of these part-time farms which was so far out of town that when strike duties kept him late in Flint he would remain overnight at Pengelly headquarters, flopping down on a bench or even on the floor and sleeping the moment he let himself go. Big, beefy, always smiling, the tall strike stave he carried at all times made you think of the man with the hoe, but there was nothing static about Ed Cronk, as he was destined soon to prove.

After poring over a rough plan of the Chevrolet area and discussing the questions of relative union numbers for several hours a tentative graph of action was finally worked out. This action was to be concentrated in the three plants where the union was strongest—Chevy 4, 6 and 9—and would take place at the change of shifts to assure the presence of a maximum of union forces. The three plants formed an almost equilateral triangle with the distance between any two of them about three hundred yards.

The initial move decided on was a decoy action—a sit-down at Chevy 9—which would serve to draw the guards away from the other plants. A big racket would be put on here to increase the illusion, with pickets outside, the sound car, the women's Emergency Brigade, and so forth. Shortly thereafter things would start in the other two plants with Chevy 6 merely mustering its strong union forces to march on the gargantuan Chevy 4 plant and help close it down.

Before the session broke up Travis made the three young men raise their right hands and give the pledge of secrecy.

"If we can put this across," he said, "it means we've cracked the backbone of GM's back-to-work movement and the strike is ours!"

Sunday evening had been set aside for a general Chevrolet membership meeting. Plant manager Arnold Lenz had presented the union with the formal excuse for strike action by discharging three union men during the week past, one for wearing a button, one for "soliciting" and one for his own "protection" against the supposed ire of anti-unionists.

We were delighted—the company was playing right into our hands! Of course we raised hullabaloo over these discharges, made veiled threats, but would have hated to see our demands acceded to just at that time. There was an overflow meeting. Mrs. Gifford Pinchot, Fr. J. W. R. Maguire and Mary Heaton Vorse warmed the boys up with sparkling talks.

Then the meeting was closed to all but Chevrolet workers and Travis took the platform amid a rapt silence. It was strange how the workers could sense the imminence of a grave decision. Travis was no orator. In fact, he seldom took the platform except to discuss some organizational matter and was delighted to be able to shirk this activity through division of labor with such excellent speakers as Roy and Vic Reuther and, more recently, Powers Hapgood, a CIO representative who had joined the strike staff.

"Men," he began, "when the unstruck plants reopened last week we gave our pledge that we wouldn't interfere. We saw no reason to. We knew that you boys could use the money. Besides, your working wasn't going to weaken the strike anyway. Then too we didn't want to antagonize the fence-sitters by a dog-in-the-manger attitude. However, it seems that Arnold Lenz took this as a sign of weakness. He's fired several men already and intimidated hundreds of others. If this continues every union man in the shop can kiss his job goodbye."

There was a stir of acquiescence and cries of "That's right!" and "Amen!" which never failed to punctuate the speeches at our strike meetings.

"Lenz is the spearhead of General Motors," Travis resumed, "and General Motors is now definitely out to smash the union by force and violence. You saw what happened this week in Anderson and at Cadillac and finally the cowardly attack of the murder squad on Joe Ditzel and the other boys in Saginaw. I've called Mr. Lenz and asked him for a conference. Now I haven't asked you yet what you want me to tell him but I'll tell you what I *think* you want me to tell him. You want me to say: '*Mr. Lenz, these three boys and Bill Roy and Howard Tolles and Walter Reed and all the other fellows who were fired before have got to be taken back—or else!*'"

The windows at the rear of the hall seemed ready to shiver into splinters with the roar coming from fifteen hundred throats. Travis continued:

"The organizers have worked out some plans that we're going to discuss with the stewards. You know why we can't just merely talk about them in the open though we'd like to do that. All I'm going to say is keep your eyes and ears open. When it comes time for you to act you won't be able to mistake what you're supposed to do."

The stewards and volunteer organizers were kept on after the meeting, a group of a hundred and fifty or so. From these a more select number were to be chosen. Travis had another one of his super-dramatic ideas for making these choices. The stewards were lined up in the hall and allowed to pass one by one into the darkened adjoining room where Travis, Roy Reuther and I by a quick exchange of eyes

195

passed on the trustworthiness of the candidate. The thirty men thus designated were given a signed slip of paper which they were told to present at the Fisher One plant at midnight. The others Travis merely shook by the hand, imparting to them some abstruse instruction such as "Follow the man who takes the lead " or "Watch for the American flag."*

The main purpose of this elaborate procedure was to eliminate any chance that details of the new strike plan would get to the company.The careful timing of the strike, which was to start ten minutes earlier at Chevy 9 than at the other two plants, was the secret substance of the whole design to draw off the armed guards at Chevy 4 and thus lighten the task of the union forces at this crucial plant. But everything depended on keeping the company in ignorance.

On the way to Fisher One, however, doubt struck us. How could we be sure that there was not a stoolpigeon even among those we had so carefully selected? All had been active in the strike but the time had been far too short for any final estimates. Moreover, the LaFollette Committee reports abounded with instances of spies who had done excellent, constructive work over a period while seeking to establish their reputations. Roy Reuther and I particularly disagreed about two or three individuals whom Bob Travis had approved over our veto. We questioned him about these choices.

Travis smiled. "I wanted to get them in," he said, giving us an enigmatic look.

*Travis always played consciously on the love of mystery and adventure shared by most Americans. It was part of his "style."

And then he went on to explain an amazing sub-plot that he had worked out.

"We're not going to tell this meeting the whole plan," he said. "It'd be dynamite. Even if there wasn't a couple of stoolpigeons among them, how would you keep thirty men from telling their friends or their wives? By tomorrow morning the whole town would know about it."

He paused, studying our faces quizzically. Did we understand? Of course we understood! But how were we going to get around *that* barrier?

"So here's what we'll do," Travis continued, coolly. "We'll tell them only that we're going to strike Plant 9 and the rest we'll keep secret. Except for the three boys that know about it already, naturally, and who have to take the lead. Your stoolpigeons are going to be there. They'll run right back to Arnold Lenz with this false dope. Okay. Lenz is pretty shrewd but he'll believe this is the McCoy all right because of all the trouble we went to to get this group chosen. That means tomorrow at 3:20 he'll rush his armed thugs to Chevy 9 and fall right into our trap!"

Slowly, as Travis unfolded the brilliant plan, smiles dawned on our faces. When he finished, Roy Reuther clasped him in an appreciative bear-hug. It was a bold and ingenious conception. Instead of the impossible course of trying to keep critical information from the company spies, this element would be drawn in as part of the whole plan, to play an unconsciously supporting role. The false intelligence that was made available to the unknown stoolpigeons would then, presumably, get back to Arnold Lenz, leading him to elaborate self-defeating counter-moves. It was my feeling that Travis got a personal gratification out of the role he had worked out for the whip-cracking Chevrolet plant manager against whom he was especially eager to pay off old scores.

As the selected men appeared at the Fisher One plant they were silently escorted through a dark corridor to one of the department offices. The room was small and many of the men had to sit on the floor. Travis stood looking them over searchingly for several minutes and then solemnly he began to talk. He told them how the contemplated plan would be the crowning action of the strike. It would mean certain victory—or defeat. When, however, he announced that the project entailed the "taking" of Chevy 9, it fell like a dud. One of the men ventured a question. Couldn't General Motors get bearings* from other places? He was quite sure that the plant at Muncie, Indiana, could supply all the corporation needed.

"We've checked into all that," Travis said with authority. "Besides we're not really interested in the importance of the plant. General Motors isn't going to put out cars anyway so long as Fisher One and Cleveland-Fisher are kept tight. This strike is merely to show that the union hasn't demonstrated all its strength yet and that there's more to follow unless the company comes to its senses. The reason we chose Chevy 9 is because the union group is strong there. Also the plant is on the street which will make it easy to feed and defend. Do you get the point?"

The men thought they did. They perked up a little.

"One more thing. You boys in the other plants aren't to rush out and help Plant 9. The boys in 9 can take care

*This is what Chevy 9 produced chiefly.

of themselves. Stick to your own plant and—*watch for developments.*"

After the meeting Travis drew Ted La Duke and Tom Klasey, a couple of the Chevy 9 men, aside.

"I want to tell you fellows that everything depends on the fight you can put up. We don't expect you to win out but it's absolutely necessary for you to hold the plant from 3:20 to about 4:10. Then you can walk out. You see, we're not really after Chevy 9. We couldn't tell all those fellows our real plan or it would be sure to get back to Lenz. What you guys are going to accomplish by your fight is to draw off all the company guards while the boys are taking *Chevy 6.* That's the plant we really want!"

And thus was the plan laid for the "capturing" of Chevrolet No. 4—with checks, double checks and triple checks.

The following morning, Monday, Arnold Lenz called off the meeting he had granted Travis for that day, telling him to call on Tuesday for another appointment. This was as much as to say that the union plan had worked thus far —Lenz had evidently been forewarned by company spies and was busy preparing his "reply."

Nevertheless, Travis kicked up an awful fuss at the postponement, alleging that he saw in the action a subtle connection with the story that was being carried by some Canadian papers that the corporation was going to repossess its plants by force on this day. He told reporters of another Chevy man having been fired that day for wearing a union button, a chap with twenty years seniority, and he left the impression that the revolt among the rank and file of Chevrolet men was getting out of hand. At about 11 a.m. Kermit Johnson, one of the three key men in the strike plan, showed up at the union office, looking sheepish. Travis transfixed him with a cold stare.

"How come you aren't in the plant?"

"I overslept," Johnson laughed self-consciously.

"Can you get in at noon?"

"Sure."

"See that you do!"

But the noon hour passed and when Travis ran into Johnson again he was fit to be tied. This time the young chap had simply "forgotten" to go down in time.

"Listen," Travis told him, "you're going to get into that plant at the change of shifts if I have to throw you through a window! Even so you're not going to be able to hold back many of the day men. We can just about write them off."

It was a case of funk—one of the chances of war—but it gave us some awful misgivings. So much depended on three or four individuals just like this scared kid! At 2:30 a meeting opened in the Pengelly auditorium. It had been called ostensibly for the purpose of organizing a protest march on the courthouse where the injunction hearings had started that afternoon. At this hour also the union's two sound cars, each under heavy guard, began making devious tours of the city, advertising the meeting at Pengelly that evening but all the time drawing closer and closer to the Chevrolet area where each one had its part outlined for that afternoon's activities.

A little after three o'clock one of the cars took up its post on Bluff Street overlooking Chevy 6 while the other with a considerable group of pickets had swung about finally to Kearsley Street in front of Chevy 9. Many of the men with this car were from the Westside local of Detroit—fellows from Kelsey Hayes chiefly—whom Walter Reuther had brought up in response to a request by Bob Travis who was anxious for as large a mustering as possible for the afternoon's events.

At 3:10, while Travis was speaking at the Pengelly meeting, my wife came suddenly dashing into the hall, looking very excited. She handed Travis a slip of paper. It was blank but Travis drew his eyes over it as though he were reading. Then he said quietly:

"Brothers and sisters, I don't want you to get excited, but I've just gotten word that there's trouble at Chevy 9. The guards are beating up on our fellows inside the plant. There are some pickets down there already but they can use some reinforcements. I suggest that we break up this meeting and go right down there."

The audience, more than half of them women, pushed their chairs back and made a mad rush for the stairs. You weren't fooling them—they had expected something like this. Their foresense was confirmed when, on arriving outside, they met a long line of cars waiting with motors running. The transportation of the pickets to the plant was accomplished in a few minutes. In fact it was so expeditiously done that when they arrived, nothing had yet begun to "happen" inside the plant.

The reporters had also been tipped off that there would be "something doing" at Chevy 9 and there were dozens of them, including movie trucks from Paramount and Pathé News, already on the spot. The photographers called on the pickets and particularly the women to pose for them in innumerable arrangements but always with clubs brandishing. The newsmen weren't sure whether or not they were witnessing something amazingly new in strike strategy—where the whole plan was told in advance and then carried out inexorably.

But all this display was hardly necessary. For a "leak" to the company from the previous midnight's "secret" meeting had had the proper results. The entire armed force of the Chevrolet division had been concentrated in the personnel building right next to Plant 9, awaiting the union "attack."

The first visible move came shortly before 3:30 when a large group of blue-uniformed company guards filed out of the personnel building, crossed the narrow driveway and entered Chevy 9. The pickets, assembled on the opposite side of the street, booed lustily. From time to time thereafter additional guards came running from different directions; latecomers from the other plants. Then an ambulance came clanging down the street and was admitted through the factory gate. Arnold Lenz was prepared for all eventualities.

But no violence had as yet taken place inside of the plant, from what could be made out on the street. Evidently the strike had begun since the outside windows of the factory which opened right to the street sidewalk had been ominously shut a few minutes before. Suddenly the pickets were conscious of fighting going on inside behind the little opaque square panes. The crowd grew excited and when one of the windows was pushed open and a worker's bloody head appeared, gasping for air, Geraldine Klasey recognized her husband, let out a yell and dashed across the street, screaming:

"They're smothering them! Let's give them air!"

All the other women followed immediately and the men started to go also but were held back by their leaders who fought to quell the hysteria. Walter Reuther had to sock one of his irate unionists on the jaw to quiet him. Meanwhile the women began smashing the plant windows with their sticks, revealing indistinct snatches of the inside fighting, vague forms milling about eerily in a thick fog.

Reuther and my wife finally managed to get the women quieted and away from the windows and marching in a line. Sullen, boiling with indignation, they marched around and around while their leaders admonished them to: "Keep union discipline! Don't be provoked!" For standing nearby was a large contingent of the hated city police, riot clubs in hand, seemingly prepared for action at any excuse.

All union sympathizers were going through a hell of doubt and indecision. What was happening inside? Could the workers win with all that mustering of power against them? To everybody, of course, this plant was the actual union goal. After what seemed an era of waiting, it was suddenly evident that the fighting had ceased inside. The city police, with surprising gentleness, began wedging the women's picket line slowly back along the street.

A strange quiet settled on the union crowd, a quiet of conscious defeat and apprehension. Thus did the verisimilitude of this phase of the union plan fool even its own adherents. The leaders, after conferring with each other, decided to abandon the field just as some of the men from inside, a number of them hurt and bleeding, started coming out. The outsiders picked up several of the wounded men and took them along. It was a little after four o'clock.

All through these exciting events the injunction proceedings were taking place at the county courthouse with the union attorneys holding the forum. There was drama here, too, for the partisan audience that packed the courtroom and hallways outside. The union had based its position on the "unclean hands" theory, arguing that the corporation had sacrificed all claim to equity in the case because of previous multiple violations of the Wager Labor Act. The company's plea was built entirely on the argument of the priority and sanctity of property rights—"if these rights can be challenged, all rights are gone"—and was glitteringly studded with citations and precedents, one of which went as far back as 1898.

Lee Pressman, CIO counsel, singled out this citation to ask if General Motors were approaching the case "in the light of doctrines of 1898 or in the light of doctrines approved by the people of Michigan in 1936?"*

"We are not considering economic questions," Judge Gadola rapped out, halting him abruptly.

"We claim that we can show that the action of the management was of a nature which would forfeit their right to the plants," Pressman asserted, holding to his guns.

"Do you mean that you claim the right to seize property as you see fit?" the judge demanded angrily, fairly rising in his seat.

"We mean that we can show a most ruthless and blatant disregard for the laws of the United States as they concern relationship between worker and employer," Pressman responded.

*Reference to the overwhelming pro-New Deal vote in the November elections.

"Do you claim that one wrong justifies another?" persisted the judge who frequently forgot that he was not one of the corporation's counsel.

"No, but I do claim that to get an injunction the appellant must come into court with clean hands, free from any blame for illegality."

Roy Brownell, General Motors counsel, momentarily forgot the necessity of observing the outer forms and expressed the corporation's cynical confidence of judicial favor by rising with sudden anger during Pressman's presentation and exclaiming:

"If this longwinded argument continues I'll walk out!"

Pressman called the contemptuous outburst to the attention of the judge and Brownell flushed an apology.

On another occasion when attorney Maurice Sugar was presenting evidence of anti-union actions of the police in other General Motors centers, he told how he and Vice-President Ed Hall had gone to Indiana following the outbreak of violence in Anderson with the intention of reestablishing the union headquarters. On the news of their coming, the GM Delco-Remy plant was closed down by the management and a big group marched to the station under command of the supervision. Fortunately Sugar and Hall had been forewarned, leaving the train at Muncie, and the Anderson mob went through the train in fruitless search of their expected prey.

Suddenly Gadola broke sneeringly into Sugar's recital:

"The police don't seem to like your union."

"No, they don't!" the lawyer snapped back. "The police in Anderson, Muncie and Flint don't like the union because they take orders from General Motors."

The judge said nothing.

Sugar was continuing the union's argument when someone handed Pressman a note. He glanced at it and quickly interrupted Sugar's talk:

"I have just received word of the latest General Motors violence. This message says that seven men have been killed in rioting down on Chevrolet Avenue."

The announcement naturally created a great hubbub in the courtroom and quickly spread to the crowds in the outside corridor. Gadola rapped his gavel and said somberly:

"I have known about the riot for some time but I have no proof as to who is to blame for it. I wish I did know who was to blame and could have the chance to deal with them as completely as is possible under the law."

Bob Travis and I had remained at headquarters behind closed doors, each at one of the phones. Several scouts had been assigned to different sectors of the "front" with a handful of nickels and instructions to call every five minutes. Our function was to coördinate the actions of the several groups through issuing proper orders in line with the developing situation. This was all the more essential since so few of even the leaders knew the exact nature of the plan. It was not a question of mistrust but just an additional assurance against the human weakness of gossip.

It was a quarter of four and still we had no news of Chevy 4 except that the day shift had left the plant at 3:30 and there was no sign of a disturbance or other happening inside the plant. Organizer Ralph Dale was keeping us informed about this sector. The sound of motors and machinery seemed to indicate that work was going on full-force, Dale said. Reports from Chevy 9 showing that everything there had gone off smoothly and exactly as planned left us cold. We felt desolate as we admitted to each other that apparently our brilliant plan had fizzed.

Finally we couldn't stand the suspense any longer and Travis sent me down to Chevrolet to reconnoiter. It was around 4:15 and I was hastening with the driver toward the volunteer car that was to take me when I heard a din of shouting and cheering coming from up the street. It was the union caravan returning from Chevy 9. The boys had been told as they were passing police headquarters to sing out as though in triumph and they did so well, hanging two deep on every vehicle and with pickets upraised, that they might easily have impressed observers that they were returning from victorious battle. I dashed to the sound car.

"How come you're back already?" I shouted to Walter Reuther above the din. "How about Chevy 4?"

"It fell through," was the reply. "The plant's working full force."

We went back to headquarters. The men emptied their hats of the paper they had stuffed into them in anticipation of meeting up with police clubs. We stood looking at each other disconsolately.

"Well, Bob, it was a noble effort anyway," Powers Hapgood said with invincible good humor.

The phone rang. It was Ralph Dale. We could hear his excited voice rattling through the receiver:

"We've got her, Bob! The plant's ours!"

"What the hell are you talking about?" Travis yelled. "Are you crazy?"

"Honest to God, Bob! I've just been talking to the boys on the inside. All the scabs have left already. The boys have begun to barricade the back doors. We're going in to help them."

For a moment we were too stunned to express our joy. How had it all happened? How was it that we hadn't heard about it sooner? It was evident that we had underestimated the time that would be needed to shut down the enormous plant. Also, because of Kermit Johnson's absence the strike had not been launched until the second shift was underway—that especially played hob with the original plan. And there were other miscalculations and misadventures. But the workers had made up for them all with a remarkable spontaneity.

11

Capture of Chevy 4

AND YET in its broad outlines the original plan had worked out surprisingly well. At 3:20, ten minutes before the end of the first shift, the night shift men of Chevy 9 who had gathered in the cafeteria in the southwest corner of the one-story plant lined up three abreast and entered the plant proper. They circled the shop, shouting: "Strike! Strike!"

A majority of the day workers immediately shut down their machines and joined the parade. Others hastily made for the plant exit, some without stopping for their wraps, but were halted by a cluster of plant guards who had been stationed near the door. Almost simultaneously the doors opened from outside and a throng of company guards came running in, all armed with big hickory sticks. This was the battalion that had been waiting in the adjacent personnel building. Storm trooper Arnold Lenz himself was in the lead, closely followed by personnel director Floyd Corcoran and other top managerial and supervisory officials.

Lenz's army swarmed into the plant and followed in the

wake of the union parade, shouting: "Reds! Communists!"
For a while only a row of machines separated the two
groups. The unionists shook their fists furiously at Lenz.
"You bastard!" they cried. "We ought to tear you apart."
A flying wedge of guards split the workers' line up in the
center of the shop and then an attack with clubs and black-
jacks began. The workers were outnumbered but they had
put defensive weapons in handy places. They spread out to
break the attack up and began firing oil pump blanks and
pulleys, anything that came to hand, at their attackers.

Dozens of individual fights were soon taking place in
scattered parts of the shop. Several guards would isolate
a striker and go to work on him. Two union men, Russel
Hardy and Morley Crafts, were beaten unconscious, then
tramped on while lying on the ground. Some of their buddies rushed to them, fought the guards off and carried the
injured men to the cafeteria. Many others were hurt,
less seriously, including a number on the company's side
also, the captain of the plant police among them. These
latter were taken outside and treated in the plant hospital.

The 3:30 whistle blew while the fighting raged at its
fiercest. Little by little the guards retreated to the back
part of the plant where Lenz and a few others had gathered to watch the spectacle. The remaining workers were
assembled at the opposite side of the plant facing the
street.

Suddenly, at an order from Lenz, the guards produced
riot guns and fizzing shells began to explode among the
workers. All ventilation having been shut off, the gas took
immediate effect and the men began coughing violently.
But they held on doggedly. When the women began break-

ing windows from the outside the company group seemed to get scared. For a while the two sides merely stood glaring across at each other. Then the company forces began planning to make a final attack to drive the by now greatly reduced union group out of the plant. But the men spared them the trouble. At 4:10 sharp they marched out in unison, having fulfilled their task with exemplary courage and determination.

In Chevy 4 meanwhile the day crew had gone home and the night crew had started working. Kermit Johnson had managed to get in at the change of shifts but was able to keep only a handful of his buddies from leaving the plant. With these few he hid in the balcony toilets, undecided what course to take. Finally the small group determined to make a stab at closing the plant. The lines were going full speed when the men descended the stairs into the pit and began shouting:

"Shut 'er down! Shut 'er down!"

But nothing happened. The shouters were too few to attract any notice. A worker here and there joined them but it made no real impression—the great toiling city continued its infinite, interlocking activity: drills and presses and punches pounding and vibrating, cranes swinging back and forth, supply trucks threading the aisles. And everywhere, men crowding the machines with an intense concentration.

The little band finally reached the rear northeast gate leading on to the plant grounds. Here Ed Cronk was scheduled to come with his Chevy 6 men. Everything depended on him now since the day crew at Chevy 4 had failed to start the ball rolling.

In Plant 6 as the 3:30 whistle blew and the machines started up Ed Cronk went to his press, set it going, shut it off again in one minute, picked up a piece of lead pipe, took an American flag from his pocket and holding it above his head began running through the plant, shouting:

"Shut 'er off and follow me!"

This plant which made heavy steel parts like fenders, running boards and splash guards was extremely noisy. Cronk banged his pipe on things as he ran to attract attention, jumping over stationary conveyors and supply stacks that were in his way and heading for the exit. The plant superintendent and a group of four or five foremen sought to stand him off but Cronk swung his pipe and they backed away. He was a big, husky baby and was clearly in no mood to frolic. However, he travelled too fast and by the time he reached the door he had only about thirty-five men with him.

Cronk decided to go on with this group anyway, figuring that there was no time to go back for more. It was but a short jog to Chevy 4. When the men got there, Kermit Johnson and his group were waiting at the door with the bad news that their part of the little plan had failed to come off.

"Well," Cronk said, "let's go back and get some more men then. I would have waited for more but I thought you'd just about be shut down here by this time."

They hotfooted it back to 6. When they got there, things were really stirring. Carl Bibber's powerful group of a hundred men from the dock—all union—were working through the plant and another bunch of fifty were marching and shouting in a different section. With the newcomers adding a spirited third force the union men succeeded in shutting the entire works down in no time.

"All right, boys," Ed Cronk shouted as once more he raised aloft his crumpled American flag, "everybody over to Chevy 4 now!"

The entire plant moved in force.

The Chevy 4 workers had been waiting meanwhile with agonizing tenseness. Kermit Johnson's belated little sally had hardly been noticed by more than a few hundred of them. The plan as given out by the union—that Chevy 9 was the objective—had not fooled these men. Many of them felt that their own plant was to be involved in the action but where it would start and what it would be nobody could guess. Without getting definite instructions a number of the men had taken certain little precautions before leaving home, packing an extra lunch or pocketing several packages of cigarets. Now they worked nervously with one eye over shoulder as it were.

At about a quarter to four Bob Barrett, general superintendent of the motor division, came running through the plant, tapping several men on the back as he ran. These were all well-known "company stooges," pets and favorites of the bosses, and each man thus designated immediately left his work and made a dash for the east exit toward the rear of the plant, evidently bound for the battle at Chevy 9. Thus did the union's strategy cause the company to strip this crucial plant of even its few allies among the workers.

As the workers from Chevy 6 surged into the plant, they spread into two groups, one going into the motor test division and the other proceeding down the aisle toward the motor lines, threading in and out among the machines, yelling, exhorting, reaching for switches. One of the Chevy 4 men, Joe Sayen, proved quite an acrobat. With hammer in hand he leapt from one stationary conveyor (roller) to another, shutting them down as he went along. The entry of the Chevy 6 group was the signal to the union men on the lines. Thus, in "crankshafts," Gib Rose chose that moment to step up to his buddy.

"Smith, you said you was with me no matter what happened. How about it?"

"Sure!"

"Okay, as soon as I pull that button you get into the aisle and start parading and hollering."

He reached up and pulled the switch and conveyor A-1 was dead. This was the signal for Dow Kehler who headed conveyor A-2. In five seconds she was down too. When Kenny Malone saw that he pulled the switch on conveyor A-3 and the entire division was frozen.

But the real job had only begun. A few of the stanchest unionists got into the aisles and began marching around, shouting to the rest: "Strike is on! Come on and help us!" Many of the workers stood waveringly at their posts, struggling with the shackles within them. And meanwhile the superintendents and foremen and straw bosses tore about, starting the conveyors up again, yelling to the men to "get back to work or you're fired" and at the same time carefully avoiding the union groups.

Some of the men began working again or at least made a desperate effort to do so under the tumultuous circumstances as they were still anxious to differentiate themselves from the strikers. But the ranks of the latter grew inexorably. Courage added to courage. There was practically no physical violence. The men would merely act fierce and holler threats. There was huge Kenny Malone with wrench in hand tearing down the lines and yelling: "Get off your job, you dirty scab!" Yet he never touched a man—all melted with fright before him.

Again and again the union men returned to shut the switches. The more timid non-unionists were beginning to leave. Many of them had run up the stairs to the balcony and gathered there as though to find strength in their collective fear. The foremen and superintendents on the floor saw themselves more and more isolated.

By this time the several union groups which had been going through the plant had joined forces, now many hundreds strong. Carl Bibber's gang from the Chevy 6 dock looked pretty terrible with their claw-hammers in hand. Ed Cronk's group, including big "Polack" Joe Stoyall and his buddies, came down one of the other motor lines.

Everywhere at key conveyors squads of union men were now stationed. Others were set to guard gates and mount lookout. Among the last departments to be halted were "connecting rods," "pistons" and "cylinder heads." They were working spasmodically when the united union forces started through them. Like a swarm of locusts they passed among the machines, leaving silence and inertness where they went.

They drove the supervision and the non-strikers before them, shouting to the former that they had fifteen minutes to leave the plant. The foremen now yelled to the non-union men to mount to the balcony, hoping to organize a big enough group there to take back the plant. Superintendent Barrett was upstairs already talking excitedly to them when Joe Sayen ran perilously along the narrow balcony railing and leaping to a cafeteria table right in the midst of the listeners began shouting to drown the plant official out. The workers were almost too dazed to know what it was all about. They were milling around, looking for their coats, and many began heading for the exits.

Most of the foremen retreated to the superintendent's office and locked the door. Ed Cronk, accompanied by his gang, kicked the door in.

"You've got five minutes to get out!" he commanded.

Bob Barrett tried to joke with the men while one of the top officials of the entire works, M. K. Hovey, was talking over the phone to the central office in the personnel building, frantically calling for reinforcements. Cronk pushed Barrett aside and ripped the phone from the wall. The company officials fled, this time all the way to the shipping department which was located in a small building adjoining the plant at the rear.

The fight was over; the enormous plant was dead. The vast complex with its dizzying profusion of conveyors and machines was sprawled out like a wounded giant. The unionists were in complete control. Everywhere they were speaking to groups of undecided workers.

"We want you boys to stay with us. It won't be long and everything will be settled. Then we'll have a union and things will be different."

Many of the workers reached their decision in this moment. Others went home, undeterred by the strikers. About two thousand remained and an equal number went off. But as they left by the rear exits the majority of them, following an impulse of incipient solidarity, dropped their lunches into huge gondolas, half filling several of them with what proved to be a much needed extra supply of food.

As soon as the men had driven the foremen out they began barricading the plant exits, starting with the wide shipping department doors. The plant guards returning from Chevy 9 after the battle tried to enter by the northeast gate but the men drove them off with pistons, connecting rods and rocker arm rods while others brought fire hoses and squirted water and foamite at the would-be invaders.

By this time, also, the high main gate on Chevrolet Avenue had been locked and the outside pickets and men from Fisher Two had erected a shack, carried salamanders over, parked a sound car in front of the gate and in no time, a singing, cheering picket line, including many of the Emergency Brigade girls who had engaged in the Chevy 9 events, was marching hundreds strong before the plant. Many workers who had left the factory were still hanging around. A number of sitdowners stood at the top of the stairs with arms pridefully folded. Others had mounted to the roof and were leaning over the ledge.

Joe Sayen, the acrobatic young chap, climbed the tall fence at the foot of the stairs and standing between the spikes delivered an impromptu oration to the crowd. It was already dark and the flickering of the salamanders and the sudden silence of the listening people gave a stirring sense to his fantastic words.

"We want the whole world to understand what we are fighting for. We are fighting for freedom and life and liberty. This is our one great opportunity. What if we should be defeated? What if we should be killed? We have only one life. That's all we can lose and we might as well die like heroes than like slaves."

The pickets cheered.

In the hours that followed, many from the outside climbed the gate to have a peek at the plant and to help with the barricading. Among these were several hundred from the Detroit Westside local with George Edwards* in charge. It was the back part of the building that needed the defenses most. Electric trucks were hitched on to hauling gondolas full of stock, each weighing 8,000 pounds, and these were then dragged into position against the doors. Others were lifted and set upon the first layers of gondolas and then a third level would be added to the huge defense piles.

The plant resembled an enormous beehive of organized activity. Groups formed, self-designated, some to make tours of inspection, some to guard strategic points like the communicating under-street tunnel to Plant 5, some to mount to the roof to watch against a possible attack from the top of the old hospital which was situated on the second floor of the adjoining shipping department building. Most were occupied with the barricade work, filling bins, dragging, pushing and adjusting them. The job was so thoroughly done that after the strike it required several days for the maintenance crew to undo it.

Finally the plant was secure and the men gathered at the rear windows watching the movements of the foremen

*This young man, just out of college, had planned a labor career, hiring in at Kelsey-Hayes and being promptly involved in its sitdown. His continued rise to prominence has been phenomenal. At present Edwards is president of the Detroit Common Council.

and guards who were marshalled in Plant 8 across the narrow court. They shouted imprecations at them and every so often shot a bolt or a connecting rod at some dim form seen mounting the stairway behind the glass wall of the nearby factory. A crash of glass and the figure would scurry down again. Finally the company men gave up. They came furtively out into the court and dashed around the corner of the plant out of sight. They were all carrying clubs but the fight was over for them. It was the company's admission that the sitdown had succeeded.

The far-reaching consequences of the new sitdown which exceeded all our imagining had certain harsh and unexpected early features. Governor Murphy, who had been preparing the diplomatic ground for the resumption of negotiations (or at least such was his belief), thought that the new hostilities would again throw all his efforts into disjoint. Apparently he did not realize that it was exactly such a defeat for the corporation that would now force it finally to agree to negotiate seriously and with the purpose of terminating the drawnout struggle. He was furious with the union, regarding the new action as almost a personal affront.

He called Colonel Joseph H. Lewis, who was in charge of the militia in Flint, and at 9 p.m. twelve hundred troops mounted into army trucks and moved on the Chevrolet area. They took possession of all streets and approaches. Guards with fixed bayonets were strung around the entire vast rectangle. Eight machine guns and 37-milimeter howitzers were mounted at strategic points overlooking the tract. And thus at last did the pro-corporation crowd at city headquarters see one of their tenderest plans accomplished—the National Guard in possession of the plants (two of them anyway) and the sitdowners subjected to virtual martial law.

How far would the troops go? The first order issued by their command was to stop all those seeking access to Chevy 4. Even the union food car was turned back as the colonel announced with military severity:

"When the men get hungry they can go out and eat. Nobody is keeping them from going out."

These actions of the Guard opened the question of a possible attack by them on the plant. A meeting of several leaders who had come into the plant after the sitdown to help organize its defenses was held to discuss this question. What to do in case? Walter Reuther felt that the workers should be told not to resist the Guards actively but to sprawl out on the floors and force the troops to carry them bodily out of the plant. I disagreed strongly with this viewpoint. However, nothing was settled at the time. The same question came up again and again during the following day and reached a final disposition by the board of strategy. It was merely decided that night that the question of an attack by the Guard should not be discussed with the men since it might result in a moral paralysis. Moreover, since it was to be expected that spies could get word of all plans to the company or Guard, an overt decision on the subject would be like an invitation to the troops to walk in.

Around 1:30 a.m. the lights suddenly went out in the plant. And the heat blowers likewise went dead. For a moment it looked as though a panic would result as the men began milling about in the dark, stumbling over each other and crashing against things. Was it an attack? The men thronged to the front gate and shouts sped up and down the enormous plant:

"On your toes! Everybody on your toes!"

But nothing happened and calm was slowly re-established. Joking and laughing began to break out here and there. Eyes grew accustomed to the dark and the men roamed about the plant by match-light looking for places to settle for the night. It grew mighty cold inside.

At about 4 o'clock Walter Reuther and Powers Hapgood crawled under the boxcars standing along the loading dock and got past the military blockade. The National Guard had set up headquarters in the personnel building near Chevy 9. Here the union men found troops mingling with foremen and company guards, some of them wearing bandages from that afternoon's battle. They told the officer in control:

"There are three thousand men in the plant. We are assuming the responsibility of keeping these men disciplined. But the lights have been shut off and the men are making torches out of old waste. If that plant goes up in flames the company itself will be to blame."

Shortly afterward the lights came on again. But the heat still remained off. Once more Hapgood and Reuther went through the blockade and told the Guard that the men were fixing to build open fires in the plant. And the heat was turned back on, though not for long. The blockade on food was strictly maintained, however. The strikers grew hungry. Nevertheless, the candy bars, peanuts and sandwiches that were stacked in the company commissaries remained untouched as the men resolved to demonstrate in this manner their discipline and responsibility.

Toward morning the picket line had dwindled to a handful, which included several inconquerable women of the Emergency Brigade. Reinforcements had of course been prevented by the Guard. Nothing was known of outside developments until a union sound car appeared at the crest of the hill just outside the military zone and a singular loudspeaker dialogue between it and the sound car in front of the plant took place. However, the Guard later pushed back their blockade to well beyond all approaches from the south. Then a squad moved on the plant, tore down the picket shanty, confiscated the sound car and arrested the last five pickets. The sitdowners were now completely isolated.

All the next morning efforts were made to get the governor to allow food into the plant. Shortly after noon, John Brophy came up from Detroit just as I arrived at Pengelly headquarters from the plant. I told him of the situation. Brophy immediately got the governor on the phone and a long and heated conversation ensued.

"The good people of this country did not expect to see the governor of Michigan condemn to starvation hundreds of workers who are fighting for their elementary rights," Brophy said, his face deeply flushed with anger. "I'm sure you will be able to win the strike for General Motors that way....Well, I don't see how their taking the Chevrolet plant breaks faith with you. After all, these workers are fighting a vicious, unscrupulous corporation and it's asking too much to expect them to accept violence and attacks with meek submission.... I don't say that two wrongs make a right, governor, but the cases aren't at all similar. General Motors broke its word and the workers merely took steps to defend themselves.... We appreciate that, governor, but it will all be meaningless if at this late date you break this strike by martial rule!..."

Travis and Roy Reuther had gone to confer with Col. Lewis. Brophy and I prepared to join them at the armory. Just as we were leaving, Kermit Johnson breezed into the office and calmly announced that he had gone over the fence to argue with the Guard about some silly matter and was run out of the military zone. And last night, with our help, he had been elected chairman of the strike! In despair we took him along with us to the armory. Maybe somehow we could get him back in.

The colonel seemed to have undergone quite a change in attitude since we had last called him. We wondered why. Had Brophy's little talk with the governor actually helped? Later we were to learn that it was something much more exciting—the corporation, overwhelmed by the new union victory, had finally agreed to negotiate.

The colonel didn't tell us about it, however; but he was very gracious.

"You see, gentlemen," he said, "the governor has been receiving information all night from certain sources that the entire new strike was executed by out-of-towners who just went in and seized the plant. We understand now that isn't entirely correct."*

"I should say it isn't!" I broke in. "I've just come from

*This story was probably fabricated by the same National Guard officer who had given the press fantastic tales that the strikers were holding five hundred "loyal" workers as hostages.

the plant after spending the night there. There were a few outsiders but we asked them all to leave this morning. Outside of two organizers every last man in there now is a Chevrolet worker."

"I'm glad to hear that," the colonel commented. "Otherwise, you can understand, it would be putting the governor in an impossible position."

"We're willing to go in there with you and inspect all occupants," Brophy offered. "Any man who can't show a Chevrolet badge will be asked to leave."

"That wouldn't be necessary," the colonel replied. "If you will do that yourselves I will take your word for it."

"And the men will get food?" Travis asked.

"I see no reason why not once that point is clarified."

Delighted, we rose to leave. It was clear that something was in the wind but we were too anxious about getting food in to the men to worry about such subtleties. However, Roy Reuther hung back wanting to be satisfied about a doubtful point.

"What I can't understand," he said, "is if that was the only reason for the governor's action why couldn't he have let us know hours earlier so that we could have satisfied him on that score?"

The colonel smiled a bit wryly.

"Gentlemen," he adjured, "let us not embarrass the governor."

He gave us a pass for five to enter the plant and four to leave as I had specified in an opportune moment that I had brought Kermit Johnson out of the plant for the conference. We were aware by this time that Johnson wanted to be quit of his responsibility but we also realized that his absence at this time might prove demoralizing to the men in the plant.

We hastened to the factory where a meeting was quickly called in the cafeteria. The plant was quite frigid. The men were asked to show their badges and all those who wanted to leave were told to do so at this time. Not one took advantage of the offer. Then we sang "Solidarity," bade the men goodbye and left. As we were climbing the fence back into Chevrolet Avenue, a car drove up and a tall personage got out accompanied by an army officer, evidently intending to enter the plant to check on whether we had carried out our promise. The army man indeed explained in a few words that that was their purpose. Brophy turned to the man in civies.

"And who might you be?" he asked. Brophy was standing on the top of the fence, one leg on each side. The man replied haughtily:

"H. E. Coen, the assistant plant manager."

Brophy bristled with anger. "Well, that wasn't our understanding with Col. Lewis!" he snapped. "We agreed that the National Guard could come in with us but nothing was said about a representative of the company."

"That's all I wanted to know," Coen said, turning away with evident satisfaction.

As soon as we got on the pavement the officer placed us all under arrest. Brophy and Travis went into the personnel building where the officer in charge accused them of having broken their pledge to Col. Lewis, maintaining that it was part of the union's understanding with him and with the governor that a company official be allowed into the plant to make an "inspection."

"You mean count the number of men and snoop around generally," Brophy countered.

Travis grew impatient, thinking of this additional delay in getting food to the cold and hungry men.

"Let's get Col. Lewis on the wire," he said.

They did and the matter was quickly straightened out as originally agreed upon. Coen fumed to reporters when he heard of it. The newsmen took down some of his angry words.

"What did you say your initials were, Mr. Coen?" one of them asked.

"H.E.—and you spell the name *without* an h!" the husky company official (at present head of the corporation's labor relations department) replied pointedly, proving that the incident had not discommoded him sufficiently to make him forget his religious prejudices.

The governor had also ordered that the union's impounded sound car be released. Roy Reuther drove it out of the yard while I sat in the rear seat. And we had a military escort all the way out of the zone, consisting of a squad of Guards who marched along stiffly as we jogged slowly after. The lieutenant in charge of the squad rode with us to the zone boundary and we all had a big laugh at the high honors accorded the lowly labor men.

And this too, we felt, might be some kind of a sign.

12

Final Jitters

THE CORPORATION understood fully the significance of the Chevy 4 events. And so did John L. Lewis who heard about them directly from strike leader Bob Travis over the long-distance wire. Travis, concluding that the climax of the great drama had been reached and that it was time for the CIO head to come out from behind the scenes and give the union everything he had, dramatized his viewpoint by waiting until 3 a. m. before calling Lewis, routing him out of bed. Lewis grumbled but held Travis on the line for over thirty minutes and the next morning's papers carried his announcement that he was entering the negotiations in Detroit immediately.

During the previous day, while reports of Chevy 4 were still incomplete and contradictory, President Roosevelt had summoned the CIO leader to the White House to discuss possibilities of a settlement. But the chief executive's proposals were still the same as had been repeatedly made before—they were, in fact, the manufacturers' terms —i.e., the workers would leave the plants and negotiations would then begin. Lewis answered with a flat no. With what pleasure accordingly did he hear that evening confirmation of the brilliant new union victory.

The miners' leader was given credit (or blame) for almost everything that took place during the strike. And now to his account was also put the working out of the Chevy 4 scheme. This had a humorous sideline when "Frenchy" Dubuc reported the next time to Arthur Pugmire, his Pinkerton superior.

"See, what I tell you, you dumb sonabitch," "Frenchy" upbraided the spy-herder with amiable profanity. "I tole you Travis was askin' 'bout Chevy 4 and you say I was crazy. Who's crazy now?"

Pugmire didn't lose his composure. Evidently he had kicked all self-reproach out of himself already. "Naw," he came back, "that wasn't Travis' idea. It was too good. I happen to know it was John L. Lewis who figured that one out from start to finish."

Actually, not only Lewis—who sent a wire to Travis congratulating the Flint workers on their triumphant maneuver—was unaware of the plan beforehand. Most of the board of strategy in Detroit were in the same situation and this was particularly true of the nominal head of the union, Homer Martin. We had made special efforts to keep the scheme from coming to his notice prematurely. For we felt certain that he would try to countermand it or at least, given his insane love for publicity, would blurt out something about it to the press.

Two other events, occurring simultaneously with the new Chevrolet sitdown, undoubtedly gave added emphasis to the union's greatly strengthened position. Vice-President Ed Hall flew back from Milwaukee to announce that he had obtained consent of the AFL local at the A.O. Smith Company, sole source of frames for all General Motors cars except Chevrolet, to demand that its management stop immediately all shipments to GM plants.

And in Detroit, at the key Chevrolet Gear and Axle plant, a hundred and twenty welders had walked out when the company sought to discharge Jerome Ziolkowski, a union man. This was one of the plants where the back-to-work movement had made the most noise. Hence the strike here gave special cause for sober thought. Were even the corporation's "loyal" workers becoming infected by the union bug? Would this union horror be like the head of the monster with several new strikes shooting up at every successful company counter-stroke?

The change of front which these incidents and especially the Chevy 4 action forced on General Motors was a terrible blow to that insubstantial but despotic entity—corporation pride. Knudsen sought urgently to save face while accepting Murphy's now peremptory request that negotiations be reopened in a circumstance that the governor's letter had seemingly made available for the purpose:

The request you now make for a conference is stated to be "in accordance with the wish of the President of the United States." The wish of the President...leaves no alternative except compliance, and therefore we accede to your request for a conference with Mr. Lewis in the morning with a view to formulating a basis for negotiation.

Naturally it could not be expected of Knudsen that he would publicly admit the real reason for the corporation's sudden bending. The governor in his letter had actually said "with a view to formulating a basis of agreement and settlement." But Knudsen's verbal change was not significant. For the mere decision of the great corporation to retreat on its thus far adamantly upheld position had the inescapable implication that it had finally decided that coming to terms with the union was now unavoidable.

Previously it had been assumed that the union must make a major concession—i.e., give up the plants—before the corporation would consent to serious negotiations. But now it was apparent that the corporation would be forced to make the fundamental initial grant—recognition of the union—before it could regain possession of the plants. Therefore, when Knudsen shook hands with Lewis at 9:30 on Wednesday morning, February 3rd, in Judge George Murphy's* private offices the ultimate fate of the strike was sealed.

Which did not of course mean that the battle was yet over. The question of degree of "recognition" was still moot. In fact it took a week of conferences to decide it, during which time the corporation never lost sight of the fact that the extent of its concession would still be very much influenced by its continuing toughness, particularly "down below." General Motors never for one moment gave up the offensive. Everything it finally "gave" had to be fairly torn from it—the rewards of union victory had always to be won over and over again. Hence the strikers in Flint, rather than experiencing any relaxation of the struggle during these last days, went through a period of extraordinary tension and marshalling of forces.

The continuing struggle now centered around the new injunction which Judge Gadola had granted, as expected,

*Judge Murphy was a brother of the governor.

230

the day after Chevy 4. As soon as defense counsel had completed its argument the judge unashamedly reached for the law books that lay ready on his desk with plugs in them at the citations he wished to use and read his opinion. That the decision would be against the union was a foregone conclusion and yet its content was so fantastic that its reading created a great stir of surprise.

The judge had computed the value of the corporation's property that was occupied, added to that the losses in business General Motors was supposed to have sustained since the strike and arrived at the astronomical sum of $15,000,000 which, he asserted, could be levied on the union's funds or on the "lands, goods and chattels" of any individual who violated the injunction.

And the incredible magistrate, not content with a single role, next announced that he would see to it personally that the writ was put into practice and to prove his authority for such action he quoted a certain obscure statute on the state books which ostensibly gave him jurisdiction —together with the sheriff and independently of the governor—over the National Guard!

It all seemed beyond serious consideration but yet the union leaders in Flint took the threat soberly enough and sought to come to some decision concerning what the attitude of the sitdowners should be in case the National Guard were actually to attack the plants. Several members of the strategy board happened to be in Flint the night that the writ was issued and the discussion on the subject went on at some length. The proposal that had been made on the first night—that of passive resistance to forceful evacuation—was again urged. And finally someone made the amazing suggestion that the men be told to resist for a short time—as a sort of "protest" against superior forces —and then surrender.

Bob Travis who had listened in silence all the while broke in at this point and brought the discussion back to reality.

"You're not going to tell workers to fight five minutes by the clock and then stop," he said. "Either they won't fight at all or if they once get started nothing you've agreed to beforehand will mean a damn thing. They've either got to fight or give in—there's no two ways about it. Well, suppose we tell them not to fight because it's impossible defeating such a superior force? Do you know what will happen? They'll march out of those plants like whipped dogs. Not all the talk in the world afterwards is going to change that. By taking the plants away from those boys now it would mean tearing the heart right out of them."

He paused. Would he take the responsibility of endorsing the terrible alternative? Several times before the question had been raised by leaders who had shown dauntless personal courage: Would *you* be willing to tell the men that they had to face the attack of bullet and shell? It was the cross of leadership bearing down at its heaviest.

"I think we've got to tell them to be prepared to fight," Travis went on. "Not that they'll really have to do so. I don't think it'll ever come to that point because Governor Murphy isn't going to be responsible for bloodshed at this late date. But the only way to assure that is to take the attitude that we won't surrender to anybody. We fought the cops, we fought the company thugs, and we can fight the National Guard, too, the way we did in Toledo...."

There seemed to be a definite feeling of relief after he spoke, as though everybody had been waiting for someone to say what he did. And no one challenged the correctness of his viewpoint.

That night the sitdowners in Fisher One and Two* sent long wires to Governor Murphy. Composed at a tense moment they were filled with a harsh and defiant courage:

> We feel it proper to recall to you the assurances that you have given many times publicly that you would not permit force or violence to be used in ousting us from the plant. The police of the city of Flint belong to General Motors. The sheriff of Genesee County belongs to General Motors. The judges of Genesee County belong to General Motors.... It remains to be seen whether the governor of the state also belongs to General Motors. Governor, we have decided to stay in the plant. We have no illusions about the sacrifices which this decision will entail. We fully expect that if a violent effort is made to oust us many of us will be killed and we take this means of making it known to our wives, to our children, to the people of the state of Michigan and the country, that if this result follows from the attempt to eject us, you are the one who must be held responsible for our deaths!

As the deadline set by Judge Gadola for the evacuation of the plants approached, rumors were current throughout the city that the men were to be ejected by force. Exactly where that force would come from few bothered to consider. The sheriff might deputize hundreds of men or he might even accept the offer of the Michigan Sheriffs' Association of 1,300 deputies for the purpose. The Flint Alliance could furnish a couple of thousand men possibly— there were that many foremen alone in Flint! Or, finally,

---

*The injunction did not cover Chevy 4 and hence the men in this plant were theoretically independent of Judge Gadola's order.

233

perhaps the governor would decide to use the National Guard.

Francis O'Rourke, the Fisher Two diarist, told of the tension inside his plant:

> Injunction has been granted and Sheriff Wolcott is coming down to take us out. We're not coming out. Waiting, waiting, won't he ever come? We can't get news from the outside and can't get news out. It's nervewracking. Just waiting for the sheriff and wondering when we go into action. I do hope none of us get hurt. All good men they are and don't want violence. We're not coming out though....

The city had an enormous case of jitters. And the union prepared itself for the worst. Bob Travis had contacted Detroit and other union centers the night before and asked for mass assistance for the showdown. The locals in his own city of Toledo began immediate arrangements for sending five hundred to a thousand men who could remain in Flint for a week if necessary. Auto-Lite and other plants shut down in the city as a result of the withdrawal of large proportions of the workers. The same was true of several plants in Detroit as hundreds and even thousands of unionists poured out on the road to Flint that morning. The reinforcements were hardly needed, however, as Flint workers themselves prepared incomparably for the deadline, massing from fifteen to twenty thousand strong at the two plants.

But as though to demonstrate its pacific intentions despite the extraordinary mobilization the union declared this day to be "Women's Day." Several hundred women came up from Detroit, Toledo, Lansing and Pontiac for the occasion. Those from Detroit were wearing green berets to match the red tams of the Flint girls as the idea of the Emergency Brigade had spread swiftly. It had originated after the Fisher Two "battle" in which the women had engaged so courageously. The following day a petition on the table in the Women's Auxiliary room gathered signatures: "I wish to join the Emergency Brigade and be on call day and night." The women of Flint had conceived the function of the Brigade as one of serving as a bulwark of defensive femininity against any violence that might threaten their husbands.

"We'll form a line around the men and if the police want to fire then they'll have to fire into us," they explained. The Brigade members were organized along semi-military lines. Each squad captain, usually with home phone and car, was responsible for her group and upon notice was expected to round up her women and transport them to the scene of "action." One failure to answer a call automatically suspended the truant from membership in the Brigade though she could continue to give service to the strike in the less exigent Women's Auxiliary. The pledge that was required of all members was undertaken in dead earnest by these women as was sufficiently demonstrated on numerous occasions during the strike.

And now the women decided under the critical existing circumstances to demonstrate right in the heart of the city, many of them with their children. Thousands of people lined the streets to watch them, wide-eyed. They read their placards: "We Stand by Our Heroes in the Plants." One tot was carrying a sign reading: "Our Daddies Fight for Us Little Tykes." So this was the "unruly mob" that the *Flint Journal* spoke of. These were the women who had

"rioted" at Fisher Two and Chevy 9. Were they tough?
Were they vulgar? They seemed just simple, decent, ordinary American workfolk. They sang union songs and yelled union cheers:

> We're the wives,
> We're the mothers,
> Of our fighting union brothers.
> We'll fight for our kith and kin.
> And when we fight, we fight to win!
> Rah! Rah! Rah!

After the parade the women hastened out to Fisher One as the dread "deadline" approached. The picket line here was the biggest in Flint's history. Down the entire great length of the plant the loop formed, six abreast going both ways, an anxious but determined throng. They were here to defend their hard-fought victory. No last-minute surprise was going to wrest it from them. All carried slender wooden braces ($1\frac{1}{2}$″ x $1\frac{1}{2}$″) used in car windows which the insiders had handed out to them. Others had brought defense weapons from home, stove pokers, crowbars, pipelengths. Piles of small metal parts had also been dumped on the lawn from the plant and the inside protective agencies were keyed for action.

All sitdowners wore neckcloths made of material that went into the backcloth of auto cushions. These could be dipped into water and rubbed protectively over the eyes in case of gas attacks. Quantities of a glycerine solution for the same purpose were everywhere available throughout the plant. Continuous arrivals added to the already huge crowd and as the traffic jammed on the main highway in front of the plant while motorists slowed to watch the demonstration, the pickets themselves, in absence of any police, had to manage an impromptu traffic corps to keep the cars moving.

The attack did not come off, however, and the great mustering of defenders gave joyous expression to their feelings of relief. A singing antiphony between inside and outside groups developed new choral effects on the everlasting theme of "Solidarity." A signal corps of war vet sitdowners mounted to the roof and gave an exhibition of their art. Wives had long visits with their sitdown husbands.

"Are you warm? Have you got enough to eat?"

"Sure, sure!"

If the wife was querulous the husband would try to use stronger assurances: "They can't beat us, sweatheart. We ain't going to leave this building. Everything is going to be okay, so don't worry."

The union women had learned much since the beginning of the strike. At first there had been only a small group of them. But the spark of unionism lay dormant in many others—daughters of miners, for example, from southern Indiana and Illinois, in whom, as in their husbands, childhood memories began to stir under the impact of the struggle.

During the first days the union had begun receiving urgent letters from sitdowners expressing concern over their wives. "She hasn't been down to see me and she won't answer my letters," a typical note complained.*

The fact was that some of the wives simply boycotted

*Early in the strike, the Fisher One meeting-of-the-whole had resolved "that an article be published in the paper addressed to wives and sweethearts advising them of the importance of the men's staying in the plant."

the strike which had come without warning to them and constituted a great shock, particularly when their husbands failed to return home. They often regarded this as equivalent to desertion and there were stormy scenes enacted at the "Information" window of the plant with threats of "going home to mother" and even divorce expressed. But most of the angry wives merely brooded, trusting that if they made no initial move their husbands would be the first to break and then they would be able to keep them home.

It caused a critical situation and gave rise to one of the most important committees of the strike. The auxiliary women called it the "Goodwill Committee." They would visit the complaining wives at their homes and try to explain the meaning of the strike and their husbands' and their own stake in it. Yet often they couldn't get past the front door.

"We're the sisters from the union auxiliary," they would begin.

"Don't you sister me," the angry response would come. "I ain't no sister of yours!"

"We have a message from your husband," the visitors would persist.

"If my husband wants to talk to me he knows where he can find me. Tell him that. And tell him he'd better come soon or maybe I won't be here when he gets here. If he cares more for his filthy union than me and the kids he can keep it!"

And the door would be slammed in their faces.

The "goodwill" visitors changed their approach. They would have to use salesmen's tactics to disarm the angry wife and to get into the house. Then suddenly the distraught, bewildered woman would break down, burst into tears and reveal the fullness of her misery and fear.

"My husband was always a good man till this union trouble started. Now the company won't take him back and we'll have to go on the county. What'll become of us?"

The visitors would explain that they too were facing the same difficulties and yet they were standing by their husbands, trying to make their task lighter, to help where they could. Quietly they'd look around and delicately they'd inquire. Was there enough food in the house? Was the coal bin empty? Often it was some worry of this kind that had broken the woman down though it might have been anything. One striker's wife grew almost hysterical about her canary for which she had not been able to buy the proper bird food. Indeed the little creature peeped pitifully during the interview and the visitor went away wondering which to do first, buy food for the wife or the canary.

It was mainly the older auxiliary women who undertook this work, women like Mrs. Bessie Lamb, mother of seven children and several times a grandmother. Mrs. Lamb's husband and three or four sons and sons-in-law were union members. Her father had been a miner and she had witnessed many strikes before. She was big and strongly-built, vital and exuded confidence; there was no element of doubt in her. If on one of her goodwill trips the wavering wife would ask: "But what if they lose?" Mrs. Lamb's eyes would open wide as though in amazement that such a thought could even occur to anyone.

"But they can't lose," she would say. "We're all going to fight this fight through to the end!"

Often the goodwill visitors would get the wives to accompany them to the plant where reconciliations were effected. Many would agree to visit the Pengelly strike headquarters and were amazed to find the strike leaders and others not at all like the ogres they had pictured from descriptions of radio and press or of the foremen and other company agents—usually posing as salesmen—who indefatigably contacted the wives of sitdowners all through the strike, systematically cultivating their panic.

And everywhere in the union they found an intense, an irresistible sincerity and a friendliness without reserve. Here was no "looking over" of new arrivals; everyone "belonged." As the wife of a worker and a union man, the woman's welcome was assured, her membership and ability to contribute taken for granted. After this there was no returning to the dismal, pessimistic thoughts of before.

If on undertaking any work a woman showed some leadership, her development was pushed and fostered. She was given more responsible tasks and encouraged to speak at meetings. This was a difficult step for many and even Mrs. Lamb had faltered momentarily on her first trip to the platform. "I never made a speech in my whole life," she began, glancing suspiciously at the microphone. "I never spoke into one of them things before either." She put her hands behind her back and picked her head up and told her story. "Mother of seven children ... always believed in unions ... knew we had to have one ... me and my man ... gotta fight this fight through to the end...."

The auxiliary received many glowing letters from delighted sitdowners, thanking them for having "won over" their wives. But it meant more than that in many cases. For the strike was often to prove the beginning of life to these women, at least the beginning of a conscious social life.

A few hours after the demonstration at Fisher One, reports started pouring into union headquarters that City Manager Barringer and Police Chief Wills were organizing a civilian army for the purpose, as they had announced, of "shooting it out if necessary to repossess Flint for the forces of law and order." The mass picketing during the demonstration, the blocked traffic, the pickets' sticks and alleged bellicose acts against passersby served as the immediate arguments for the mobilization.

"The strikers have taken over this town and we are going to take it back," Barringer told reporters. "We have asked for the state police and the National Guard to keep order and have been refused; so we are going down there shooting!" And Wills parroted his superior:

"When officials and authorities of the state whose duty it is to protect life and property fail to do so, organization of the good citizens is all that we can do."

The fighting city manager announced that he would have five hundred men in "an army of our own" by morning, young, unmarried men preferred. There was a tremendous hubbub in all city buildings as the "good citizens" came to register, carrying guns under their hunting jackets. They were sworn in and a high official told them what their duties would be. They were to keep themselves in readiness twenty-four hours a day. Silver-colored tape was wound about their arms to serve as an identification in case of "night duty." All police shifts had been called in also and the cops ran around excitedly with helmets and riot guns.

Actually Barringer had been organizing the "special reserves" on the q.t. for several weeks now in anticipation of an inevitable need. A number of his political lieutenants were engaged in this work; men like Charley Pratt, an inspector in the city's health department, Ed McLogan, Ray French and other leaders of the so-called "Allied Veterans."

The "reserves" were recruited from among company foremen and the most active elements of the back-to-work group. Also the city's racketeer reservoirs were opened for the purpose of preserving "law and order," with bootleggers Chauncey Downes and "Monty" Montague helping to swell the lists. Similar aid was given by two violently anti-CIO priests.

As the night wore on Barringer and the chief became more and more inflamed. Wills threatened:

"Unless John L. Lewis wants a repetition of the Herrin, Illinois, massacres he had better call off his union men."

The next day the city manager called his "civilian police reserves" (vigilantes) to a dress rehearsal at which he promised them prompt action. At the same time Judge Gadola entered into the baleful mobilization by issuing a writ of attachment addressed to the sheriff for the "bodies of all occupants of Fisher Body plants Numbers One and Two," as well as of the international officers and organizers.

This action following a plea of General Motors attorneys came as a great surprise to the union conferees in Detroit since the corporation had promised only the day before not to proceed further with the injunction ruling, "pending negotiations." Lewis accused the General Motors ne-

gotiators of "sicking" their dogs on the strikers while hypo-
critically engaging in peace conferences. The situation
became strained and Murphy had his hands full to avert
a break.

Nevertheless, the corporation heads agreed to put a
damper on their over-zealous agents in Flint. These people
were becoming desperate as the strike neared its end. Their
fate was so intimately linked with that of the corporation,
they knew that many of them could hardly survive a General Motors defeat. The strike had early seemed a great
political opportunity to these men. Their thought had become dominated by the fixed idea of pulling off some brilliant coup; in particular, of getting the men out of the plants.
Perhaps one might even attain national fame that way.
It had happened before.

And now the great opportunity was surely and swiftly
slipping away. Couldn't they do *something?* Perhaps there
was time yet for one great blow that would shift the course
of things. Men high in office later told us that discussions
went on interminably as to how this blow could be struck.

National Guard officers entered into the discussion of
hypothetical stratagems, a major suggesting the flooding
of the plants with vomiting gas sent via the ventilation
system. A number of variations on the "Trojan Horse"
idea which later attained fame in the Fansteel (Chicago)
sitdown were also aired while one doughty Amazon offered
to marshal five hundred of her sex to lead in the forceful
evacuation of the sitdowners. And everybody cursed Sheriff Wolcott who as a lone Democrat and political friend
of Murphy was refusing to lend himself to any of these
schemes, having placed himself strictly under the governor's orders.

It was a sure sign of the approaching end when the controlling local political machine, Barringer's machine, exploded with a truly pitiful fizz and crackle. The background of this blowup was the bitter opposition between the so-called "reform" group, the "Civic League," and the "Green Slate" men. Heretofore the former—under control of such individuals as Harry Gault, militant General Motors counsel—had thoroughly dominated the nine-man city commission in whom was vested complete power of government and choice of administrative officers, among them the city manager himself. But something happened to this stanch majority after the "taking" of Chevy 4 when it suddenly dawned on the politicians that the union might actually win. It was a foreshadowing of the widespread political upheaval that resulted in all parts of the state and chiefly in the auto centers in consequence of the strike and the subsequent upshooting of the UAW.

Joseph Shears, leader of the opposition "Green Slate" group in the city commission, though a worker in the Chevrolet plant, was certainly not an early friend of the union. He had in fact vigorously opposed it at first both as commissioner and as a representative on the Chevrolet works council. As late as January 28th at a meeting of that company union, he had outdone most others in denouncing the union, assailing the leaders as a bunch of "outside agitators" who he said were "educated in Russia."

"If John L. Lewis wants to do something for somebody why doesn't he do it for the miners who are starving?" he demanded.

But then came the breath-taking union coup at Chevrolet and suddenly Shears realized that, his own views of the union apart, the moment had definitely arrived for him to overturn the clique in power which had been trying to cut his throat for years. It would be sweet revenge, indeed. He forced the calling of a special meeting of the commission for the announced purpose of investigating the formation of the "special reserves." And Shears now made the first overt play for union favor of any major political figure in the city. He said:

"As commissioner I do not intend to stand by and allow innocent citizens to be mowed down by a group of prejudiced and irresponsible people."

Jim Barringer defended himself heatedly against these charges. "I have prevented anything in the city that would bring on further controversy," he brazenly asserted. "Every effort is being made to coöperate with the men conferring in Detroit."

"After the agreement the other night," Commissioner Ollie Tappin, a pool room operator and a supporter of Shears, contradicted him, "everything was peaceful and then you come in and make statements and organize the reserve police and that starts the trouble. Do you remember coming back to the chief's office that night, pacing back and forth, and then telling the chief that 'I'm going to call out all the men and clean out that goddam place?'"

Barringer denied this but Tappin persisted:

"And you said that Murphy ain't running this town and that you were, didn't you?"

"I said that and I still say that," Barringer retorted.

There were hundreds of delighted workers who witnessed these proceedings, men and women who had discovered a dramatic interest in the one-time cut-and-dried meetings of the city commission since the union had begun to use them as a forum. Here UAW speakers repeatedly emphasized the political aspects of its program, voicing sharp comment on a variety of issues. But nothing had as yet quite equaled this decisive interplay. The upshot was that Mayor Harold Bradshaw clamped down a strict censorship on all city officials. This was, to Barringer, the cruelest cut of all, for Bradshaw, a Buick official for years, had always stood very close to him.

On the other hand, it was not too surprising when George Boysen condemned the setting up of the "special reserves" as "inflammatory and provocative" since the new development had taken the play out of his hands. His one great opportunity now past, Boysen quickly receded to his normal position—a smalltime businessman with frustrated political ambitions. In fact one heard little of the organizer of the back-to-work movement thereafter, until some time following the strike when he threatened to sue General Motors for expenses incurred by the Flint Alliance.

Two days later the intra-commission jockeying for power was resolved when Joseph Shears won a majority of his colleagues to his side and got Bradshaw, who had evidently visualized the rise of his own political star in the decline of his friend Barringer's, to string along with him. (Shears later claimed to have turned down a five thousand dollar bribe to take a "vacation" in Florida.) At a second stormy session the mayor was granted virtual decree powers over the city government for the duration of the strike while Barringer was practically stripped of all authority. Prolonged cheering of the packed chamber greeted the announcement of Barringer's fall. The latter was wounded to the depths of his soul. The following day reporters found him packing his papers as though in preparation for a move. Soon after the strike, he was indeed ousted from office and dropped out completely from public life.

Gloom reigned in the police chief's office also. Jim Wills would not even see reporters. He felt deserted and lost following the demise of his super. For several years he had been chief in name only since Barringer had assumed all of the actual authority inherent in the post. This had been even more true during the strike, the old Calumet strikebreaker having found the rush of events too swift to keep up with. He always seemed to be in the way and even lost his own swivel chair in the end to a mysterious personality known as "Mr. Addison" to reporters (Chris Addison, a Chevrolet executive), who was the corporation's leading representative in the behind-scenes braintrust that worked out strategy for the strike. Wills was likewise fired following the settlement when his post and that of the city manager were filled by men friendly to the union.

The union did not go into any ecstasies over these events. They were certainly confusing enough. Most minds were full of the strike and it was hard to see why the new group in power could be trusted any more than the old. Wasn't Bradshaw a "GM stooge" the same as Barringer? The danger of violent attack on the sitdowners seemed to remain just as immediate with the new man at the helm as it was before. The strikers continued their vigilance.

The "Union War Vets," under "commander" Marion Hawley, detailed bodyguards to trail the strike leaders through day and night and to stand watch over their hotel doors as they slept. When the second injunction was issued, the Fisher One boys offered to give the organizers asylum inside their plant. The latter continued to be threatened with death by gun and rope, sometimes even by feminine voices on the phone. After the crisis the "Vets"* told us of a fantastic plot that had been secretly planned in all seriousness against the possibility of the outside leaders being arrested in keeping with Gadola's writ. They would muster an armed force among their own number and in defense of the U. S. Constitution, of "real patriotism" and the union, would take over the city hall, the courthouse and police headquarters, capture and imprison all officials and release the union men!

The union was in receipt of all kinds of unsolicited advice on its conduct of the strike as well as complaints, pleas, praise and threats. One wire announced oracularly:

My friends, do you men really want to see how quickly this thing can be settled right now? Evacuate, but make it understood that all are coming out of their own free will.

Another telegram asked the men to leave if General Motors would agree to establish "the principle of profit sharing." A letter, from "A Catholic Mother," suggested that "the men ought to name a day of settlement—to be decided: Yes or No." "An observer" in Connecticut upbraided the strikers for falling prey to Lewis' ambition,

*The "Union War Vets" had been set up early in the strike at my suggestion when the local American Legion leadership was reported to be making anti-union preparations. The proposal was inspired by the successful work of a similar organization that had been established during the Goodyear strike in Akron, early in 1936. And, indeed, after many hundreds of Flint's unionists signed the "Vets" roster, we never heard of any strikebreaking Legion activities again.

248

asking: "Among you is there one chin like that of Lewis?" Sympathetic strategists had innumerable suggestions to outwit the police and the militia, such as feeding the Chevy 4 men by dropping food to them by airplane (Bob Travis himself had considered this plan) or by shooting it into the plant by means of giant slingshots. One letter addressed to "John Lewis, Esq." arrived from Buenos Aires.

There were letters from religious fanatics and crackpots of every style. A fifty-page poetic document by one calling herself "The Human Mother Power" proudly subordinated the sitdown and all the other problems of mankind to that of procuring "a legal duplicate preferential ballot by universal written referendum civil service suffrage." And Homer Martin, who seemed already to have caught the imagination of the public as the "new type of labor leader," began to be swamped with fan mail from languishing middleclass females. One wrote:

Mr. Martin, I wish we had somebody like you in South Carolina to battle for women who are the victims of sex-minded ignoramus politicians. Not even a divorce law in South Carolina! Women here are worse than Negroes ever were—except a favorable few—mostly concubines.... I wish I had the right words to say—I think you're wonderful.... If you have some person in mind who should have a cause to champion, please let it be known there are fields waiting!

These were signs of the universal interest as well as confusion that the strike had aroused. An early note of the fashion that was soon to sweep the country was played on a humorous key when an unsuccessful wooer sat down outside his girl's home while some Brooklyn tenement dwellers went on a rent "sitdown." Only the Ohio Valley floods could drive the Flint strike temporarily from the nation's spotlight.

The National Guard in ten days issued press passes to over three hundred reporters desiring to get through the military lines. Every newspaper and magazine with a reputation to uphold had its frontline correspondent on the scene while the London Daily Herald's stunning female reporter created a precedent of some kind when she crossed the big water to write eye-witness stories of a mere strike. She was not the only foreign visitor attracted to Flint by the strike. "Wee Ellen" Wilkinson, sprightly Labour Party M. P. of England and member of the present Labour Government, came for a day to reveal a vivacious sympathy and understanding. "This is the revenge of the man they tried to turn into a cog," she commented.

We were at first very strict about allowing outsiders into the plants until we realized the immense publicity value of such visits. The decent, peaceful conduct of the men and their extreme care of the plants and machinery were very impressive to people whose prejudices often prepared them for a different picture. Numerous clergymen, writers, professors and public figures made the union's Baedeker tour only to emerge with glowing praise for the high spirits of the strikers and the businesslike efficiency of their inside organization.

Such interest often resulted in more substantial aid. The Church Emergency Relations Committee of New York donated a hundred dollars and the Michigan Council of Churches, representing all of the state's three hundred Protestant churches, delegated Rev. Owen Knox to urge the Flint city officials to refrain from violence against the sitdowners. One General Motors stockholder proposed a vote of all corporation stockholders in answer to the demand for a vote of the workers; while others sent wires assuring support. Owners of General Motors cars did likewise. Evelyn Preston, president of the League of Women Shoppers, following the violence at Fisher Two announced that she was trading in her Buick for another make. "Riding a Fisher body at the present time would cause me intense moral and physical pain."

However, word from Detroit was still the same: no progress in the negotiations. Mortimer called us every evening merely to report that absolutely nothing had been accomplished. Only the one question of "recognition" was being aired. And that not seriously. Perhaps the negotiators would break up once more? What then? We could foresee what would happen. The vigilantes would run wild. And our people—seriously demoralized—would be more vulnerable to their attacks.

We gave orders to tighten all defenses. A close guard on Pengelly headquarters was instituted and cots were laid in all available parts of the building where defense squads slept, ready at call. All-night dancing, singouts, recitations and amateur theatricals kept an added number of younger people always on hand. One night it rained and the dancers carried umbrellas to ward off water from leaks in the roof and wove around the pails receiving water on the floor. "Tiny" Wahl proved an indefatigable swingster at the piano. A late "supper" was served at 3 a.m. by the union kitchen.

The men at Fisher One were put through regular defense

drills for several days. These were conducted by the "Officer of the Day" who was to be in command in case of attack. A certain signal given by the crane whistle would mean a call to arms. Everybody had his orders. Nobody was to leave his group or the specific post that was assigned him. Upon the signal four men would run to each hose and drag it to the window where a pane had been removed and a double thickness of protective sheet metal with a hole for the nozzle adjusted in its place.

The hoses were kept at full pressure at all times by arrangement with the union powerhouse men who likewise assured the sitdowners a constant supply of heat and light throughout the strike. Others would roll the foamite guns (electric fire extinguishers) into place. These were mounted on two big wheels and looked like small cannon. There were also some deer rifles and revolvers in the plant, though these were officially banned and were confiscated if discovered. However, during the height of the vigilante scare, when an armed attack was expected at any time by Barringer's reserves, a room was rented above a restaurant across the street from the plant and strikers with gun in hand sat before the sealed windows watching twenty-four hours a day.

Despite these extraordinary measures the morale of the Fisher One sitdowners remained at a high level. The secretary's books during this period show such items as a collection of eighty-six dollars made inside the plant for the family of an hospitalized member and thirty-five dollars for the flood victims in the south. The conviction of the strikers was never stronger. Repeatedly you heard them say: "I'll never go back to work under the conditions we had before. I'll never go back to that speedup!" A "fight-to-the-death" pledge proposed by the strike committee at the time when there was uncertainty as to the actions of the National Guard was signed by a majority of the men. The plan was to fight any and all attackers from floor to floor up to the roof which the strikers felt they could hold indefinitely. A two-week supply of canned food, always kept inside, was shifted upstairs for this contingency.

The situation of the Chevy 4 men who were isolated by the Guard was considerably more difficult. Despite constant complaints by the union to the governor, the company with the collusion of Guard officers played a continuous tattoo on the physical endurance of the strikers by manipulating the plant's heat and light supply. It would allow the temperature to drop to slightly above freezing, keep it at that low point for some time and then turn the blowers on again. This process went on incessantly. The men bundled up as well as they could. Their wives and the union sent in flannel underwear and blankets in quantity and the men made chest warmers from shop towels. They looked strange walking around the plant all bulged out with blankets over their shoulders and dragging at their heels.

The strikers worked on all the valves and conduits beneath the plant trying to get heat in. One amateur electrician blew out the big panel causing an explosion that shook the whole plant. The resulting electric fire created much excitement until it was put out with foamite extinguishers. In anger at the heat blockade, the men shot brass bolts across the river aimed at the powerhouse where, contrary to the situation at Fisher One, the workers did not coöperate with the union. The strikers rigged up giant slingshots, one man holding the crotch bar as another would pull the sling back. On another occasion they closed the valve outlets of the radiators and opened the windows wide, threatening to freeze the pipes and machinery. But when the Guard began to gather in force on Chevrolet Avenue, the men shut the windows again.

A minor flu epidemic resulted from this constant exposure to low temperature, a circumstance that almost ended in the breaking of the strike in the plant. Art Moore, a chap who had been given charge of the first aid department when he testified to having had that kind of experience in the army, began all of a sudden to act very agitated and gave orders to call in a certain Dr. William T. Finkelstein who put the men through hasty examinations and immediately sent a number of them home. On the following day, the physician took an even larger number out. "Anyone who has the slightest hint of a cold or a cough or any kind of respiratory ailment should evacuate the plant immediately," he ordered. "Strep throat is assuming epidemic proportions." As the committee protested weakly the doctor grew angry:

"I'll take every last man out of the plant if necessary!" he shouted.

One can imagine the effect of such a situation on the already jittery men. These goings-on when reported to headquarters aroused our suspicions. Dr. C. C. Probert, who had serviced the Fisher One men from the beginning of the strike, was asked to check over the four last men whom Dr. Finkelstein had ordered out. Three of these were found to be without any temperature while the fourth merely had a slight fever and cold. Thereafter we were more careful of the physicians we sent into the plants. Drs. Eugene Shafarman and F. C. Lendrum of Detroit, who later helped found a medical research department for the union, aided by Dr. Probert, soon had the situation under control.

Art Moore, the first aid man, had other tricks up his sleeve. He had the guards waken the men early one morning, asserting that he had discovered that the oyster stew which had been served for supper was poisoned. As the guards ran about striking the soles of the men's shoes and yelling: "Get up! Emergency!" a near panic resulted.

Moore had prepared an emetic, consisting of a mixture of bicarbonate of soda and soap suds and every man was ordered to drink a cupful of the vile brew. Some did and they began to retch and vomit when Gib Rose, now a member of the strike committee, put an end to the tragi-comedy by offering to eat three more bowls of the suspected stew to prove that nothing was wrong with it. The men then began talking of running Moore out of the plant, but he spared them the trouble by leaving voluntarily, claiming illness.

The men were on edge and worn out with fighting the hard conditions of the plant. One older fellow, a former preacher from Missouri, suddenly becoming distraught, mounted on a table and began to hold forth fervently to the effect that the men ought to leave, organize the workers on the outside and then return to resume their strike. He carried on in the impassioned revivalist's manner and some of the strikers began to respond emotionally, shouting: "Amen! Amen!" Joe Sayen who happened to be passing by at the moment suddenly called out:

"Sing 'Missouri Farmer,' Elmer! Go ahead, sing 'Missouri Farmer!'"

It was the ex-preacher's favorite song. He paused and a smile broke out on his face. He began to sing the song. When he finished Sayen started the boys going with "Solidarity" and the danger was past. He took the old man down from the table and quietly convinced him to leave the plant.

An unfortunate circumstance in Chevy 4 was the weakness of Kermit Johnson's leadership. He sent repeated hysterical notes to Travis.

"Is there some reason why you can't write to me?" he would demand. "I find time to write to you and I haven't slept over three hours a night since I've been here because of the growing dissension among the boys in here. These boys don't need democracy, they need a king...."

The jitters of Kermit Johnson could hardly have failed to affect the men under him. However, when Rose Pesotta* and my wife, in the name of the union, finally wheedled permission of the National Guard to pay a visit inside the plant, they found things not nearly as bad as the hysterical young strike chairman had painted them. Other leaders seemed to have the situation well in hand. As the two women were leaving they asked Dow Kehler who accompanied them to the gate if there was anything he wanted from outside, anything they could tell his wife.

"Naw," Kehler, stout and good-humored, replied. "Unless you'd want to tell my old lady to send me my red flannels and woolen socks." And he burst into laughter,

*Formerly a vice-president of the International Ladies Garment Workers.

wheezing with a hoarseness which seemed to have afflicted most of the sitdowners in the plant.

But the women went straight to a department store and bought out almost its entire supply of men's warm underclothing.

At Fisher Two, meanwhile, Francis O'Rourke intensified his prayers and sought surcease in "make-believing" a Sunday with his family. O'Rourke's fellow-diarist at Chevy 4, Roscoe Van Zandt, the only Negro sitdowner in Flint,* also frequently "went off into [his] secret place for prayer."

The company did not stop with working on the nerves of the men. Their wives also were the recipients of such attention. The chief method of intimidation used was the personal call. This campaign met with some success as a number of letters with fabricated stories began to arrive from the men's homes seeking to draw them out of the plants. Union headquarters also were bombarded with such letters as the wife might think that her husband would be too canny to fall for the ruse.

"I am asking you for the second time to get my husband out of the plant," one said. "I am sick and I need him bad. No if-or-and about this!"

Also there was a sudden epidemic of births which often caused hilarity in the supposed "father." One case touched a moral low when a sitdowner received an anonymous letter telling him that his wife had taken another man in to live with her during her husband's absence.

*Buick had the only large group of Negro workers in Flint who were not, of course, on strike. Chevrolet employed very few Negroes while the ban on colored workers in the corporation's body plants was absolute.

On investigating these reports, the union found them almost always fictitious or at least highly colored. The fact was brought to the attention of the sitdowners who decided that no action would be taken on any word from a man's home till headquarters had had time to look into the matter. This decision was reflected in such letters as the following written by a sitdowner to his wife:

They are having the boss go round to all the homes and telling the wifes that they had better write and tell your husband you are very sick or we will lay him off they will try and give you money for doing so. Honey what ever you do don't let them tell you what to do. if any one gos to the house ask him their name and we will do the rest. if they don't want to leave shot the basterd. they will try to get yous to go with them mabe they will do anything to get us out.*

The men sent a steady stream of encouraging letters to their homes. For a week this was the only contact allowed by the Guard between a man and his family. A number of these letters have been preserved and reveal in inglorious but tremendous detail the profound meaning of the struggle to the common folk who were engaged in it. Here was that anonymous courage—"I faced the guns and I'm still here"—that determination "to stay till hell freezes over" —"to do battle to the very end if necessary"—which had made possible the union's surprising victories.

One might so easily forget the simple truths that sustained these men, the modest sources of their pride, the thought even that one's young son "has big things to say about me," or the admiration of a friend! To one home-loving worker victory would mean more time to be with

*Original spelling and punctuation are retained in all quoted letters.

his family and to play with his kids, Lary and Suzanne, "as I will not have to work so hard or long." Another found thrilling satisfaction enough in the mere struggle: "I am having a great time—something new, something different." The spirit of adventure was uppermost also with the young fellow who wrote to his girl to call off a date and to playfully suggest to her that she "find a temporary boy friend" until the strike was over. And always evident was the potent force of emulation, the fact that one could not do less than one's buddies:

Hunny Wayen and Sim and Pat is all in here. I could of came out wen they went on strike But hunny I just thought I join the union and I look pretty yellow if I dident stick with them....

In this manner the wives were encouraged to bear the struggle with their men. Remaining at home as they did, they were the ones to face most immediately the problems of material want, the shortage of food and coal and the threats of creditors. Their prompt concern about these matters as revealed in letter after letter showed the narrow ledge of economic security upon which Flint's worker-families lived.

Yet, though some of the wives might complain bitterly about their loneliness or their added burdens, though they might express the wish that the union "would hurry up and settle" the strike or even pass judgment on it, perhaps in mystical fashion—"if the people hadn't forgot God there would not be what is going on"—nevertheless, the question of their loyalty to their husbands' cause was seldom in doubt. And, indeed, often the women made a great contribution to the spirit of resistance as the following letter from wife to husband will illustrate. This letter is by no means exceptional among those that have been saved, in courage, in understanding, in its undoubted power of enhancing that priceless quality of morale:

I am just fine. Of course, I worry about you but other than that I am OK. GM. is putting up a stiff fight, all over the Union demanding sole right to bargain for all strike closed plants. Of course, we don't know the outcome but we think we will win. Pop saw Frankie yesterday and he said Helen's brother, a foreman at Fisher says GM. is licked and might as well admit defeat. Her three brothers in Saginaw are anxious to join the Union. Pop gave Frankie a card and he may go with Pop to the Mass meeting tonight....

No my dear, I won't sent in for you unless I get sick. But if *you* get sick *come home*. Honey I miss you dreadfully but I know you are fighting for a good cause. My fair weather friends have left me pretty much alone. But they don't make our living for us. I can live without them!...My coal is holding out OK. But dear me I must carry out ashes tomorrow Boo Hoo....Lucille and I had an argument with the cottage cheese man yesterday. No more cheese will I buy from him. He is scabby!...I guess I will quit the Ladies Aid. Those old hens make me sick. Don't think for one minute I can't live without them....I think of you constantly I am praying for you....Keep a stiff upper lip Honey Boy!

Final recognition of the major role played by the women in the strike came when a car carrying a group of Emergency Brigadiers from a visit to Lansing was sideswiped off the road by three other cars. The technic used was the same as that of the earlier attack of the Saginaw vigilantes. Two of the women were thrown into the windshield, suffering bad lacerations, and three others received severe sprains and bruises.

But the women took this attack as a matter of course.

They outdid themselves during this tense final period of the strike when the threat of vigilante action was rampant in conceiving novel methods of relieving the strain, of deflecting the hovering fears. One day they enacted "living formations" outside the Fisher One plant and the sitdowners had to guess such symbols as "Solidarity Wins" or "Sole Collective Bargaining."

On another occasion they conducted a three-hour dance on the lawn outside this factory. Dozens of couples whirled about on the frozen turf as the approaching night, the flurries of snow and the leaping flames of four salamanders gave atmospheric background to a scene that almost made one think of a medieval carnival rather than a strike. Women of foreign birth gave exhibitions of the folk dances of the countries of their origin. When night had fallen, coffee and sandwiches were served at the salamanders and the celebration ended in a "singout" led by the sitdown orchestra.

One of the dancers on the plant lawn was 72-year-old Rebecca Goddard who boasted of six children, twenty grandchildren and ten great grandchildren—and all *union*, she insisted. Her husband, she told the reporters with queenly pride, was a union pioneer, having gone on strike with the Au Sable rivermen 52 years ago.

The men had been working twelve hours a day and were striking to cut their working time. The militia was called then too. One man was shot. And the troops were run "right out of town." Her youngest son was sitting down in the Fisher One plant and Mrs. Goddard said she also had several grandchildren and other relations inside but she had apparently lost count of them. She wore the red tam and arm band of the Emergency Brigade and watching the wonderful old lady tramping around on the picket line with her American flag or gayly dancing now in the deep and festive twilight, one thought joyously: "The strike is won." And then one felt a slight pang of impatience at the procrastination of the negotiators in Detroit.

13

"Solidarity Forever!"

THE negotiations in Detroit meanwhile had circled around and around the single subject of "recognition" which in its abstract quality seemed terribly distant from the grim realism of the battlefront. Yet the profound content of this subject meant everything to the life and future of the union and consequently to the welfare of the hundreds of thousands for whom it spoke or sought to speak. The basic fact of union recognition had of course been practically accepted when the corporation agreed to negotiate while the Flint plants were still occupied. The only question remaining was the degree or concrete detail of that recognition.

For the union this meant under what minimum practical conditions would its bargaining relationship with the corporation be assured reality insofar as the solution of the day-to-day grievances of the workers was concerned? What safeguards would have to be provided to avoid the tragic sequel of 1934? How could the almost certain resurgence of the Flint Alliance be blocked? If these problems were not satisfactorily determined the strike would have been fought in vain and the doom of unionism in the industry would have been written for many years to come.

The necessity for a compromise on the union's initial demand for corporation-wide recognition as sole bargaining agent was accepted by the strategy board who early instructed the negotiators to offer an important concession for a quick settlement. This consisted of a demand for exclusive bargaining in only the twenty struck plants where the union had demonstrated its strength. Once this had been granted the plants would be evacuated, work would be resumed and negotiations would proceed on the other union demands.

But the corporation representatives made no sign of bending to the offer. Their arguments were technical, legalistic. Both law and equity, they insisted, demanded that they protect the rights of workers who refused to accept the UAW as their bargaining agent. Of course they could not be unaware that this would leave the way open for some company-spawned organization to intrude its challenging claims and thus strip any paper recognition of the union of all real value, the same as had occurred in 1934.

For days the negotiations stiffened along these lines and the settlement remained as far away as ever. The strain of the waiting hours grew increasingly great. The two groups sat in separate rooms at opposite ends of Judge George Murphy's court, killing time, never meeting, while the governor hastened back and forth between them, keeping the thin wisp of the "discussions" alive.

Homer Martin was the first to break. It had been coming for weeks. Following the calling-off of the initial "truce" he was found one night delivering a stirring speech to an astonished crowd in the downstairs drugstore of the Hofmann building where the international offices were located.

Tears were streaming down his cheeks. A doctor was called and he was given a "shot" and put to bed.

His condition had hardly improved since then. He was nervous and absent-minded. Even in the conference room he couldn't sit still for more than an hour at a time. He'd get up, excuse himself, and then be gone—no one knew where—for an hour or two or maybe more. While negotiating he smoked incessantly, kept a constant smile on his face but seldom added a word of his own to the discussions.

This had become a manner of self-defense with him. Company negotiators were always shrewdly throwing up to him his lack of experience in the industry. And it was true that he would sometimes show pathetic ignorance of the technical phases of the union's demands when he tried to discuss them, embarrassing the other union negotiators and causing company representatives who had frequently enough "come up from the ranks" to smile.

Lewis now drew him aside.

"Homer, this looks like a stalemate to me," he said. "We've got to get our story before the public. I suggest that you tour the country and hold mammoth meetings in all the GM centers. Let them know what it's all about."

Martin was delighted to be able to escape the hateful conference room, to listen to the applause of the thousands of new friends that the union had won, to feel his full worth as a man again. An extended tour was arranged for him to keep him away for at least ten days and Vice-President Ed Hall was designated to accompany him and to keep him out of mischief.

That the union head could make his most positive contribution in this manner, besides, was undoubted. Before leaving he engaged in a debate with a company apologist, R. L. Lee, priest of the Protestant Episcopal Church, before three hundred and fifty ministers of the Michigan Council of Churches and Christian Education. By all accounts Martin won a spectacular victory. Lee had made the initial mistake of stating that he was not empowered to answer any questions whereupon Martin quickly replied that it was General Motors' policy to keep the true issues in the dark. If they were brought to light, the strike could be settled in three hours.

The UAW president got great applause when in reply to Lee's old chestnut about General Motors being like a big family of 250,000 people, he asserted: "It's the kind of family where father eats the bacon, mother eats the gravy and the kids can lick the skillet." He showed how the corporation could pay an annual wage of $2,000 to each worker and still make close to a hundred-fifty million dollars. The meeting, attended by ministers of all faiths, including the Catholic, voted a resolution pointed at the new injunction, asking Governor Murphy to do everything in his power to avoid violence in its handling.

The "negotiations" continued to languish and Murphy had to have frequent recourse to phone calls from the "White House" to keep the corporation principals interested. It was a magnificent game of bluff at which the Wall Street men were past masters. But the union negotiators seemed equally prepared to wait things out. They studied the production figures for the week past and smiled. Ford had registered 28,825 units; Chrysler 25,350; and General Motors a mere 1,500.

"If they want to build cars they will have to come to

terms sooner or later," John L. Lewis told Mortimer and Lee Pressman, his co-negotiators. "We can wait just as long as they choose to make us."

Often this grim game of stretching nerves, of the silent confronting of immovable wills grew too much for Governor Murphy himself. His state of mind sometimes bordered on the despondent and despite his efforts to preserve an atmosphere of hopefulness the situation—according to his own later description—had begun to take on for him the overwhelming impression of a nightmare in which hands were perpetually reaching for hats and overcoats, threats "never to return" were being shouted and doors slammed for the last time.

A systematic intimidation campaign of vast proportions, including a recall movement, reached the politician in Murphy with staggering blows. Every morning he would greet the union negotiators with: "Well, I got four thousand letters and telegrams yesterday, most of them calling me anything but a gentleman." He'd throw a few samples on the table. Some of these letters were in fact amazing, even going so far as to threaten violence against the governor—"a bullet through your damn Bolshevik brain"— if he would not take action to evict the sitdowners.

"Now, governor," Lewis would say, "if it's telegrams of support you want I can see that you get a million of them!"

"Oh, no!" the governor replied with forced gaiety. "I merely wanted to keep you current."

In a public statement he said: "It is futile for anyone on either side to attempt to intimidate or coerce me. It will not make the slightest difference in my judgments nor cause

me to alter my pledge to work in the public interest...."
Because of the almost traditional anti-union prejudice
of many public servants in the past, the governor now
gave an impression of rabid partisanship on the other side.
But his acts thus far consisted largely of a series of absti-
nences—refusal to obtain evacuation of the plants by force,
refusal to help serve three hundred John Doe warrants
against the sitdowners, refusal to publicly condemn the
sitdown, and so on. Not that even these strictly negative
acts did not under the circumstances require great courage, because they did.

At times Murphy would chat with the union representatives concerning the underlying implications of the strike.
In these private talks, he violently castigated the use of
the new strike tactic and employed increasing pressure on
the union leaders to abandon it during the crisis. He refused to recognize in the sitdown the sole possible recourse
of the auto workers in their struggle against the law-defying employers, contradictorily urging upon them a unilateral legalism.

"But governor, isn't it actually illegal even to picket in
Michigan?" Mortimer asked him on one occasion.

"Yes," Murphy replied.

"Well, then, since there's nothing the workers can le-
gally do, we must do that which is most effective and at
the same time least violent."

Always the governor returned to the personal dilemma
in the situation.

"I've taken an oath to uphold the laws of this state and
my oath will compel me eventually to enforce those laws."

Then Lewis broke in.

"Does that mean," he asked quietly, "that you would order your troops to shoot down these defenseless men, fathers of families?"

"Oh, no, no! I don't mean that at all!" the governor replied quickly as though anxious to erase the terrible vision before it had established itself. As the union negotiators were soon to learn this violent method of clearing the plants was not the only alternative in Murphy's mind.

And one day Bill Green phoned Murphy demanding that the AFL craft unions be given a voice in the negotiations. It was the sixth attempt at "intervention" in the strike by the AFL, all but one of the others having been kept secret. Green supplemented his call with a telegram. Murphy brought it in to the union conferees. And then Lewis blew up.

"Well, governor," he said with abysmal irony, "maybe you're talking to the wrong people. Maybe we shouldn't be here at all. Maybe you ought to call a conference with Mr. Green and Mr. Frey and get them to open the plants for General Motors!"

Murphy disclaimed any personal interest in the AFL wire.

"Then why bring it up?" Lewis demanded with uncloaked disgust.

"Because the other side is always bringing it up," the governor replied wanly. "I'm merely carrying their arguments to you so that you'll know their viewpoint."

The AFL request went disregarded. The kickback resulting from this intrusion at so critical a stage was so immediate and great that Green was forced to "clarify" his position which actually amounted to a sudden retirement from the field. "We want to see General Motors organized and a coöperative relationship established which will mean better wages and working conditions for the men," he said. "We don't want to be charged with being an ally of General Motors in this thing."

Green took a back-handed slap at Roosevelt in answer to a reporter's question as to whether the AFL's position hadn't prevented the President from making a more positive contribution in behalf of the strikers. "He's done everything he could for them but call out the Marines!" he replied.

The rebuke was thoroughly undeserved as the Administration's careful policy in the strike had certainly found an excellent motivation in the threat that any other course would antagonize the AFL leadership. This was a fact of which Green was well aware and a chief cause of the sharp criticism which President Roosevelt had received from Lewis. Green's remarks hence actually constituted a continuation of the AFL provocation in different form. For it would certainly have the effect of still preventing Roosevelt from doing anything more direct in behalf of the auto workers. Since the AFL through Green's denial was now supposedly giving up its imaginary claims in the situation, even the excuse of immediate self-interest was no longer applicable.

The union was not unaware of the difficulty of Governor Murphy's position. From the beginning of the strike he had strained every nerve to keep it free of violence. To Flint Alliance representatives who had early sought protection of "loyal" workers by state troops he replied by accusing them of having caused the first breakup of negotiations. "I know of plans recently in Flint to manufacture riots to get the militia involved," Murphy told them. "If the Flint Alliance had not entered the scene, you would all be back at work today."

"That was a nice speech but an awfully poor answer," said Sanford Rasbach, a former company superintendent and General Motors stockholder, who made a strange head of the workers' delegation.

"May I say that you asked an awfully poor question?" Murphy shot back.

Murphy held firm when a second, statewide, committee tackled him. The governor said that he would not sanction the use of bullets and bayonets "even if ten thousand men marched up here and asked me to do it." The delegation got tough and threatened a sitdown in his office and the governor made them welcome. But the anti-sitdown sitdowners gave up their demonstration after a few hours of discomfort. Murphy then spoke of "agents provocateurs" in connection with these demonstrations and announced an intention of starting an investigation "to determine whether General Motors is behind a sinister, vicious, skillful attempt to force me to use violence in this strike."

And now, even more than ever the governor was determined to keep bloodshed from the struggle. He assumed full responsibility for the situation, indicating that if any overt act were attempted by the Flint officials he would declare martial law, suspending all civil authority, including such acts as Gadola's injunction and writ.

Murphy made direct appeals to the people of Flint, as though over the heads of their unregenerate officials. His statements were redundant in the vocabulary of peace, with such words as "restraint" and "calmness" and "moderation" and "forbearance" always coloring his remarks. "Any inflammatory act or suggestion will imperil our hope to end this conflict without bloodshed, without tragic incident of any kind," said the governor, in whom stern public service had not destroyed a flair for graceful English.

On February 8th the complete breakdown of negotiations seemed unavoidable. When the conferees left at one in the morning no arrangement had been made for their return. The corporation representatives had stated that there was no further purpose in conferring and issued a lengthy statement telling "all the facts," the first since the conference had opened. Despite the heavy sense of finality the statement nevertheless left a narrow chink open as the corporation officials promised to respond to an early call of the governor for resumption of the conferences, "if in his judgment any good could result therefrom."

The implication was that he must have something new to offer and was actually a reminder of the supreme responsibility of the governor to correct the condition of "violence, disregard of the law and order and contempt of the courts" which the union hordes had visited upon the state. "Naturally, such a situation is entirely beyond the province of General Motors," the corporation asserted. And yet there was a strong hint that more imperious demands were in store to force "those charged with authority" to deal with the situation "according to their responsibility."

The union also issued a statement and Lewis supplemented it with a press conference. He put the matter in the most succinct and concrete terms:

The situation is actually this. The plants are shut down. Production is suspended. General Motors and the governor are now recognizing the UAW as the bargaining agency. We are the only agency being consulted. No one else is in the conference. No one else is qualified to negotiate. If we are the bargaining agency to start these plants in operation, we must be the bargaining agency after an agreement is reached. We insist that next week, as well as today, we shall be the bargaining agency. That is very simple, very concise and perfectly understandable.

Murphy had exhausted his best efforts to keep the conference from breaking up, knowing that an end to the discussions would inevitably result in a call for final measures. His entire energy had been directed to avoiding such a contingency not only because of the compelling political motive of a peaceful settlement but also because the very thought of violence was abhorrent to him. He tried to keep face to the public, insisting that there was peace in the family despite the angry shouts and the crashing of dishes that were audible to all beyond the closed doors and sealed windows.

"The parties are closer together than at any time," he white-lied. But his optimism needed bolstering: "Of course, everybody must remember that this largest industrial conflict of our time has not been marked by any fatality."

As a matter of fact the governor was steeped in the depths. What an outcome after all the herculean efforts for peace! A firm decision asserted itself. He would have to act—it was time. As the negotiations broke up he told the union representatives that he would like to see them within an hour at his apartments. His manner was extremely cold as he indicated that he had a major announcement to make to them. There was something ominous in his words.

Lewis who had come down with the grippe during the day went to bed but the rest of the strategy board kept the appointment with Murphy.

They found the governor in his bathrobe and house slippers, lounging in a deep chair. Though he looked utterly exhausted his attitude had apparently changed again. He was very intimate and friendly as he told of having just spoken to the General Motors heads and found them still adamant.

Then he went into a lengthy discussion of the situation, emphasizing again and again his own predicament. He had kept things going just as long as was possible, he said. He had been eminently fair to the union—no one could deny that. But the time had come for a change of policy and the union would now have to make an important sacrifice unless it wished to invite an attack of volcanic proportions upon itself, the Democratic Party and him. The point, of course, was that the union was to voluntarily evacuate the plants. The governor's plea was ardent and eloquently worded. He felt that he had made an impression on the union men and putting his hand on his former classmate Maurice Sugar's knee, asked confidently:

"Morrie, what do you think about it?"

The union's legal adviser felt that the situation was more than delicate since all the arguments of propriety bade him not to take the lead. Yet his conscience would not permit him to evade a grave responsibility on a mere personal scruple. He started with apparent hesitation: "It's hard for me to say, Frank, being a lawyer—but...." Then he outlined the situation in perhaps unlegalistic but highly humanistic terms, his argument summing up to the point that he thought the men ought to stay come hell or high water.

"Who is General Motors anyway that they should dictate to you or to these thousands of workers?" he demanded.

Murphy was pained and tried to brush Sugar's opinion aside as being dictated by "principle" rather than by legal necessity.

"Well, I'd like to ask you a question, Frank," Sugar persisted. "What exactly do you propose to do if the men don't come out?"

The governor proceeded to give a long, circuitous answer which led up to this: he would go into the plants personally and ask the men to leave voluntarily!

"And I would expect you boys to help me," he concluded.

It was a simple answer quietly given but it contained the possible destiny of the strike as the sudden silence of the union leaders upon hearing it indicated. Murphy knew this perfectly well. He was fully aware of his great personal authority with the workers—a mere report of the contents of the outgoing letters from Chevy 4 which the National Guard insisted on being allowed to read would tell him this. Only the question of the future of that great authority hung in the balance and caused him to temporize. And there was another circumstance. Before this meeting he had had a secret conference with Lewis alone, had imparted to him his decision and had received an unequivocal reply.

Emphasizing that it had the full knowledge and approval of President Roosevelt the governor had read a letter to Lewis which was to be directed immediately to the auto union and presumably would be made public simultaneously. It was a formal and final demand that the union "restore possession of the occupied plants to their rightful owners." It was more. It was a direct threat that Judge Gadola's injunction—"lawfully entered after fair and open hearing had been accorded to both parties"— and his writ of attachment for the bodies of the sitdowners would in case of a refusal be put into force by the National Guard in Flint.

"I shall exhaust every means to obtain such obedience peacefully," the governor ended ominously, "but I must and will be faithful to my oath of office."

To which Lewis responded:

"I do not doubt your ability to call out your soldiers and shoot the members of our union out of those plants, but let me say that when you issue that order I shall leave this conference and I shall enter one of those plants with my own people."*

Murphy undoubtedly had thought hard over Lewis' words. Very probably he called Roosevelt and discussed the formidable predicament in which they had placed him. The fact remains that the letter was not sent and was not even read to the auto union leaders. Only two years later was it made public when the now ex-governor of Michigan and candidate for U. S. Attorney-General sought through it to allay a charge of legal irresponsibility.

Murphy kept to his bed all of the following day. In the morning Sheriff Wolcott called to tell him that the vigil-

*As quoted by Lewis himself at the St.Louis convention of the UAW in July 1940.

antes were beginning to stir again following the breakdown in negotiations. He asked the governor to order the troops to Fisher One to prevent the hotheads from taking action. The governor agreed that if he was not able to get the conference reopened that day he'd give the desired order in the evening.

But the negotiators were back at Recorder's Court at 8:30 p.m. and the order to the troops was not given. The pleasure of striking final poses had been a short-lived one for the corporation bigwigs. Perhaps they had gotten wind of the little surprise bomb that the Chrysler Corporation was timing for the following day in the form of an announcement of a blanket ten percent wage raise for all its employees. Such a declaration would surely mean the *coup-de-grâce* to further General Motors resistance and create an awful eagerness in the corporation to get the strike over with as quickly as possible.

And, indeed, it is not at all unlikely that Chrysler should have picked this strategic moment to assure its competitor's submission to a fate that now seemed sealed for itself. Only a few days earlier, so-called "representative" elections in the Chrysler Corporation plants had been held and the union had made a spectacular showing, capturing 84 of 109 places. The clean-sweep record of the workers at the Chrysler Kercheval plant threw their leader, R. J. Thomas, into the union spotlight, where he has remained ever since.

The union was of course delighted to be the beneficiary of this animosity between the titans of the industry. Earlier the Ford Motor Company had scotched a reported attempt of General Motors to get a mutual agreement of all auto manufacturers to halt production with the promise of reciprocal action in case of further dislocations. The fact that the effort had been made was most significant, however, indicating that with the pyramiding strength of the union, concord of action by the great manufacturers was not out of question in the future.

In a couple of hours that evening the negotiators made more ground than in all the eight days previous. The corporation had finally agreed in principle to granting sole recognition for the struck plants. James Dewey, the federal conciliator, had hit on a satisfactory expedient—that this point not be included in the agreement proper but in a supplementary letter that the corporation could address to the governor, thus "saving face."

The question of wearing union buttons in the plants made some trouble. Knudsen seemed ready to concede this point too but his associates regarded it, the same as every other question, from the purely legalistic viewpoint. To them every demand of the union no matter how insignificant constituted an invasion of the fundamental rights of employers. Their backs ruffled at the mere thought of discussing these things with "outsiders."

Knudsen on the other hand looked at the matter more practically. He had a terrible headache—his plants lying idle—and he wanted to get rid of it. At times it seemed that he grew impatient with his colleagues for their failure to understand this basic issue. On one occasion when the actual working of some proposal inside the shop was being discussed and the technical phases of the problem left all the negotiators but Mortimer and himself high and dry

Knudsen gave a little laugh and exclaimed to the former, "This is a hell of a conference! A lot of lawyers, preachers, coal miners and only two auto workers!" (Meaning himself and Mortimer.)

Finally the button question was also settled with Knudsen agreeing to give the union a personal letter on the subject from which the other corporation negotiators could abstain.

Another snag was the question of discrimination against strike leaders. Naturally the company desired to keep the most militant strikers out permanently.

"What are you going to do with a fellow who hits his foreman with a club?" Knudsen demanded.

"What are you going to do with a foreman who kicks a worker in the face?" Mortimer countered.

Knudsen seemed to be honestly surprised.

"Who did that?" he asked.

And Mortimer explained that if a successful relationship was to be established after the strike was over both sides would have much to forget. The point was granted.

The only remaining question was the duration of the sole bargaining agreement. The union had asked for a year originally but had come down to six months. The corporation set the limit at three months. The question was still unsettled on the afternoon of February 10th when Pressman and Mortimer got Bob Travis on the phone.

"We'll leave it to you, Bob, as to how tough we can be. How long do you think the Flint people could hold out if there was a breakdown now?"

"That's hard to say," Travis replied. "It depends a good deal on what Murphy does. Otherwise I'd say we can still keep going for a couple more weeks but the strain is getting pretty strong."

"Well, we think you ought to come down here then."

When Travis and I arrived in the evening the negotiations had shifted to the Statler Hotel. Lewis was in bed and there was a steady come-and-go in and out of his suite. Everyone was extremely hopeful. Most issues had been disposed of and the conferees were hacking out the final forms. James Dewey moved back and forth between the suites on soft swift soles carrying successive copies with further slight corrections and amendments between the conferees. When a semblance of finality was attained Mortimer and Pressman brought us a copy of the wording.

"Read it over carefully and see if we've left anything out," they enjoined, both almost bursting with inner joy.

They hung over us possessively as we read. Despite the tenseness of the moment one experienced a feeling of letdown as one read the few wispy words. Was this all? Only this bit of thin paper after the stupendous struggle?

It was a list of the plants that were to come under the sole bargaining agreement. The two sides had finally agreed on a group of sixteen.

"Where's Guide Lamp?" Travis asked suddenly.

We also noted that only Chevy 4 had been listed while Chevy 6 and 9 were not. The Flint boys would like that!

A pained look came over Pressman's face like that of an artist whose precious work has been slurred.

"Which of those points are sticking points?" he asked. "Let's keep it down to the absolute minimum so we don't kill our chances for the six-month clause. We haven't settled that yet!"

"That's right," Travis agreed. "Guide Lamp is the only one I'd insist on. We can take care of Chevrolet. But Guide Lamp means a wedge in Anderson. That's goddam important. It means Muncie, Indianapolis, Kokomo. That's key for GM."

So the union negotiators went back and in a half-hour returned wreathed in smiles. The governor came down, looking gay and heartfree though terribly worn. Lewis was in bed in the next room. Ora Gassaway, the mine leader's shadow, stood silent guard at the door. Murphy took a call on the room phone. It was from some political lieutenant with whom he discussed at length certain appointments that were to be made for a party convention that was scheduled to take place that weekend. The governor always stressed the "progressive" qualities of his recommendations.

"Why, many people call him a Communist!" he said about one of his choices, making a naïve play at us, we felt.

Reporters kept rapping at the door always with some new question of no importance. Gassaway pushed them gently out. The six-month question had been turned over to Lewis and John Thomas Smith by the other negotiators for final adjustment. Smith came down from the twelfth floor, a tall, portly gentleman, and as he entered Lewis' room, Pressman whispered:

"I'll bet he comes out without his shirt."

There was a considerable strain for the next half-hour though John Brophy beguiled the time with jokes in a rich Irish brogue that came natural to his tongue. Finally Smith came out again and though we all studied his face anxiously we could not tell from his manner how the thing had gone.

He strode over to where we were lounging on the twin beds and as Brophy continued with a story he addressed his narrative to the new arrival.

Smith didn't seem to be exactly heartbroken or perhaps he was just a supremely fine poker player. I studied his face curiously as he stood just a trifle aloof at the foot of one of the beds with a faint smile on his lips.

The governor came out of Lewis' room, beaming. There was a mischievous sparkle in his eye as he caught sight of the GM bigwig standing by us.

"Why, Mr. Smith," he exclaimed, "aren't you afraid of getting infected, hobnobbing with all those Bolsheviks!"

After the governor and Smith had left Gassaway came out of Lewis' room. "The chief wants everybody inside."

We filed in quietly and stood about his bed. The tough public figure had quickly melted to the courteous personality that was Lewis' private self. He told in a few words of the final conversations with Smith, dramatizing the last exchanges for us.

"So I just got up on my elbow and I looked at him and said: 'Mr. Smith, do you want your plants reopened?'— 'Of course!'—'Well then, it's six months!' And so it was."

It was as simple as that! No, we silently thought, all of this would have been meaningless if not for the courage and devotion of the thousands in Flint and Detroit and Cleveland and the other cities where the real battle had been fought and won!

"Well, boys, I think you've got something that you can work on," Lewis summed up the agreement.

Before we left he shook hands with each of us, then pulling the covers to his chin and turning on his side, said:

"And now I'm going to have a good night's rest."

Outside there was a mob of photographers wanting to get a flash of Lewis in bed. Gassaway was holding them off good-naturedly.

"Mr. Lewis won't see anybody tonight," he said immovably.

An eager young fellow rushed up to us. "Is it true Lewis is wearing red flannels?" he asked in all seriousness. We burst out laughing.

The negotiators were pledged not to divulge the terms of the agreement until the next day when it was to be formally signed. But in five minutes reporters were in possession of all the facts and were dashing through the halls and seizing any phone available.

The settlement, aside from the recognition question (the union was recognized for its members only at plants other than the seventeen named for sole bargaining), specified that negotiations on the other questions would begin Monday, February 16th, and the union agreed that no strikes would interrupt the procedure of these conferences. Besides the no-discrimination-against-strikers clause the company also agreed to dismiss the injunctions obtained or pending, and though having gained a pledge that there would be no solicitation by union members on company property it conceded that "this is not to preclude individual discussion."

The direct recognition granted the union was limited only to its members but the far more important phase of recognition as contained in Knudsen's supplementary letter to Murphy carried the following crucial company pledge:

...we hereby agree with you that within a period of six months from the resumption of work we will not bargain with or enter into agreements with any other union or representative or employees of plants on strike in respect to such matters of general corporate policy as referred to in letter of January fourth, without first submitting to you the facts of the situation and gaining from you the sanction of any such contemplated procedure....

This periphrastic language in effect and fact constituted exclusive bargaining since it was understood that the governor would fully support the union's trust. Everybody followed Murphy up to the Presidential Suite, the governor's headquarters, for the official announcement to the press. As Smith and the governor were leaving Lewis' rooms the former had paused a moment and whispered in a patrician tongue to a friend among the reporters:

"*C'est fini.*"

Up in the green-upholstered room the governor posed for photographers and newsreel men as Knudsen, Smith and Donaldson Brown stood stiffly aside, unapproachable as ever (except for Knudsen who had his ineffaceable pleasant smile), watching Murphy with a noticeable mistrust.

"Smile, will you, governor? Give us a smile!" the photogs coaxed.

"How can you smile when you're as tired as we are?" the governor replied in a slightly overdone tragic-Hamlet manner.

He stood erect, nevertheless, always the perfect showman, his eyes looking far out beneath their heavy brows. This too was a different man from the one we had just known downstairs in Lewis' suite. He began speaking or rather words began to flow from his lips, independently, effortlessly. "An agreement has been reached." His beautifully modulated voice sang the hymn of peaceful victory in soft and guarded phrases. "This will be an enduring peace," he ended. Then reporters stood about him, firing questions in their almost disrespectful manner, which the governor answered with the same abstracted graciousness.

Martin and Hall were enroute to Janesville from Grand Rapids on their speaking tour when the agreement was reached. They were changing at Chicago the following morning when they picked up some papers and found them all announcing the end of the strike.

"They can't do that!" Martin exclaimed. "Brother, they did it!" Hall replied characteristically. Imagine ending the strike without notifying the president of the union! Martin called Detroit and asked that the official signing be put off until his arrival but the corporation principals saw no point in the delay. Accordingly, the agreement—the most important possibly that the union was ever destined to compact—failed to bear its president's signature. It was not always that poetic justice overtook this amazing man with such haste and appositeness.

The great strike after forty-four days of strain and struggle was hardly over when the papers were already telling of the wild reaction in Wall Street. General Motors leading, stocks had leapt up one to three points since the previous day's closing and after a delay in opening due to overnight orders heavy trading was resumed. Announcement of a 5-cent general raise by General Motors, calculated to strip 25 millions from the coming year's profits, seemed to have no discouraging effect upon the expectant buyers.

This increase, clearly necessitated by Chrysler's steal-the-show attempt, also had the purpose of discouraging the union's wage demands in the supplementary negotiations. It was an announcement to GM workers that the corporation had not yet surrendered its role of independent benevolence. Thus the corporation heads continued to give evidence of a queer ivory tower existence while the workers and all other normal people tied the raise up with the strike and the union where it of course belonged. Alf Sloan's statement on the settlement made an even more ridiculous effort to evade reality:

"Terms of the agreement are in complete accord with the principles upon which General Motors has stood since the beginning of this unfortunate controversy."

Only Bill Green purported to agree with him in words of continuing disingenuousness and treachery: "Reports indicate that the original demands of the UAW for exclusive collective bargaining for all GM employees were abandoned. The whole of labor is injured when one division of labor's army sustains defeat."

President Roosevelt glowingly commended Murphy, his worthy protege: "Yours has been a high public service, nobly performed, for which I desire to express the thanks of the Nation."

And the governor stated with Olympic repetition: "The agreement, and the manner it has been worked out, is an exaltation of reason and justice over brute force and violence."

"Another milestone on labor's march," said terse John Lewis, foreshadowing still greater things to come.

On arriving in Flint that afternoon we stopped first at

Fisher One for a prearranged meeting. As Mortimer read the pact and explained the individual points the faces that were glued on his were serious almost to the point of somberness. These men had given too much to be carried away by a gust of enthusiasm. The night before when told of the "settlement" by reporters, Bud Simons had snapped: "This strike isn't over till these boys say so." And now "these boys" fired questions at Mortimer. Did that mean everything else stood where it did when they started? How about the speed of the line? How about the bosses—would they be as tough as ever? "I'll be goddamned if I ain't gonna smack the first one that looks the least bit cockeyed at me!" one chap said and was cheered.

The announced raise was hardly mentioned or even thought of. These other things were what the strike had been fought for. All questions were answered painstakingly. It was not that the men didn't know the answers themselves—they had discussed these things hundreds of times. But it was part of that toughness that had grown up in them, of that new self-reliance that spoke so well for the future, that was reflected in this seeming skepticism. Finally one of them defined the settlement with basic clarity:

"What's the use of kidding ourselves? All that piece of paper means is that we got a union. The rest depends on us. For God's sake let's go back to work and keep up what we started here!"

When the vote was taken not one hand was raised against accepting the pact. Then a great cheer burst from the throats of the sitdowners and demonstrative joy broke through their restraint.

These experiences were repeated at the other plants. After all, none of these men had any criterion to go by to understand exactly what they had won. At Fisher Two the discussion went on for several hours before the pact was ratified. At Chevy 4 there was disappointment among the fellows from the other units who had engaged in the sitdown because the entire plant had not been included in the sole bargaining agreement. But all pledged earnestly not to consider their work completed until the entire Chevrolet division had been completely unionized and had received equal recognition.

The strike whose character in Flint was as much a social upheaval as anything else found its full and immediate vindication in the reaction of the whole people to the settlement. We had outlined an extensive plan for the evacuation ceremonies but the explosive spontaneity of joy and freedom that seized the city late that afternoon and evening made a chaos more glorious and significant than anything mere organization could have contrived.

The evacuation began at Fisher One at about 5 o'clock. All day the plant had been filled with an immense turmoil that was probably not unlike the excited but grave preparations of a pioneer people before a great trek into an unknown land. How did the men feel about leaving this home, scene of the birth of an exciting new freedom? One of them* recorded his feelings with beautiful simplicity:

As the exhilaration of our first union victory wore off the gang was occupied with thoughts of leaving the silent factory which for [forty-four] days had been our home.

*John Thrasher of Standard Cotton, a small feeder plant for Fisher One, whose sitdown closely paralleled that of the major unit.

One found himself wondering what home life would be like again. Nothing that happened before the strike began seemed to register in the mind any more. It is as if time itself started with the strike.

What will it be like to go home—and to come back tomorrow with motors running and the long-silenced machines roaring again? But that is for the future....

One must pack. Into a paper shopping bag I place the things which helped make my "house" a place to live in: house slippers, extra shirts, sox and underwear; razor and shaving equipment; two books; a reading lamp; and the picture of my wife that hung above my bed....

It is near time to go. Already there is a goodly number of cars and people outside, brother workers who have come to escort us out of the plant. The first victory has been ours but the war is not over. We were strong enough to win over all the combined forces of our enemies and we shall continue to win only if we remember that through *Solidarity* we have been made free.

Now the door is opening.

The factory whistle blew a full blast and the men began marching to the door. The crowd of thousands that was gathered outside let out a great hurrah as Bud Simons appeared heading the line. Following him came the "Bearded Brigade" carrying their placard: "We Shave When Victory Is Ours." Long stogies were in their mouths, a sign of their new prosperity and importance. Every striker toted a big bundle on his back. The lines formed immediately in the street for the two-mile parade to the other plants where the chief celebration was scheduled. Four color bearers with large American flags were in the lead. Tiny flags were carried in every hat. The massive jam of sitdowners, sympathizers and hundreds of autos began their singing, cheering, honking way toward town.

Night was beginning to close down on Chevrolet Avenue when the Fisher One contingent appeared at the crest of the hill. A combined roar from the two great crowds down the street—one before Chevy 4 and the other in the hollow at Fisher Two—greeted the long-awaited marchers. The Chevy 4 leaders were standing on the high landing above the gate, a tall American flag on each side, and their men were gathered inside the doors. As the Fisher One parade reached the plant, great flares suddenly lit up, confetti flew and the enormous gates of the plant opened slowly.

Lungs that were already spent with cheering found new strength as the brave men whose brilliant coup had turned the strike to definite victory began to descend the stairs. They looked haggard with exhaustion. The mark of suffering was on them. Yet their collective joy and pride submerged all this. As they came out, wives and children rushed to husbands and fathers who had not been seen for ten fear-filled days. Strong, heavily-bearded men were unashamed of tears. Then someone began to sing "Solidarity"

> Solidarity forever!
> Solidarity forever!
> Solidarity forever!
> For the union makes us strong!

and as all joined in, the moment was carried beyond its almost unbearable tenseness and emotion.

The crowd was so great at the Fisher Two plant that the thousands coming from up the hill had to stop by the bridge fifty yards away. On the Chevy 2 roof across the street, sixteen National Guardsmen stood watching. The cheering and noise exceeded all the bounds of hearing as the small group of Fisher Two men came out of the plant which they had defended so valiantly against police gas and bullets for the first great victory of the strike. A narrow path had been left open for them and then they were swallowed up in the mass. Hardly anyone paid any heed to the speakers at the sound car. The people needed no further words for their drunkenness.

They surged into Third Avenue bound for the center of the city. It was hardly a parade, it was more like a great migration. And to some who watched from the windows of the ritzy Durant Hotel as the human flood poured into the main street of the city, it must have seemed an ominous invasion. Crossing the river on Saginaw Street right in the heart of the city the parade halted momentarily while four bearded sitdowners solemnly bore a dummy tagged "Boysen" to the parapet and with ex-preacher Homer Martin pronouncing last rites for the deceased, tossed it into the river.

Not a policeman was in sight anywhere yet thousands of people lined the street and—for the first time in Flint—applauded and cheered a union parade. "Come on in!" the men and women shouted. Many responded. Union buttons were visible everywhere along the route.

Passing the Ritz theatre the marchers gave a cheer, remembering the friendliness that Maxie Gealer, the manager, had shown their cause. The nearby Strand theatre on the other hand which had been pronounced "unfair" to the Motion Picture Operators got a salvo of boos. Never had a boycott appeal of an AFL union in Flint received such an impressive approval. It was a first sign of the new union consciousness and solidarity that had been forged in this struggle, a spirit more earnest and profound and far-reaching perhaps than any that had preceded it and which was destined to sweep from coast to coast in the wake of the splendid victory of the auto workers.

The Pengelly auditorium was jammed beyond the last inch of space. The vestibules on all floors and the stairs and the long hall downstairs were packed also and when the crowd couldn't get into the building anywhere the people began to mass outside. And still more came. Sound apparatus was strung down to the second floor from the hall and was hung out of the auditorium windows facing the street. Five thousand people were gathered outside. No one could estimate the number that had crushed and fought their way into the building.

In the hall an original play with two hundred actors, mainly from the Women's Auxiliary, was being given. It had the significant title—"The Strike Marches On." It had been several days in preparation by writers Josephine Herbst and Mary Heaton Vorse and though the players had had the benefit of a final going-over by Morris Watson, director of New York's famous "Living Newspaper," the performance was exceedingly crude.

And yet one did not require a special gift of loyalty to see something there. The mere numbers on the low stage: their exuberant, infectious vitality; the audience prompting and responding across the hardly distinguishable break; the universally-shared rock-bottom terms of the enacted message...were these not amply expressive of the class awakening, of a mass soul in birth?

In the general merry-making that went on all night in

celebration of the victory one might have found cause to doubt the reality of this significant social fact. Particularly as the heavy drinking that went on everywhere gave the workers' hilarity much of the loose and uninspiring character of a Rotarian shindig or American Legion convention whoopee.

Around two in the morning I was in the Pengelly auditorium. The crowd had thinned out considerably but there were still some dozens of people in the hall, men and women filled by the glamour of the great strike and reluctant to abandon it finally for the humdrum of everyday life. The music dragged on wearily, playing for a handful of indomitable couples. Tired faces were unnaturally flushed, eyes ringed and blinking with immense fatigue.

Leaving, I noticed two young fellows near the door. They had been drinking and one of them was trying to explain something to his buddy. His words came garbled and as though realizing that he was not making himself understood, he shook his head violently several times. Finally, almost tearful, he exclaimed as from the very depths of his being:

"Emmet, you gotta believe me! It ain't me that's talkin', it's the CIO in me!"

This little expression delighted me despite the unworthy circumstances in which it was spoken. For it seemed to give a flashing insight into the great depth of meaning that this magic entity—the CIO—had so swiftly attained for the workers. It was not yet the millenium, as this poor sodden fellow reminded one. It was chiefly significant rather for its tremendous implications—of an immense collective unity and power based on simple loyalty to group interest.

A Note on the Author

Henry Kraus received degrees in mathematics and psychology from Western Reserve University and taught school for a time in Cleveland. He first became involved in union activities in 1933, with the American Federation of Labor, and moved to Detroit in 1936 as international editor of the *United Auto Worker,* a monthly tabloid that he had founded in Cleveland the year before. He is the author of several other books, mainly on medieval art. These include *The Living Theatre of Medieval Art* (Indiana University Press, 1967) and *Gold Was Mortar: The Economics of Cathedral-Building* (Routledge & Kegan Paul, 1979) and, with his wife Dorothy, *The Hidden World of Misericords* (Braziller, 1975) and *The Gothic Choirstalls of Spain* (Routledge & Kegan Paul, 1985). In 1984 he was the recipient of a fellowship from the MacArthur Foundation. He presently lives in Paris, France.